poems,

4/94 Ed Kaplan

BAUDELAIRE'S PROSE POEMS

EDWARD K. KAPLAN

BAUDELAIRE'S PROSE POEMS

THE ESTHETIC, THE ETHICAL, AND THE RELIGIOUS

IN

THE PARISIAN PROWLER

THE UNIVERSITY OF GEORGIA PRESS
Athens and London

Athens, Georgia 30602

Designed by Louise M. Jones
Set in 11/13 Bodoni Book
The paper in this book meets the guidelines for permanence and durability of the Committee on Production Guidelines for Book Longevity of the Council on Library Resources.

Printed in the United States of America
94 93 92 91 90 5 4 3 2 1

Library of Congress Cataloging in Publication Data
Kaplan, Edward K., 1942–
Baudelaire's prose poems : the esthetic, the ethical, and the religious in The Parisian prowler / Edward K. Kaplan.
p. cm.
Includes bibliographical references.
ISBN 0-8203-1218-5 (alk. paper)
1. Baudelaire, Charles, 1821–1867. Spleen de Paris.
2. Prose poems, French—History and criticism. I. Title.
PQ2191.S63K3 1990 841′.8—dc20
89-27410 CIP

British Library Cataloging in Publication Data available

Frontispiece: Portrait of Baudelaire by Etienne Carjat, 1866.
Private collection. Giraudon.

My thanks also to Michael Bishop for permission to reprint part of an article which appeared in *Dalhousie French Studies* of which he is the editor. A revised form of "Baudelaire's Portrait of the Poet as Widow," *Symposium* 34, 3 (Fall 1980): 233–48, published by Heldref Publications, 4000 Albemarle St., N.W., Washington, D.C. 20016, copyright © 1980, is reprinted with permission of the Helen Dwight Reid Educational Foundation.

To
Yves Bonnefoy
and
IN MEMORIAM
John Porter Houston
(1933–1987)

CONTENTS

PREFACE

This book strives to resurrect Charles Baudelaire's neglected masterpiece, a collection of fifty "prose poems" first published together posthumously under the title *Le Spleen de Paris. Petits Poèmes en prose.* (I have translated it as *The Parisian Prowler* [1989] and all my quotations are taken from that work.)[1] Of course individual pieces have hardly been forgotten and recently have stimulated astute literary theorists. Yet most current critical methods, which can illuminate significant details, often obscure the whole. I analyze the structure and meaning of the entire collection, with a dialogue with deconstruction as the most explicit theoretical complement. This is not a random assemblage of melodic rhapsodies, but a coherent ensemble of "fables of modern life" that joins both lyricism and critical self-awareness.[2]

The collection includes a number of subgenres and can be classified somewhere between Edgar Allan Poe's "fantastic tales," which Baudelaire translated, and Franz Kafka's "parables and paradoxes" (Politzer 1962; Bernheimer 1982, 45–55). At first reading, *The Parisian Prowler* is comprised of enigmatic stories, many of which appear to be patently romanticist, with stock characters such as suffering clowns, princes, devils, redemptive or defiling females, dreamers, and voyagers. Several depict Second Empire society, with anecdotal details of the capital. Others develop reveries—exotic or urban—in which the narrator—simultaneously "critic" and "poet"—himself struggles to reconcile "knowledge and voluptuous pleasure" ("Richard Wagner et Tannhäuser à Paris," 1861, *OC* 2:786). Hoaxes also abound, ironic or frontal attacks against common sense. This "experimental laboratory," in Claude Pichois's terms (*OC* 1:1301), recapitulates the author's entire development.

Preface

Baudelaire considered his "prose poems" (as he tentatively called them) to be of equal magnitude to *Les Fleurs du Mal*, and scholars have recognized their importance. Sociohistoric or Marxist criticism, deconstruction, and other pre- and post-structural "readings" ratify their compelling presence, starting with Charles Mauron's psychocritical study, *Le Dernier Baudelaire* (1966). Walter Benjamin's posthumously collected articles, *Charles Baudelaire: A Lyric Poet in the Era of High Capitalism* (1973), brings them into the arena of contemporary theory.

Barbara Johnson's doctoral dissertation, *Défigurations du langage poétique. La seconde révolution baudelairienne* (1979), develops a lucid deconstructive analysis emphasizing the discontinuities between the poetry and the prose; she applies the idea of Baudelaire's "second revolution" to Mallarmé, who develops the consequences of Baudelaire's prose poems (pp. 188–91). I trace the second revolution to the second edition of *Les Fleurs du Mal*. The sensitive, but all too modest book of J. A. Hiddleston, *Baudelaire and "Le Spleen de Paris"* (1987), provides an excellent introduction, but articulates only major prose poems with the author's aphorisms and essays. Jonathan Monroe's wide-ranging, comparative study *A Poverty of Objects: The Prose Poem and the Politics of Genre* (1987) combines the latest critical methods with an appropriate focus on the fables about poor people, thus furthering Benjamin's and Mauron's approaches. Marie Maclean, *Narrative as Performance: The Baudelairean Experiment* (1988), provides valuable linguistic tools. These important books, however, all neglect the collection's unity.

I emphasize the prose poems' coherence—individually and as a collection—first, because it exists; second, in order to nuance the current preoccupation with their fragmentation and "undecidability." Barbara Johnson's elegant deconstructive analyses convinced me that the self-awareness inscribed in the texts often destabilizes their perspective. But I did not conclude that their meaning, even when intriguingly undecidable, should remain undecided. They *can* be interpreted with no loss to their true complexity, internal tensions, and originality. My first six chapters demonstrate in some detail how the groupings printed in

1862 for the newspaper *La Presse* (a total of twenty-six pieces) form the foundation of the future collection.

Baudelaire clearly envisaged a book, despite his many unfinished sketches and plans. He established a sequence of fifty titles in a table of contents, probably written in 1865, which Charles Asselineau and Théodore de Banville, who edited the 1869 posthumous edition of his complete works, faithfully followed. All subsequent editions of the prose poems retain that order. The author's handwritten memorandum does not include either the dedication "To Arsène Houssaye," normally considered to be the preface, or the verse "Epilogue," now placed, rightfully, with the projected third edition of *Les Fleurs du Mal*. This document is at the Bibliothèque littéraire Jacques Doucet in Paris (MS. 9022) (De George 1973; *OC* 1:1306; Kopp, xxviii–lxxii, 174). The prose poems' prepublication history, as I demonstrate throughout my study, confirms this definitive arrangement and reinforces textual exegesis based on a sequential reading. See appendix 2.

Baudelaire's self-reflective fables clarify some hypotheses about his development. His mature work—the second edition of *Les Fleurs du Mal* and the "prose poems" written between 1861 and 1865—is energized by conflicts between his esthetic and ethical drives. The "esthetic," his passion for plastic images and for reverie, inspires his ground-breaking "Salon of 1846" and other essays on painters, sculptors, writers, and cultural theory. The first edition of *Les Fleurs du Mal* (1857) traces an imaginative odyssey beyond the world's confines, and its ambiguous lyricism of cruelty and affliction marks a European literary revolution—a *frisson nouveau* (new shudder), as Victor Hugo proclaimed. Baudelaire's so-called "prose poems" emerge as an autonomous genre and parallel the poems added in 1861, which emphasize finite reality and its constraints, the "ethical" world of *shared* experience.[3] These "modern fables" constitute, in Georges Blin's phrase, an "absolute beginning" (1948, 143).

Both collections—the verse and the fables—evolved simultaneously from prepublications in newspapers and periodicals, as was common practice. On 1 June 1855, the prestigious *Revue des Deux Mondes* presented eighteen poems, for the first time under the title *Les Fleurs du Mal.* (Several pieces had already appeared, and in 1851 a book to be called *Les Limbes* [Limbo] was announced.) The next day a modest but momentous innovation—prose versions of two corresponding poems—appeared in an anthology of verse by Asselineau, Banville, Hugo, Gérard de Nerval, and others. These "two twilights" (as Baudelaire called them) parallel "Le Soir" and "Le Matin" (Evening, Morning), later included in *Les Fleurs du Mal,* which first went on sale on 25 June 1857. Baudelaire's poetic masterwork was confiscated by judicial order on 7 July, and six poems were condemned as immoral on 20 August.

Four days later, the first series of prose poems conceived as such—called *poèmes nocturnes* (nocturnal poems)—was published in *Le Présent* (on 24 August 1857). These consisted of two meditative narratives, "Twilight," "Solitude" (both from the 1855 anthology), and two allegorical anecdotes, "Plans" and "The Clock" ("Les Projects," "L'Horloge"). This sequence added an ironic voice to the verse "models," although the author apparently did not anticipate their radical originality.

Critical reflection nourished both projects. Baudelaire defended *Les Fleurs du Mal* against obtuse government prosecutors, as had the author of *Madame Bovary* the previous February, but he did not neglect his already impressive production. In 1855 alone he published translations of Poe's tales, "The Universal Exposition," "The Essence of Laughter," art criticism, and theory. His far-reaching reflections on modernity, the "Salon of 1859," and his germinal essay on Constantin Guys, "The Painter of Modern Life," probably written between 1858 and 1860, completed this program. On 1 January 1860 Baudelaire sold to Poulet-Malassis and De Broise rights to the second edition of *Les Fleurs du Mal;* an anticipated collection of prose poems; his translations and critical biography of Poe; *Artificial Paradises;* and other "esthetic curiosities." Motivated in large part by a desperate need for money, this contract also certifies his ambition to immortalize himself by publishing, with proven friends, his complete works.

Yet the man embodied an intriguing paradox. During this period of spiritual triumph, his intimate life—his loves, his health, and his finances—were a shambles. On 13 January 1860 he experienced a first brain hemorrhage, his nervous system being undermined by previously dormant syphilis which had periodically disturbed him. He was fearful of going mad, and on 23 January he noted: "I felt brushed by *the wingbeats of idiocy*" (*Fusées, OC* 1:668). Yet we cannot agree with Suzanne Bernard that his prose poems show "a short-windedness, a drying up of the creative imagination . . . a sort of sinking into prosaism" (1959, 119). More perceptive is Maurice Blanchot's defense of the poet's victories against Sartre's autopsy of the man's existential "failures" (Blanchot 1949; Sartre 1947).

The narrator of Baudelaire's fables seems to typify the author's inner struggles. An artist and a thinker, whose complex personality remains consistent, he continuously frustrates his passion for absolute Beauty with his yearning for affection. He begins his journey alienated from reality, becomes aggravated by conflicts between his "ethical" and "esthetic" drives—to the point of despair—and ends by expressing loyal companionship. Later fables surpass these binary thematics by intermingling or even confusing them. The most advanced ones—which I call "theoretical fables"—through ironic puns on their own form, further undermine idealist constructs.[4]

I have borrowed my heuristic categories from Baudelaire's contemporary, the existential theologian Søren Kierkegaard (1813–55), whose work he did *not* know. Both authors, reacting against their respective establishments, wrote under Socratic personas in order to wage war against the trivialization of ultimate values. Kierkegaard's spiritual radicalism, his relentless satire of Denmark's state religion, anticipates Baudelaire's uncompromising repudiation of the Second French Empire's bourgeois norms. But choosing to concentrate on the texts, I have kept most comparisons implicit or relegated them to notes. Kierkegaard's rigorous and detailed distinctions might divert us from the relative simplicity of Baudelaire's fables.

Three dimensions of experience inform *The Parisian Prowler* from beginning to end. The *esthetic* includes art, ideal beauty, and especially the intense immediacy of sensations, fantasy, and dream; it is the domain of subjectivity and solitude. The *ethical* includes principles of right and wrong, relations between intimates or between individuals and the community; broadly speaking, the "ethical" is the domain of shared reality. The *religious* —not to be confused with church or dogma—points to ultimate reality, whether it be God or a pure standard of truth, justice, and meaning.

The "religious" is a perspective from which the narrator judges the self-serving world and its rationalizations. Like Kierkegaard, Baudelaire was driven by a passion for integrity that accepted no compromise. The proxies of both often wear ironic masks so as concretely to engage readers in dialogue. Kierkegaard's interpretation of Socrates provides a hermeneutic model for these polemic positions: "Thus he elevates himself higher and higher, becoming even lighter as he rises, seeing all things disappear beneath him from his ironical bird's-eye perspective, while he himself hovers above them in ironic satisfaction borne by the absolute negativity within him. Thus he becomes estranged from the whole world to which he belongs" (Kierkegaard 1965, 221).

Kierkegaard's categories inspired my approach, but contemporary debates helped bring it to fruition, though not in a way that rallies behind one flag or another. In the course of my work it became clear that "the esthetic, the ethical, and the religious" can define the collection's thematic armature but not its ambiguities. In fact, the potential violence of theory becomes one of its principal subjects. Baudelaire's eloquent preamble to "The Universal Exposition" (1855) reflects my position in the critical arena:

> I have tried more than once, like all my friends, to lock myself up in a system in order to preach there at my ease. But a system is a kind of damnation which forces us to a perpetual recantation; one must always invent another one, and the drudgery involved is a cruel punishment. And my system was always beautiful, vast, spacious, convenient, clean and smooth everywhere; at least it appeared to be. And always a spontaneous unexpected product of universal vitality would come to give the lie to my infantile and obsolete knowledge, that lamentable daughter of utopias. . . . To

> escape the horror of my philosophical apostasies, I haughtily resigned myself to modesty: I became content to feel; I returned to seek refuge in an impeccable naïveté (*OC* 2:577–78; Baudelaire, *Art in Paris*, 123).

My task was to reconstruct the stable foundation of Baudelaire's irony and contradictions. An elemental (or "naive") respect for literary context reveals how his fables can interpret themselves and each other. Textual analyses should be philologically "impeccable," historically accurate, without losing sight of literature's "universal vitality," its literal content. But I quote from his essays only when they formulate views more transparently than his fictive stand-ins. The poet-critic wears many masks, but his dramas of consciousness—his "modern fables"—reach a clarity that his criticism confirms only at second hand.

The present study straightforwardly interprets Baudelaire's collection of fifty fables such as he arranged them in his autograph table of contents. But first I relate his most relevant critical writings to the changes represented by the 1861 edition of *Les Fleurs du Mal*. Then I follow the sequences of "prose poems" as they were published in periodicals before the definitive book took shape. It is decisive to our analysis that Baudelaire generally retained the sequences as they originally appeared. This historical correlative objectively confirms an integral analysis of *The Parisian Prowler*. A complex but coherent itinerary emerges from these readings, one which follows the progress of its dynamic narrator.[5]

The problematic guide who gives *The Parisian Prowler* its title is a "*misunderstood man*" (Baudelaire's italics) who absorbs traits of Delacroix, Edgar Allan Poe, Thomas De Quincey, and Constantin Guys—each one with whom the poet identified:

> A half nervous, half bilious temperament . . . , a cultivated mind, trained by studies of form and color; a tender heart, wearied by misfortune, but still ready to be rejuvenated; we will . . . admit to old failings, and, what an easily excitable nature should produce from it, if not concrete remorse, at least the regret of time

> desecrated and badly used. The taste for metaphysics, the knowledge of different philosophical hypotheses about human destiny, are certainly not useless complements,—nor that love of virtue, of an abstract, stoic or mystical virtue, which is defined in all the books which nourish modern youth, as the highest summit to which a distinguished soul might ascend. If you add to that a great sensitivity of the senses I omitted as a supplemental condition, I believe I have assembled the most common general elements of the modern sensitive man, of what might be called the *banal form of originality*. (*OC* 1:429–30)[6]

Baudelaire's fables of modern life are dialogical in that they radically challenge us to examine our presuppositions.[7] They are not quite "polyphonic," as Bakhtin uses the term, for their various points of view are ultimately submitted to the narrator (1984, esp. chap. 1). This persona exercises the poet's volatile dialogue with his public: "Hypocrite lecteur, mon semblable, mon frère" (hypocritical reader, my peer, my brother). Sometimes, often, he betrays self-destructive anger, rebelling against injustice or stupidity—or against women who might love him. Sometimes he insults our complacency and self-deception with vicious glee. At other times he recognizes his own frailty, nurturing a sense of fellowship with the oppressed. And, rarely, he does unveil his ethical standard.

Baudelaire's narrator joins "criticism" and "poetry" in a voyage of self-discovery. He is a dreamer who seeks both to analyze experience objectively and to sympathize with isolated individuals like himself. Yet readers cannot comfortably identify with him: his irony is often too devastating, his hostility too obnoxious. Our relationship remains unsettling, both confrontational and empathic. We join his journeys on the alert.

ACKNOWLEDGMENTS

This project has its distant origin in conversations with Yves Bonnefoy, exemplary poet and critic; his insights into the modern embrace of finitude opened Baudelaire to me. Also, work with a gifted honors student, Michael Mullins (Amherst College, 1976), significantly focused my interest in the prose poems.

Several colleagues read this manuscript in its various forms, and I am grateful for their criticism and support: Victor Brombert, Wallace Fowlie, Eugene Goodheart, John Porter Houston, Virginia Marino, Laurence M. Porter, and Barbara Johnson, whose openness to different perspectives, and willingness to communicate, sharpened my professional self-awareness.

My research was supported financially by a fellowship from the National Endowment for the Humanities, 1985–86, and funds from Brandeis University. Scott Magoon and his colleagues at the Feldberg Communications Center of Brandeis University provided stability with their patience and computer expertise. Ann McWilliams helped prepare the index. Malcolm Call, director of The University of Georgia Press, and his colleagues, showed remarkable sensitivity to me at all stages of this project and in their publication of my translation of the prose poems, *The Parisian Prowler*. Their professionalism is a model for all presses, particularly university presses.

My family, Janna, Jeremy, and Aaron, created a community of love which made my efforts worthwhile.

I dedicate this volume to Yves Bonnefoy, now professor at the Collège de France, and to the late John Porter Houston, whose integrity and learning represent what is finest in the American academy.

ABBREVIATIONS

CPl	Charles Baudelaire, *Correspondance*. Ed. Claude Pichois and Jean Ziegler. 2 vols. Paris: Gallimard, Editions de la Pléiade, 1976.
Doucet	Bibliothèque littéraire Jacques Doucet [Paris]
FM	Charles Baudelaire. *Les Fleurs du Mal*. Text of second (1861) edition. See *OC*, below, vol. 2.
Kopp	Charles Baudelaire, *Petits Poèmes en prose*. Ed. Robert Kopp. Paris: José Corti, 1969.
JI	Charles Baudelaire. *Journaux intimes. Fusées. Mon coeur mis à nu. Carnet*. Ed. Jacques Crépet and Georges Blin. Paris: José Corti, 1949.
Lemaître	*Petits Poèmes en prose (Le Spleen de Paris)*. Ed. Henri Lemaître. Paris: Editions Garnier, 1962.
OC	Charles Baudelaire. *Oeuvres complètes*. Ed. Claude Pichois. 2 vols. Paris: Gallimard, Editions de la Pléiade, 1975–76.
PE	Charles Baudelaire. *Petits Poèmes en prose. Les Paradis artificiels*. Ed. Charles Asselineau and Théodore de Banville. Vol. 4 of *Oeuvres complètes*. Paris: Michel Lévy frères, 1869.

1

INTERPRETING THE PROSE POEMS

An Amalgam beyond Contradictions

Baudelaire's 1855 experiments with lyrical prose quickly faded into the background as he developed autonomous subgenres—"fables of modern life," as I call them. The formalistic problem of the "prose poem" is far less valuable in interpreting them than a focus on their narrator, a Second Empire Parisian poet—a *flâneur*, or urban stroller—who struggles with his conflicting drives. It is remarkable that Baudelaire's early critical essays anticipate, by many years, his new prose genre and the revised second edition of *Les Fleurs du Mal* (1861) which they parallel. In fact, his overall development confirms his conversion from "poetic" idealism to a literature of daily experience.

Questions of form are of course essential and we need an appropriate interpretive model: "These texts include in perfect but minimal form the *Märchen* or wonder-tale, the *Sage* or anecdote, the fable, the allegory, the cautionary tale, the tale-telling contest, the short story, the dialogue, the novella, the narrated dream" (Maclean 1988, 45). Editors have accepted—inappropriately, in my view—Baudelaire's dedication "To Arsène Houssaye," which introduces the twenty-six prose poems serialized in 1862 for *La Presse*, as a preface to the completed collection. "The Thyrsus" ("Le Thyrse," no. 32,[1] first published in 1863) is a more sophisticated model, one which surpasses the binary opposition of prose and poetry which has seduced interpreters. These two prominently analyzed texts grope toward a theory of genre but do not encompass the modern fable. "The Stranger" and "The Old Woman's Despair" ("L'Etranger," "Le Désespoir de la vieille"), which open the collection, define *The Parisian Prowler*'s dynamics more precisely.

THE ESTHETIC VERSUS THE ETHICAL

Baudelaire's early essays demonstrate the generative tension of his entire work: his personal struggle to maintain both compassion and a fervent estheticism. In 1851, his first reflections on imagination, "Du Vin et du hachisch" (On wine and hashish), warn firmly against intemperate reverie by distinguishing the "good" intoxication of wine, which makes one sociable, from the "bad" ecstasies of hashish, which alienate and enfeeble the dreamer. He concludes by quoting a "musical theoretician," Barbereau, a proxy of his implicit ethic: "I do not understand why rational and spiritual man uses artificial means to achieve poetic beatitude, since enthusiasm and free will suffice to raise him to a supernatural existence" (*OC* 1:398).[2] Baudelaire's defense of the will remains uncompromised.

The following year, in "L'Ecole païenne" (The pagan school of poetry), Baudelaire locates the problem in literature. He censures the fastidious, polished poetry of "art for art's sake," notably that of Théodore de Banville. The final paragraphs denounce an obsession with esthetic idealism: "The excessive appetite for form induces monstrous and unknown disorders. Absorbed by the ferocious passion for the beautiful, the notions of the just and the true disappear. The feverish passion for art is an ulcer which devours what remains; and, as the clear absence of the just and the true in art amounts to the absence of art, the entire person vanishes; excessive specialization of one faculty produces nothingness" (*OC* 2:48–49).

The most radical solution is to destroy all art. He goes on to cite the famous incident in Augustine's *Confessions* (6.8) when the neophyte Christian accompanies his friend Alypius to a brutal Roman circus; they refuse to watch, until the crowd's shouts rouse their curiosity. Baudelaire, as moralist, embraces the convert's asceticism: "I understand the fits of rage of iconoclasts and Moslems against images. I accept entirely Saint Augustine's remorse for his excessive pleasure of the eyes. The danger is so great that I forgive the abolition of the object. The madness of art is the equivalent of the abuse of mind" (*OC* 2:48–49). The shattering of a peddler's windowpanes, at the end of "The Bad Glazier" ("Le Mauvais Vitrier," no. 9), confronts us with a comparable idolatry.

Art—the voluntary creation of significant form—should not be confused with self-titillation. Contradicting his reputation as a dandy, Baudelaire admonishes the overly refined "mind" which denies ethics. A perverse "artist" may relish the idea of beauty and yet ignore its intrinsic rectitude:

> [The madness of art] engenders stupidity, hardness of heart and a boundless pride and self-centeredness. I remember having heard about a joker artist who had received a counterfeit coin: I will keep it for a poor man. The wretch took an infernal pleasure in robbing the poor and at the same time enjoying the benefits of a charitable reputation. I heard another one: Why don't the poor put on gloves to beg? They would make a fortune. And another: He is badly draped; his tatters do not become him.
>
> We should not consider those things as childishness. What the mouth gets used to saying, the heart gets used to believing. (*OC* 2:49)

In fact, anecdotes cited in this essay became, fourteen years later, full-fledged fables that demonstrate how an exaggerated *estheticism* can abolish elemental decency. The narrator of "A Joker" ("Un Plaisant," no. 4, first published in *La Presse,* 1862) clamors against a gloved dandy who violates the dignity of a beast; the stroller of "Widows" ("Les Veuves," no. 13, first published in the *Revue Fantaisiste,* 1861) analyzes "in the mourning clothes of the poor, an absence of harmony that makes them more heartbreaking"; and the narrator of "The Counterfeit Coin" ("La Fausse Monnaie," no. 28, first published in *L'Artiste,* 1864), speculates about his friend's false gift.

The critic's moral indignation, in 1852, contrasts sharply with the perceived obscenity of his poetic masterpiece, censored a scant fortnight after publication. Perhaps the author subverted his didacticism even more vehemently after *Les Fleurs du Mal* had been so utterly misunderstood, for the magistrates did not fathom the author's ethical irony: "One must depict vice as seductive, for it is seductive" ("Les Drames et les romans honnêtes," *OC* 2:41).[3] By 1861, when he consolidated his practice of the modern fable, Baudelaire abandoned good conscience as his narrator responds to beggars and other outcasts with cruelty, outrage, or cynicism. His anger (an ironic disguise and often hard to interpret) appears to outweigh his compassion.

There is no deeper tension in Baudelaire's mature work than the conflict of ethics and esthetics, and he grapples with a temperament driven by a powerful animus: "To glorify the worship of images (my great, my only, my primitive passion)" (*Mon coeur mis à nu,* JI, 94, 389–90nn.; *OC* 1:701). The poet feared that his enthrallment with formal grace would numb his humane concern. Despite his neurotic, self-destructive relationships, he cherished the possibility of ordinary love, while at the same time remaining driven by absolute values. A too "perfect idealization" (the phrase appears in "A Heroic Death" ["Une Mort héroïque," no. 27]) might deaden the artist's sympathy with others.

CONVERSION TO THE REAL

Baudelaire's "second revolution" integrates ethics and art. The thirty-two new poems—and especially the "Tableaux parisiens" (Parisian pictures)—added to the 1861 edition of *Les Fleurs du Mal* undermine the first edition's idealist thrust and depict a conversion to the world as it exists (Kaplan 1979).[4] Briefly stated, the first edition storms the gates of a transcendent kingdom, while the second sanctifies the finite. The three sonnets that conclude the 1857 edition—"La Mort des amants," "La Mort des pauvres," and "La Mort des artistes" (The death of lovers, The death of paupers, The death of artists)—recapitulate the journey toward immortality. The expanded 1861 closure introduces a crucial irony; "La Fin de la journée," "Le Rêve d'un curieux," and "Le Voyage" (The day's end, A curious man's dream, The voyage) reject dreams of afterdeath survival.

The initial and longest section, "Spleen et Idéal" (Spleen and Ideal), defines this conversion (Kaplan 1985, 108–14). The "Beauty Cycle" (poems numbered 17–21) can be read as a single experience which revises the philosophy of the whole. The 1857 sequence consisted of three allegorical sonnets, "La Beauté," "L'Idéal," and "La Géante" (Beauty, The Ideal, The giantess). The 1861 sequence is transformed by two major poems, "Le Masque" and "Hymne à la Beauté" (The mask, Hymn to Beauty), which denounce the idolatry enounced by the previous three.[5] The artist becomes a self-aware critic who replaces the transcendent with temporality.

"La Beauté" barricades the frontier and promotes the idealist standard. The Idol herself exclaims: "Je suis belle, ô mortels! comme un rêve de pierre" (I am beautiful, O mortals! like a dream of stone [line 1]). Beauty is a concept of which the artist can produce only a facsimile, "a *dream* of stone," while reenacting a tragic drama:

> Les poètes, devant mes grandes attitudes,
> . . . .
> Consumeront leurs jours en d'austères études
> (Lines 9–11)

(Poets, confronting my grandiose poses, . . . will consume their days in austere studies).

Artists can justify their sacrifice, since imagination can transform our perception of daily existence. Refracting the Ideal, Beauty's eyes are "De purs miroirs qui font toutes choses plus belles" (Pure mirrors which make all things more beautiful [line 13]). As "The Bad Glazier" insists with devastating irony, art should "make life [look] beautiful," *faire voir la vie en beau*, as it were, through rose-colored glass.

Then a momentous change occurs. "Le Masque," added in 1861, explodes the romantic heroism of "La Beauté," as the poet recovers reality. The poem interprets an exuberant and seductive sculpture by Ernest Christophe (to whom it is dedicated), which itself allegorizes the relationship between artifice and life. The female statue's body represents "the esthetic":

> Vois quel charme excitant la gentillesse donne!
> Approchons, et tournons autour de sa beauté
> (Lines 15–16)

> (See what stimulating magic her loveliness bestows! Let's go closer, and walk around her beauty.)

As he deliberately anatomizes his own adoration, the "critic" discovers "the mask" and translates the allegory. The drama pivots on lines 17–19, which compose one brief, but all the more striking stanza:

> O blasphème de l'art! ô surprise fatale!
> La femme au corps divin, promettant le bonheur,
> Par le haut se termine en monstre bicéphale!

> (O blasphemy of art! O fateful surprise! The woman of body divine, promising happiness, at the top becomes a two-headed monster!)

The woman's superhuman body renders even more grotesque the contradictory heads that become exposed. These two faces represent truth and falsehood. They have denied nature and its temporality, not simply embellished it. The shocked esthete recognizes the inevitable triumph of the finite.

The final section (lines 20–36) elaborates his conversion in three stages. The poet will denounce—and seemingly reject—the "lying mask" that conceals the suffering mortal. First, the woman's *real* self stands unveiled:

> La véritable tête et la sincère face
> Renversée à l'abri de la face qui ment.
> (Lines 23–24)

> (the true head and the sincere face tipped back and sheltered by the lying face)

He then identifies with her as a person, again repeating the word "beauty":

> Pauvre grande beauté! Le magnifique fleuve
> De tes pleurs aboutit dans mon coeur soucieux;

> Ton mensonge m'enivre, et mon âme s'abreuve
> Aux flots que la Douleur fait jaillir de tes yeux!
>
> (Lines 25–28)

(Great pitiful beauty! The magnificent river of your tears flows out into my anxious heart; your lie intoxicates me, and my soul slakes its thirst in the waves that Pain makes gush from your eyes!)

At the obvious thematic level—and it is of fundamental importance—the poet is roused by the woman's authentic grief. But a subtler problem arises when we try to interpret "Ton mensonge m'enivre." He is *enivré*—intoxicated or inspired—but by what? By her real inner struggle, by her pathetic attempt to mask her mortality? or by the *mensonge* itself, the "lie" of her exterior loveliness? Her "beauty" manifests her need to deny, or transcend, physical frailty. Does his imagination respond to her contradiction, her impotent denial which intensifies her suffering—in brief, from *compassion?* Or does his inspiration flow from a purely imaginative, and illusory, act of empathy—from *poetry?* This ambiguous *ivresse* will energize *The Parisian Prowler* from beginning to end.[6]

"Le Masque" might have ended here, but a third movement, comprising two stanzas of dialogue, completes his consent to the real. Unmasking the person does not suffice; we must understand her, as he asks: "—Mais pourquoi pleure-t-elle?" (But why does she weep?). The answer asserts a simple truth, the banality of which signals the poet's sincerity:

> —Elle pleure, insensé, parce qu'elle a vécu!
> Et parce qu'elle vit!
>
> (Lines 32–33)

(She weeps, mad one, because she has lived! and because she lives!)

Without any irony of qualification, the poet-critic celebrates the pathos of temporality. Disillusioned, and through a dialectical awareness of artistic illusion itself, the esthete embraces his human solidarity. The woman behind the mask is his "hypocrite lecteur," and of course "son semblable, son frère." This mature, reflective woman remains free of the ambivalence typical of his representations of idealized or frivolous females.

The famous "Hymne à la Beauté" which follows—also added in 1861—answers the "Beauty" sonnet more directly. It dwells upon art's ethical consequences as it reiterates the question:

> Viens-tu du ciel profond ou sors-tu de l'abîme,
> O Beauté
>
> (Lines 1–2)

> (Do you come from the deep sky or do you emerge from the abyss, O Beauty?)

The final two stanzas recapitulate the struggle. The penultimate one abandons the question of human justice and, provisionally, reaffirms the transcendent:

> Que tu viennes du ciel ou de l'enfer, qu'importe,
> O Beauté! monstre énorme, effrayant, ingénu!
> Si ton oeil, ton souris, ton pied, m'ouvrent la porte
> D'un Infini que j'aime et n'ai jamais connu?
>
> (Lines 21–24)

> (What does it matter whether you come from the heavens or from hell, O Beauty! monster enormous, frightening, innocent! if your eyes, your smile, your feet, open for me the door of an Infinite I love and have never known?)

This closure would typify the idealist 1857 edition, were it not for the final stanza which weds the esthetic quest to a moral imperative. Baudelaire's mature poetics subordinates the artist's anguished, unfulfilled desire to his solidarity with ordinary people:

> De Satan ou de Dieu, qu'importe! Ange ou Sirène,
> Qu'importe, si tu rends,—fée aux yeux de velours,
> Rhythme, parfum, lueur, ô mon unique reine!—
> L'univers moins hideux et les instants moins lourds?
>
> (Lines 25–28)

> (From Satan or from God, what does it matter! Angel or Siren, what does it matter, if you—velvet-eyed fairy, rhythm, perfume, light, O my only queen!—make the universe less hideous and time less oppressive?)

This presymbolist poetry, enriched with synesthesia—a confluence of music, odor, sight, and touch—preserves the Ideal within the world and renders mortality bearable. A nuanced ethics must surpass the simplistic dualism of good and evil, for these opposites are normally mixed, sometimes confused.[7] The "modern" artist still strives to redeem humanity, but his goal is modest, almost practical. Realistically speaking, Beauty can only alleviate anxiety or ennui—not cure it—as it sanctifies the possible.

Baudelaire's poems are far more subtle than his aphorisms, which retain the all-too-familiar dualistic formulas: "There are, in every person, all the time, two simultaneous postulations, one toward God, the other toward Satan" (*JI*, 62, 344–47). His concepts strained toward the notion of *simultaneity* without reaching it. His terminology, despite its affinity with Joseph de Maistre's theology of violence, remains more emotive than logical (Vouga 1957; Pachet 1976; Milner 1980). Wrestling with his experience in a necessarily imprecise vocabulary, in life as in writing, Baudelaire attempted, again and again, to mend these rifts, to become one: "Even as a child, I felt in my heart two contradictory feelings, the horror of life and the ecstasy of life" (*JI*, 96, 393–95). His Platonic, Catholic, and romantic polarities were unequal to the task.

AN ELUSIVE MANIFESTO

Baudelaire's 1862 dedication "To Arsène Houssaye," artistic editor of *La Presse*, which is normally reprinted as a guide to the subsequent collection, appears to refute my interpretive principle of unity. But the author did not include that deceptive proclamation in his handwritten table of contents, and a close analysis reveals the dedication itself to be a disguised parody of the genre: its message can be easily understood as a canny, ironic challenge addressed to a colleague whom he did not respect but needed to please (Chambers 1985; Monroe 1987, 95–101; cf. Wing 1986; Maclean 1988, 44).[8] Subversive self-contradictions emerge from the very beginning:

> My dear friend, I send you this little work of which it cannot be said, without injustice, that it has neither head nor tail, since, on the contrary, everything in it is both tail and head, alternatively and reciprocally. Consider, I beg you, what admirable convenience that combination offers us all, you, me, and the reader. We can cut wherever we want, I my reverie, you the manuscript, the reader his reading; for I do not bind the latter's recalcitrant will to the endless thread of a superfluous plot.

Baudelaire highlights the incompleteness of this inaugural series. How, at that point, could he predict their definitive conception? This "petit ouvrage . . . n'a ni queue ni tête, puisque tout, au contraire, y est à la fois tête et queue." The chiasmus *queue/ tête / tête/queue* connotes totality while the image itself opposes fragmentation to unity and suggests that each piece can be appreciated separately. Since each one is both tail and head, we must accept the collection as coherent. There is no "intrigue superflue," but there may be separate plots, or a unifying one. Whatever the case, readers should interpret them flexibly.

The imagery of segmentation derives from a traditional organic metaphor: the serpent. The author's jovial permission to "cut" cannot be completely in earnest: "Remove one vertebra, and the two pieces of that tortuous fantasy will reunite without difficulty. Chop it up into many fragments, and you will find that each one can exist separately. In the hope that some of those segments will be lively enough to please and to divert you, I dare dedicate to you the entire serpent." What author would encourage his editor to mutilate, or even surgically to excise portions of his manuscript? This was in fact the author's frustrating battle with Houssaye (CP1 2:263–64). Baudelaire waggishly elaborates conflicting metaphors, for his guiding idea is not one of disorder and irreconcilable separation but that of relative autonomy. Sparring with an authority he knew to be literal-minded, Baudelaire rejects a "*superfluous* plot" while maintaining the possibility of a sustained development (the hierarchical entity of head and tail).

An astute reader (unlike Houssaye) could restore these parts, if severed, to their rightful place within a larger, though serpentine, construction (De George 1973; Wright and Scott 1984). In the last analysis, however, this discussion is trite. Just as single poems in a collection—such as Scève's *Délie*, Ronsard's *Les Amours*, Hugo's *Les Contemplations*, and *Les Fleurs du Mal* —can be read individually or as stages of a spiritual itinerary, so *The Parisian Prowler* can mark a journey of initiation or comprise discrete experiences which readers might synthesize or not according to their concerns.

The remaining four paragraphs stress, with a playful irony, the author's originality. Baudelaire's rhetorical modesty, unanswered questions, self-deprecatory comparisons, and italics all express his pride. First he "confesses" that his project was inspired by a model: "the famous *Gaspard de la nuit* of Aloysius Bertrand (a book known to you, to me and to some of our friends, does it not have every right to be called *famous?*)." He overpraises Bertrand's commercially unsuccessful book, while the italicized "*fameux*" (which also implies "infamous") implicitly carves out the differences. Bertrand claimed to be inspired by engravings by Callot and Rembrandt, whereas Baudelaire evokes "modern life, or rather *one* modern and abstract life" in Second Empire Paris. The systematically self-aware critic exercises a far bolder ambition.

Formalistic notions of genre have only recently confirmed Baudelaire's true innovation.[9] His oft-cited definition of "poetic prose" plays only a minor role in the dedication and simply adapts conventional views of romantic lyricism: "Which of us has not, in his ambitious days, dreamed of the miracle of a poetic prose, musical without rhythm and without rhyme, supple enough and choppy enough to fit the soul's lyrical movements, the undulations of reverie, the jolts of consciousness?" It is not this "miracle of a poetic prose" that constitutes an "absolute beginning." Could not Rousseau, Chateaubriand, and Michelet, for example, better serve as models? More significantly, Baudelaire transported the lyrical narrative from nature to the city: "This obsessive ideal [of the prose poem] came to life above all in frequenting enormous cities, in the intersection of their countless relationships." The urban poet is both exemplar and theoretician of the modern self.

The two final paragraphs (surreptitiously) take aim at the main target, Houssaye himself. Baudelaire contrasts his malicious fable "The Bad Glazier" with his editor's crudely didactic anecdote, "The Glazier's Song" ("La Chanson du vitrier"), which illustrates a "democratic" reconciliation of a poor man and a poet.[10] Baudelaire pretends to admire Houssaye's effort to compose verbal music, a "poetic" idealization, from the humble artisan's "strident cry," its "prosaic" reality. He does not state that Houssaye's text only reproduces sentimental commonplaces and democratic propaganda. Nor would his postutopian prowler ever replace poetry with *une chanson,* popular ditties. Read in Erasmian tradition as "paradoxical praise," Baudelaire's compliments translate into a mockery of mediocre writing unredeemed by its lofty intentions.[11]

Baudelaire repudiates both didacticism and imitation, obliquely asserting his pride at *not* "executing *exactly* [his italics] what he planned to do." He had deliberately "remained quite far from his mysterious and brilliant model," Bertrand's *Gaspard de la nuit.* The final line of "Le Voyage" (The voyage), the final poem of the 1861 *Fleurs du Mal,* dramatizes his commitment to innovation above all: "Au fond de l'Inconnu pour trouver du *nouveau!*" (Into the depths of the Unknown to find the *new!*).[12] Quite earlier, in "Exposition universelle" (1855), Baudelaire had associated himself with Delacroix's "quality *sui generis,* indefinable and defining this century's melancholy and fervent aspect, something completely new, which makes him a unique artist, without progenitor, without precedent, probably without a successor" (*OC* 2:596–97, the final sentence). Without knowing it, Baudelaire had announced his modern fables.

BEYOND BINARY OPPOSITIONS

"The Thyrsus" (no. 32) states a theory of the Baudelairean "prose poem" more appropriately than his "dedication" to Houssaye. Commentators have differed on their interpretation of this "theoretical fable," which reflects on its own status as literature.[13] The text begins as a meditation on a caduseus (a wand or baton) entwined with flowers, which then generates an extended metaphor of multiple polarities: "What is a thyrsus? According to its social and poetic meaning, it is a sacerdotal emblem to be held by priests and priestesses celebrating the divinity whose interpreters and servants they are. But physically it is only a staff, a mere staff, a vine pole for hops, a vine support, dry, hard, and straight."[14] These ideas are not extraordinary, for any work can both mimetically represent experience and translate the story into a message, "le sens moral et poétique." But Baudelaire stresses the *combination* of "prosaic" and "poetic" elements, the interweaving of shapes, colors, and scents, which exercises a mysterious seduction—like "a mystical fandango executed around the hieratic staff."

Baudelaire further tangles the web of dualistic categories as he formulates a confluence of opposites. Interpreters should preserve the genre's integrity by applying the chemist's notion of "amalgam."[15] Baudelaire's dedication of this piece to Franz Liszt, whom he truly admired, announces his most advanced conception:

> The thyrsus is the representation of your astonishing duality, powerful and venerable master, dear Bacchant of mysterious and impassioned Beauty. . . .
>
> The staff, it is your will, straight, firm, and unshakable; the flowers, the rambling of your fancy around your will; the feminine element executing around the male its prodigious pirouettes. Straight line and arabesque line, intention and expression, tautness of the will, sinuosity of the word, unity of goal, variety of means, all-powerful and indivisible amalgam of genius, what analyst would have the hateful courage to divide and to separate you?

The rhetorical question leaves in suspense the possibility—or advisability—of destroying his prose poems' organic unity. A critic must possess a "détestable courage" in order to dis-integrate their "amalgame tout-puissant de génie" and abstract its bisexual vitality. Form is not separable from content nor can concepts replace their concrete (or allegorical) representations. Interpreters must respect the opposing elements without immobilizing their productive tensions.

Binary oppositions can distract us from the strict, condensed structure of the whole which prepares a "total effect." Baudelaire's "amalgam theory" justifies our label "fables of modern life," a plausible model of which appears in his 1857 "New Notes on Edgar Poe" (cf. Fairlie 1967). The jolts and shocks which had so impressed Walter Benjamin fit into a rigorous plan: "If the first sentence is not written in order to prepare that final impression, the work fails from the very beginning" (*OC* 2:329–30). The narrator gains in his ability to wear many masks: "the author of a short story has a multitude of tones at his disposal, nuances of language, a reasonable tone, sarcasm, humor, repudiated by poetry, and which are like dissonances, attacks against the idea of pure beauty" (*OC* 2:329–30). Both Baudelaire and Poe capture the complex dynamics of consciousness.

THE YEARNING FOR DIALOGUE

The Parisian Prowler in fact opens, not with lyrical excursions, but with two brief, prosaic fables—"The Stranger" and "The Old Woman's Despair" ("L'Etranger," "Le Désespoir de la vieille")—which form a "diptych." It is highly significant that the definitive collection of fifty retains, with their original numbering, the four series of prose poems printed in 1862 for *La Presse*. Their central characters—two outsiders, a man and a woman—establish the conflict between fantasy and reality which will consistently direct the narrator's adventures (See Kopp, 188; Guisan 1948; Metzidakis 1986, for careful studies of the symmetries). Both seek to alleviate their anguish, the one through daydreaming, the other through affectionate gestures. The "enigmatic man" of the first and the "good decrepit woman" of the second speak through the *flâneur* who begins *his* journey through them.

The stranger who lends the first fable its name is a sort of nineteenth-century Meursault, Camus's model of alienation. The narrator asks him basic questions, as might a psychotherapist who probes a patient's life history. The odyssey opens by defining a normal person's sources of being:

> "Tell me, whom do you love the most, you enigmatic man? your father, your mother, your sister, or your brother?"
>
> "I have neither father, nor mother, nor sister, nor brother."
>
> "Your friends?"
>
> "There you use a word whose meaning until now has remained to me unknown."
>
> "Your fatherland?"
>
> "I am unaware in what latitude it lies."
>
> "Beauty?"
>
> "I would willingly love her, goddess and immortal."
>
> "Gold?"
>
> "I hate it as you hate God."
>
> "So! Then what do you love, you extraordinary stranger?"
>
> "I love clouds... drifting clouds... there... over there... marvelous clouds!"

The interviewer wants to discuss love, but the stranger refuses to concede any common ground to him. He addresses him with the familiar *tu* while the other, denying any middle-class values, will not reciprocate. The stranger is indeed estranged from God, family, and country—the conventional treasures of bourgeois society. They do not really speak, just swap words.

The stranger mirrors the narrator who, in future guises, longs to participate in a community as a citizen or as an artist. He is the prototypical victim of ennui, a pathological deadening of emotion and will, the "delicate monster" leading us to despair, which threatens the narrator from beginning to end.[16] The stranger appears as an orphan who has renounced his yearning for companionship and repressed all memories, traces of the past with which he might construct a solid identity, while his apathy anesthetizes the pain of unsatisfied yearnings. This unknowable person dreams, not to foster desire, but crudely to evade reality. As he "spaces out," constantly mobile reveries waft him away from others—and from himself.

But the stranger's bleak refusals cannot bury his attachment to love. Other things being equal, he *would* pursue Beauty: "Je l'aimerais volontiers, déesse et immortelle." His use of the conditional tense does not deny a commitment to esthetic perfection. Then why does he separate this spiritual search from community values? Understandably, he repudiates the tainted (and elusive!) security of money as he equates cupidity with official religion, echoing the prophetic warning against identifying God and Mammon. His uncompromising standard of truth and beauty renders all prevailing institutions untenable.

How do we understand the stranger's final response, launching his mind into the emptiness of suspension points...? The narrator had first perceived him as "enigmatic"; he now becomes "extraordinary"—the epithet shifting from bafflement to (an ironic?) admiration. At the end, the stranger's self becomes, in Baudelaire's terms, "vaporized";[17] as Kierkegaard (1954, 164) explains: "So when feeling becomes fantastic, the self is simply volatilized more and more, at last becoming a sort of abstract sentimentality which is so inhuman that it does not apply to any person" (*The Sickness Unto Death*). Reverie relishes its narcissistic plunge into the mind's inner spaces. Nevertheless, the *esthetic stranger* (for that is what he represents) has only temporarily eluded the Other, who summons love's absence. He still dwells with ennui.

The female outsider of "The Old Woman's Despair," quite the contrary, attempts to make tender contact; she is the collection's *ethical stranger*. She too is thwarted—not by her own, voluntary aloofness but by her body. Contradicting the fierce misogyny of later fables, the narrator displays his sympathy for this female victim of time, another little old lady of "Tableaux parisiens."[18] Sweet and lonely, she seeks reciprocal affection and symmetrically contradicts the male outsider's disclaimer, in the first fable, of companionship.

> The shriveled little old woman felt quite delighted when she saw the pretty baby whom everyone was entertaining, and whom everyone was trying to please; a pretty creature, as fragile as she, the little old woman, and, like her as well, toothless and without hair.
>
> And she went up to him, trying to make little smiles and pleasant faces at him.
>
> But the terrified child struggled under the kind decrepit woman's caresses, and filled the house with his yelpings.
>
> Then the kind old woman withdrew into her eternal solitude, and she wept alone in a corner, saying to herself, "Ah, for us, unfortunate old females that we are, the age of pleasing has passed, even innocent creatures; and we disgust little children we try to love!"

The kinship of these vulnerable persons, aged and infant, at the beginning and the decline of life, is ironic, and the narrator repeatedly associates her tenderness with her age. She is "la petite vieille ratatinée," "la petite vieille," "la bonne femme décrépite," and "la bonne vieille." Baby and hag are both toothless and bald, but what is attractive in one renders the other repulsive. Beauty is relative, and the "innocent" baby has not yet learned that he has no reason to fear the old woman's smiles.

The narrator states his compassion for her "solitude éternelle"; the adjective labels her estrangement as absolute, essential to her being. And so she views herself as a puppet of biological destiny, one of a multitude of pariahs: "malheureuses vieilles femelles." Aged women, discarded by the young who perceive only exterior and transient loveliness, enter a subhuman category. Woman's superficial "gift of pleasing" is all too fragile. [19]

This tension between ethical pathos versus a compelling passion for ideal Beauty energizes the entire collection: conflicts between fantasy and reality, mental versus social space, innocence versus evil. The rigorously dialectical organization of "The Old Woman's Despair" anticipates many other pieces, and its "pivotal sentence" (Robert Kopp's term)—"But the terrified child . . ."—is the first of several brutal proxies for "the world," which will burst into a dream. Usually the narrator hides his compassion under rude poses. The male "stranger" might represent a positive model of the dandy—were it not for the journalist-narrator's deliberate probing of his intimate aspirations.[20] This diptych, which draws the lines of battle, defines the two strands of "esthetic" and "ethical" fables interwoven throughout *The Parisian Prowler*. See appendix 1.

2

FABLES OF THE HUMAN CONDITION

Dualities and Tragic Courage

The narrator takes center stage in the next, more elaborate fables. Interpretation becomes their primary focus as he explores questions of imagination and its relation to daily life. "The Artist's *Confiteor*," "A Joker," "The Double Room," and "To Each His Chimera" ("Le *Confiteor* de l'artiste," "Un Plaisant," "La Chambre double," "Chacun sa chimère," nos. 3–6) all feature a wandering male of artistic temperament who plays out a dualistic conception of the human condition. Individuals are divided antagonistically between mind and matter, spirit and body, good and evil.[1] Art and the city become parallel means of integrating them.

Although this dialectic comprises the collection's thematic frame, Baudelaire does not represent Christian faith. His sensibility is Catholic—especially his vulnerable receptivity to sin and pain—but he replaces church with art, priest with poet: writing, not liturgy, is his spiritual discipline. Nowhere does the redemptive Christ appear, and his narrator, resolutely alone, desperately strives to harmonize his intractable inner conflicts. Outside reality intrudes even more significantly as the alienated Parisian faces life as it was experienced (by intellectuals) after 1851, the Second Empire of "Napoléon-le-petit."

The narrator's multiple voices have a Socratic function: to jar the reader's habitual assumptions and to provoke self-scrutiny. Often his positions are outrageously immoral and cruel, and, like the Athenian, the Parisian prowler may feign foolishness or malice in order to engage us in dialogue, emulating, perhaps,

Thomas De Quincey, who "converses *more socratico* with all the human beings . . . that chance might throw onto his path" (*OC* 1:456). Interpreters can penetrate these masks by examining how adjacent fables reiterate themes, first in a tragic mode and then as parody—an approach we began in chapter 1. The comparison, by pairs, of fables 1–11 reveals their ethical consistency.

ART'S TRAGIC BOUNDARIES

The narrator's religion of art first emerges from a dramatic declaration and then from a comic parable of urban life. The famous "Artist's *Confiteor*" (no. 3) suggests, by its very title, a metaphysical commitment. The experience does include a confession, but not one in which a penitent humbly begs God for forgiveness. Baudelaire had analyzed the moral ambiguity of expanded consciousness in *The Artificial Paradises:* "The craving for the infinite," he warns us in the first section of "The Poem of Hashish," is "quasi-paradoxical," since it can direct desire in opposite directions, one demonic, the other benign (*OC* 1:401–404). A rigorously dialectical structure typifies the schema of these early fables.

"The Artist's *Confiteor*" wields the two-edged sword of imagination, illustrating the contradictory extremes of esthetic intensity—expansion and concentration—considered to be the heartbeat of Baudelaire's sensibility. Its four paragraphs give equal space to two antithetical movements. The first two paragraphs elaborate an ecstasy which appears to continue the stranger's escapist reveries:

> How penetrating are the ends of autumn days! Ah! penetrating to the verge of pain! For there are certain delicious sensations whose vagueness does not exclude intensity; and there is no sharper point than Infinity.
>
> Sheer delight to drown one's gaze in the immensity of sky and sea! Solitude, silence, incomparable chastity of the azure! a small sail trembling on the horizon, and whose smallness and isolation imitate my irremediable existence, monotonous melody of the

> swell—all these things think through me, or I think through them (for in the grandeur of reverie, the *self* is quickly lost!). They think, I say, but musically and pictorially, without quibblings, without syllogisms, without deductions.

The initial exclamations express a state of intensified awareness, as the dreaming self transcends space and time, loses its separateness, and plunges into the Infinite. (The capitalization denotes reverie's full spiritual potential.) Autumn, of course, was the inspirational season of early romanticism, and the modern poet renews the tradition. "Chant d'automne" and "Sonnet d'automne" (Autumn song, Autumn sonnet [*FM*, nos. 56 and 64]) relish the peculiar seduction of that moment of death and vanishing love. The "poetic" prose explodes with feelings of boundless possibility while, at the same time, and surprisingly, evaluating their painful result.

These paragraphs subtly mix ecstatic lyricism and self-analysis. The exaggerated tone prepares the dreamer's confession of fear for his liberated self. Several contradictions raise questions. How can immensity come to a sharp point? Can fantasies of open space focus and concentrate sensations? Why is this pain delicious?

The second, more complex paragraph analyzes this harmony of mental states that customarily exclude one another. A vision, comparable to the one evoked in "The Poem of Hashish," transcends the ordinary dualism of subject and object.[2] Ecstasy includes explosion and implosion, as the fantastical self both melts into the Infinite and concentrates itself back upon itself. Paradoxically, this surrender of separateness realizes the ego's greatest fullness: "toutes ces choses pensent par moi, ou je pense par elles (car dans la grandeur de la rêverie, le *moi* se perd vite!)."

Two contrary types of poetic inspiration arise. The positive one is the "pathetic fallacy" of romanticism, when the dreamer projects his feelings into the surrounding landscape and attributes self-awareness to "our friends the vegetables"—as Baudelaire waggishly called nature. An exchange of subjectivity takes place as the animate world observes the poet. Imagination converts its brute otherness into a kindred spirit, realizing the utopic reciprocity of "Correspondances":

> L'homme y passe à travers des forêts de symboles
> Qui l'observent avec des regards familiers
> (*FM*, no. 4 in both the 1857 and 1861 editions, lines 3–4)

> (Man passes through [nature] as across forests of symbols which observe him with familiar looks)

The second, negative, condition returns the dreamer to his finite and true self.

Both paragraphs prepare the critique that follows. The rich imagery of these rhythmical evocations counterbalances—but does not overrule—the narrator's skeptical self-scrutiny. Reverie is "bliss" (*grand délice*) because it realizes a narcissistic plenitude. It feels like a mystic union, "noyé . . . dans l'immensité du ciel et de la mer!" But even within the womblike symbiosis of spectator and spectacle, the pangs of loneliness increase. A delicate, though discordant, image emerges from inchoate vastness, a little boat which the narrator interprets—within the text—as an allegory of his true condition: "une petite voile frisonnante à l'horizon, et qui par sa petitesse et son isolement imite mon irrémédiable existence." His skiff is no longer the bold "three-mast schooner seeking its Icarie" of "Le Voyage," the heroic final poem of *Les Fleurs du Mal* (line 33; an allusion to the utopia of Etienne Cabet). The abandoned dreamer persists, despite his precarious autonomy, in traveling.

At the text's exact middle, an antithetical "However" returns us to earthly thinking. The final two paragraphs question the permanence, and the validity, of such boundless freedom. The ecstasy finally dissolves, for it finds no home:

> However, these thoughts, whether they emerge from me or spring from things, soon grow too intense. The force of voluptuous pleasure creates uneasiness and concrete suffering. Then my excessively taut nerves produce nothing but shrill and painful vibrations.
>
> And now the sky's depth fills me with dismay; its limpidity

> exasperates me. The sea's insensitivity, the scene's immutability appall me... Ah! must we suffer eternally, or else eternally flee the beautiful? Nature, sorceress without mercy, ever victorious rival, let me be! Stop tempting my desires and my pride! Studying the beautiful is a duel in which the artist shrieks with fright before being defeated.

The dreamer is not naive; he confronts imagination's limits because he is both "philosopher" and "artist," like Liszt and Richard Wagner (*OC* 2:782–83). First, he examines the complex makeup of his feelings of transcendence in order objectively, like a phenomenologist, to assess their genesis: "ces pensées, qu'elles sortent de moi ou s'élancent des choses." During the rapture, however, he cannot evaluate, for he has lost the anchor of his own subjectivity; he can no longer differentiate his mind from its products. Moreover, he has lost his free will—the absolute standard of Baudelaire's vision of being human. Reverie or ecstasy cannot become a way of life.

Here, and throughout these adventures of consciousness, the word *volupté* and its synonyms are ambiguous. The very joys of idealization subvert realistic thinking; sublime nature excites his fantasies but excludes companionship. "L'énergie dans la volupté" (the term stresses the visceral hedonism of inwardness) only highlights the world's otherness, when he loses his ecstatic projections: "L'insensibilité de la mer, l'immutabilité du spectacle, me révoltent." He returns to his own finitude and acute isolation.[3]

The narrator himself states the fable's allegorical import after the suspension points. Exclaiming "Ah!" he formulates an either/or alternative: suffer or flee beauty. The repeated adverb *éternellement*—and the chiasmus which magnifies it—insist that he can never include both. This artist confesses his arrogant competition with nature—a doomed rivalry, for the creature can never match God the Creator. Yet he stubbornly preserves his pride and desire (after all, a necessary self-assertion), and continues to challenge his "rivale toujours victorieuse." Art demands absolute self-sacrifice. The final sentence translates the opposition:

"L'étude du beau est un duel où l'artiste crie de frayeur avant d'être vaincu."

This audacious profession of faith, however, this quest for the Ideal, is not a divine comedy, in which the inspired poet inevitably scales the mountain of Redemption. The artist's "cri de frayeur" defies clear interpretation despite the gnomic formula. Does it signify the self's defeat or a heroic victory? This first fable devoted explicitly to the artist refines "Les Phares" (Beacons [*FM*, no. 6 in both the 1857 and 1861 editions]), at the end of which a "burning sob" symbolizes mankind's tragic contradiction —infinite desire bounded by death:

> Car c'est vraiment, Seigneur, le meilleur témoignage
> Que nous puissions donner de notre dignité
> Que cet ardent sanglot qui roule d'âge en âge
> Et vient mourir au bord de votre éternité!
>
> (Lines 41–44)

> (Because art is truly, O Lord, the best testimony that we can give of our dignity, [art] is a burning sob which rolls from age to age and arrives dying at the threshhold of your eternity!)

The Promethean artist of the "*Confiteor*" engages the Absolute in a duel, shouting, not succumbing in an introverted "ardent sanglot." He has not entrusted himself, with humility and resignation, to God's otherness. Recognizing that desire dies at the frontier, he will not for that reason relinquish his campaign to equal the Creator. He courageously maintains, simultaneously, despair and his modern hubris.

If we discard the tragic model, the ending of this "*Confiteor*" makes both more and less sense. The idealist duel is futile, not only because the goal remains transcendent, but especially because its premises are wrong. The concept of perfection can never be concretely rendered; the disparity between mind and nature is a necessary—and banal—fact.

As early as his "Salon of 1846," indeed, Baudelaire had sidestepped this futile competition between "The Ideal and the Model" (the title of section 8): "The drawing is a battle between nature and the artist, in which the artist will triumph more easily when he better understands nature's intentions. He must not copy, but interpret in a simpler and more luminous language" (*OC* 2:457). An original work of art is not a direct challenge to God, but a parallel creation, engendered by a person's temperament. Baudelaire's model of the romantic artist—Eugène Delacroix—anticipates the covert wisdom of this "*Confiteor*": "a painting should above all reproduce the artist's intimate thought, which dominates the model, as the creator his creation" (*OC* 2:433).

The brief anecdote which follows, "A Joker" (no. 4), appears by comparison to be a trivial transition piece. But it is rich in significance when interpreted in relation to its majestic prelude. The French title is ambiguous, for a *plaisant* could be someone who plays pranks or (more rarely) someone who gives pleasure. This ambiguity suggests two contradictory functions of art: (1) superficial entertainment as escape, a denial of moral responsibility; or (2) appropriate idealization, enhancement of life through fabricated beauty—an essentially ethical commitment.[4] Here the narrator witnesses a perversion of art.

The first two paragraphs imitate the dialectical structure of the "*Confiteor*" as they juxtapose intense emotion to sordid fact. The setting, this time, is not a cosmic reverie but contemporary (i.e., Second Empire) Paris: "It was the New Year's Eve explosion: chaos of mud and snow, crisscrossed by a thousand carriages, glittering with toys and candy, swarming with cupidities and despairs, official big city dementia fashioned to disturb the brain of the most steadfast solitary." The narrator, proclaiming himself to be a "solitaire le plus fort," becomes a critic who anatomizes the ecstasy. He scorns festivities which crudely evade anguish, as thoughtless citizens surrender to the "délire officiel d'une grande ville." The word "official" underlines the emptiness of this collective intoxication (or madness).

The fable's moral thrust becomes explicit, as the stroller caricatures an "artist" who further degrades the fun, which at least diverts the multitudes. This rich and pretentious dandy, who corrupts esthetic grace, inflicts a stupid trick upon a beast of burden:

> Amidst this hubbub and racket, a donkey was trotting briskly along, pestered by a lout armed with a whip.
>
> Just as the donkey was about to turn a sidewalk corner, a handsome gloved gentleman, polished, cruelly cravated and imprisoned in brand-new clothes, bowed obsequiously to the humble beast, and said to him, as he raised his hat, "I wish you a good and happy one!" then turned with a fatuous look toward some companions or other, as if requesting them to add their approval to his conceit.
>
> The donkey did not see that fine joker [*ce beau plaisant*], and continued zealously to rush along where his duty called him.

The story might end here, its "moral" only suggested by the sarcasm. The repeated adjective *beau* characterizes the joker as "handsome"—but also, antithetically, a "fine sort." Without any irony, however, the narrator admires the donkey who "zealously" fulfills its "duty" and who notices nothing. The human being, for his part, vain and artificial, insults this loyal worker persecuted by "un malotru."

Then the fable's momentous coda replaces irony with outrage. For the first time in the sequence, the narrator abolishes his distance from the event. His previously disguised moral passion now bursts forth: "As for me, suddenly I was seized with an incommensurable rage against that magnificent imbecile, who for me concentrated in himself the very essence of France's wit." The final oxymoron—"ce magnifique imbécile"—reinforces the ironic undertones of "un beau monsieur," "ce beau plaisant," which had more gently admonished him. Dignity, like beauty, is sacred, as the deftly repeated adjectives insist.

This simple sketch should alert us to the irony of all fables whose endings remain frustratingly ambiguous. "A Joker" gives readers permission to read them Socratically. The narrator's frontal attack against the nation's idiotic "wit," its self-satisfaction, reinforces his defense of truth. Yet the narrator will continue to conceal his respect for ordinary people at toil, and in some later fables, he will even act as "un malotru armé d'un fouet." These initial stories make clear, however, that he is *not* a wealthy and cynical dandy, enthralled with himself, but a lone *flâneur* who, masked as a cynic, strives to become like Baudelaire's "poets and philosophers [who] have regenerated [their] soul by consistent work and contemplation; by the assiduous training of the will and the permanent nobility of intention" (*OC* 1:441, final page).

ACCEPTING THE EVERYDAY

The next two fables are among the most famous anthology pieces. As explicitly allegorical as the preceding ones, "The Double Room" and "To Each His Chimera" (nos. 5 and 6) define the artist's inescapable responsibilities. The first one, considered to be a personal confession, echoes "Rêve parisien" (Parisian dream [added in 1861 to *FM*, no. 102]), which also evokes a writer's flights from creditors and journalistic deadlines (Kopp, 195–201). But "The Double Room" most graphically illustrates mankind's pull toward autonomous imagination, Baudelaire's "double postulation" of action and intention.[5]

Quite predictably, the text can be divided into two equal parts. Part 1 (lines 1–46 of the Kopp edition) elaborates a presurrealistic metamorphosis of the poet's living quarters; part 2 (lines 47–91) depicts the dread awakening. Its full development rigorously juxtaposes imagined and realistic images, combining lyricism and self-analysis. The writer's "double room" is an urban space corresponding to the cosmos which had provoked the utopian voyage in "The Artist's *Confiteor*" (no. 3). The opening sentence (a noun phrase, without a verb) equates the room with mental processes and places us firmly within the mind:

> A room that resembles a reverie, a truly *spiritual* room, where the stagnant atmosphere is lightly tinged with pink and blue.
>
> Here the soul takes a bath of laziness, perfumed with regret and desire. —Something like twilight, bluish and pinkish; a dream of voluptuous pleasure during an eclipse.

Paragraph 2 begins the plunge into a delicious inwardness. Thought detaches itself from perception and relinquishes the voluntary control of reason. Passivity prevails as the dreamer enjoys "un bain de paresse." (The word *paresse,* like *volupté,* signals a state of inebriation, the free self swimming within itself.) The ego again melts: "in the grandeur of reverie, the *self* is quickly lost!" (no. 3). The double room is both *like* a reverie and a *truly* spiritual space, since it actually transforms perception. We now witness a perfected Baudelairean "delight": an all-enveloping harmony of sight and odor which evokes exquisite memories spiced with sadness. The self begins to reign at the center of its mental universe.

The narrator-dreamer revels in his plenitude, but, in a simultaneous critical act, he betrays its ambiguity. Traces of external reality contaminate the ecstasy. The self is not as utterly free as it feels. The atmosphere of the "chambre véritablement *spirituelle*" was stagnant, and a poignant yearning tugs consciousness back into the past. The confluence of senses—his synesthesia—so stimulating to reverie, retains a prospective/retrospective tension, "aromatisé par le regret et le désir." Even the rarefied dream becomes sullied. The chiasmus—"rose et bleu" (line 3) / "de bleuâtre et de rosâtre" (line 6)—forcefully compromises its purity: *rose* and *bleu,* which connote mystical joy, become downgraded to *bleuâtre* and *rosâtre* in this twilight state.[6]

Nevertheless, imagination remains free in this transition between reverie and hallucination. Objects take the initiative in the dream room described next. We are reminded of the melted watches in some of Salvador Dali's landscapes, Baudelaire's rhapsodic art criticism, and of course his evocations of drugged visions:[7] "The furniture has elongated, collapsed, languid shapes. The furniture seems to be dreaming; you might say endowed with a somnambular life, like vegetables and minerals. The fabrics speak a silent language, like flowers, like skies, like setting suns." Rhythmical repetitions underscore the "poetic" (that is, the conventionally subjective) quality of this consciousness. The narrator is like the dreamer of "Elevation" (*FM,* no. 3 in both editions), an esoteric sage who deciphers "le langage des fleurs et des choses muettes" (the language of flowers and of silent things [final line of "Elévation," which precedes the famous sonnet "Correspondances"]). The animal, vegetable, and mineral realms join in harmony, as synthetic imagination realizes their vivid associations. The "setting suns," with tender melancholy, evoke a poetry of days gone by.

The following two paragraphs of "The Double Room" convey Baudelaire's most advanced theory of imaginative autonomy. An extraordinary melding of images rises above imagery itself; the dreamer envisages the possibility of a completely abstract painting, though he does not specify its nonrepresentational content:

> No artistic abomination on the walls. Compared to pure dream, to unanalyzed impressions, a precise art, a concrete art, is blasphemy. Everything here possesses the abundant light and delicious darkness of harmony.
>
> An infinitesimal scent of the most exquisite choice, mingled with the lightest wetness, swims in that atmosphere, where the drowsy mind is lulled by hothouse sensations.

Why does the dreamer so brusquely denounce ordinary realistic painting, "l'art défini, l'art positif"? The religious terms "abomination" and "blasphemy" announce an absolute value, for pure art might be compromised by its sensory connection with daily life. Although sights and smells achieve great refinement, the slight dampness he feels within this artificial atmosphere ("des sensations de serre chaude") reinforces previous hints that a troublesome admixture of matter still clings to the ideal.

The narrator then introduces his most pervasive emblem of art: the female Idol. She is an awesome mediator, here appearing in paragraph 6, as we approach the finale of part 1. The dreamer's expanded mind now faces the incarnation of his Ideal. The meeting of these two allegorical figures is an icon of the artist's dualistic universe:

> Muslin rains abundantly over the windows and before the bed; it pours in snowy waterfalls. On this bed lies the Idol, the sovereign queen of dreams. But how did she get here? Who brought

> her? What magic power settled her onto this throne of reverie and voluptuousness? What difference does it make? Here she is and I recognize her!
>
> These indeed are the eyes whose flame pierces the twilight; those subtle and terrifying *peepers*, which I recognize by their frightful malice! They attract, they subjugate, they devour the gaze of anyone reckless enough to contemplate them. I have often studied them, those black stars summoning curiosity and admiration.

This postromantic fable radically revises the idealist (1857) *Fleurs du Mal* and anatomizes its lyrical enthusiasm. The admirer stealthily subverts his hommage. He does not kneel before "la souveraine des rêves," as would a loyal subject, and the italicized slang term *mirettes* carves out his ironic distance.[8] Are the Idol's eyes truly "spiritual," as in the final line of the sonnet "La Beauté" (Beauty [*FM*, no. 17]): "Mes yeux, mes larges yeux aux clartés éternelles" (My eyes, my vast eyes, with their eternal light)? or do they deceive? He is bedazzled, but immediately inquires how she arrived. Skepticism overrides awe.

The next two paragraphs celebrate the transcendent world and appear to overcome the foregoing reservations. The narrative continues by advancing the value of those windows of the soul, from "eyes" to "peepers" to "black stars." Ecstasy reaches the perfection of "béatitude," a religious hyperbole, and another Baudelairean synonym for *volupté*—both conveying emotional plenitude. Part 1 ends with an inward victory:

> What benevolent demon has thus surrounded me with mystery, silence, peace, and aromas? O beatitude! What we usually call life, even in its most favorable expansion, has nothing in common with this supreme life of which I am now conscious, and which I relish minute by minute, second by second!
>
> No! There are no more minutes, there are no more seconds! Time has disappeared. Eternity now reigns, an eternity of delights!

The ecstatic self experiences the present as absolute duration. Ultimate esthetic pleasure feels as if it were truly supernatural, a gift from "un démon bienveillant." The mind, during such moments, discovers its sharpest focus, as it had at the beginning of "The Artist's *Confiteor.*" Self-consciousness intensifies the senses and realizes "cette vie suprême dont j'ai maintenant connaissance et que je savoure minute par minute." The intellect observes how imagination abolishes time by its acuity, "une éternité de délices!"

Yet at that very moment the idealization collapses. It is characteristic of Baudelaire's modern fables for a restrictive conjunction —this time "But"—to obliterate the utopia. Daily responsibilities invade:

> But then an awful, heavy knock resounded on the door, and, just like in a bedeviled dream, I felt a pickax strike me in the stomach.
>
> And then a Specter entered. He is a bailiff come to torture me in the name of the law; a loathsome concubine come to bemoan her poverty and adding the trivialities of her life to the sorrows of mine; or even a newspaper editor's errandboy calling for the manuscript's next installment.

The woman disappears when the pressing world returns. We learn, for the first time, that the narrator is a writer (with overdue manuscripts!). Significantly, he is violently reminded of his stomach, the organ of our most primitive dependencies. The male Specter embodies his obligations to people like debt collectors, his frustrated mistress, and the deadlines of journalism that allows him the semblance of a living.

This parallel summarizes the obvious: "The paradisiacal room, the idol [*now lowercase*], the sovereign queen of dreams, the *Sylphid,* as the big René used to say, all that magic disappeared at the Specter's brutal blow." Baudelaire definitively rejects the "chimeras" of Chateaubriand's protoromantic adolescent, the "little René," and the stylistic symmetries of "The Double Room" deliberately reinforce this demolition. Now he confronts the inescapable dread ("l'horreur") of daily existence. The "realistic" description which follows contains the same number of lines (in the Kopp edition) as the "magic" one and retranslates the décor point by point. The broken cheap furniture replaces the fluid, self-conscious phantoms; the cold hearth abolishes its former comfort and intimacy; the dirty windows deny the potentials of gazing into the Infinite; the incomplete manuscripts and datebook testify to the writer's inhibitions.

The extended metaphor of imagination as a *chambre double* contracts into the "narrow world" of consciousness constrained. Mankind's antagonistic duality is condensed in the opposition "une éternité de délices!" (line 46) and "ce séjour de l'éternel ennui" (line 61). Ecstasy has metamorphosed into despair; "délices" has become "désolation" (line 71). A disgusting olfactory antithesis explains the lesson: "And that scent of another world, which I used to intoxicate myself with a perfected sensitivity, alas! it was replaced by a fetid odor of tobacco mixed with some sort of nauseating mustiness. Now you breathe a rancid smell of destitution."

The "ethical"—in its broad sense, as socially acknowledged reality—takes over in the remaining five paragraphs (lines 72–91). The dreamer had temporarily sojourned in a paradise protected by friendly, and perhaps natural illusions. In his essay "Du Vin et du hachisch" (1851), Baudelaire considered that both drugs provoke an "excessive development of mankind's poetic faculties" (*OC* 1:397).[9] Now the unidimensional mind requires chemical assistance: "Here in this world, narrow but so filled with disgust, only one familiar object cheers me: the vial of laudanum, an old and terrifying friend [*amie*], and, like all woman friends [*amies*], alas! fertile in caresses and betrayals!" "La souveraine des rêves" is a deceitful mistress. Reverie has degenerated into inebriation, like the "délire officiel" of the Parisian New Year (no. 4), a programmed warping of judgment in the service of escape. "The Double Room" appears to confirm the essayist's denunciation of artificially induced creativity: "The next day! . . . Hideous nature, deprived of the illumination of the day before, resembles the melancholy debris of a feast. . . . Every person who does not accept life's conditions sells his soul" (*OC* 1:437–38; also the end of "Du Vin et du hachisch").

"That hideous old man," who directs "the whole diabolical

procession of Memories, Regrets, Spasms, Fears, Anguishes, Nightmares, Rages, and Neuroses," is the proxy of his unfulfilled obligations. His hope falls victim to the clock that cries, " 'I am Life, unbearable, relentless Life!' " Death appears as the only solution in the next-to-final paragraph: "There is but one Second in human life whose mission it is to announce good news, the *good news* that causes everyone such inexplicable fear." We might consider this suicidal wish in earnest, were it not for the italicized "*la bonne nouvelle*" (alluding to the Gospels) which may redeem the narrator's defeat.

The final paragraph of "The Double Room" formulates an ambiguously heroic allegory. Whether the unreal room was induced by drugs or by reverie, it is not his true home. The awakened dreamer identifies with the zealous donkey of "A Joker" (no. 4), victim like himself of menial jobs and illusions, whose abusive master forecasts the "le hideux vieillard" of the present story. He exits with these shouts: "Yes! Time reigns; it has recaptured its brutal dictatorship. And it drives me, as if I were an ox, with its double goad. —'So gee'up! donkey! So sweat, slave! So live, damned one!' "

How do we interpret this powerful response to his own compelling servitudes? Humanity is like an ox coerced by relentless leaders, exploitive labor conditions, urged on solely by the threat of hunger. The penultimate paragraph depicted a hapless writer enticed by death. Now he projects himself into three avatars and challenges "la Vie, l'insupportable, l'implacable Vie!"

The Littré dictionary—a standard of mid-nineteenth-century usage—confirms the lucid courage of this closure. The list of four types of enslavement begins with passive resignation and ends by stoically accepting finitude. The cattle prod (s.v. *Aiguillon*) which drives the ox is, figuratively, "anything that stimulates action"; the definition of *boeuf*—the narrator's first proxy —defines the urban proletariat as a dumb and sterile brute: "A castrated bull, urged to plow fields and produce food for human beings." (Baudelaire's comparison reflects a Marxian sensitivity, although certainly not its theory.)[10] The narrator then becomes a *bourrique*, a female donkey, or a feeble donkey of either sex;

figuratively, the *bourrique* is a stupid person. Its human form is the *esclave,* whose body (if not the spirit) are the property of the powerful. Finally, he translates them all into the *damné,* who recalls mankind's metaphysical exile on earth as fallen angels. The worker has accepted the real.

This concluding paragraph, in form and in content, affirms a vitality that allows animals (and human beings) to survive and even to produce. A stylistic symmetry in the final lines reinforces the positive implications of the ambiguous images. This closure is "poetic" in form, consisting of three parallel exclamations, each of which (after the initial *Et*) contains four pronounced syllables and repeats internal rhymes:

> Et hue donc! bourrique!
> Sue donc, esclave!
> Vis donc, damné!

The writer protests against his condemnation while, at the same time, he embraces his harrowing life. "The Double Room" affirms his forthright solidarity with economic captives. He has fallen from Paradise, his dream room, into social degradation. But he labors. Yet we wonder if this pit is Inferno or Purgatory? Is his will free? Does he truly continue to hope?[11]

A COURAGEOUS FAITH

"To Each His Chimera" (no. 6) begins where the preceding fable ends, at the crossroads of suicide or rebellion. For the first time in the sequence, the narrator specifies his interpretive task; as the reader's proxy, he observes and questions his own journey. His ideal, the sylphid or goddess, becomes a beast, a Chimera, traditionally pictured with a lion's head, a goat's belly, and a dragon's tail; the cliché *chimère* signifies illusion or unattainable dreams (Littré, s.v. *Chimère*). Based on well-known allegories, graphic and literary, the title itself evokes a philosophical frame of mind.[12] The narrator becomes a sort of cosmic *flâneur* lost in a wilderness, the negative counterpart of blissful dreamland, anticipating T. S. Eliot's "The Waste Land": "Under a huge gray sky, on a huge dusty plain, without paths, without grass, without a thistle, without a nettle, I came upon several men walking along bent over."

Noticing that each one carries an enormous Chimera on his back, the stranger is moved to seek contact. He feels a personal need to understand their travails and to probe the allegory before his eyes:

> I questioned one of these men, and I asked him where they were going like that. He answered that he knew nothing about it, not he, nor the others; but that obviously they were going somewhere, since they were driven by an irresistible need to walk.
>
> A curious thing to note: none of these travelers seemed bothered by the ferocious beast hanging around his neck and attached to his back. They seemed to consider it as a part of themselves. All their weary and serious faces expressed no sign of despair. Under the sky's splenetic dome, their feet immersed in the dust of a terrain as ravaged as the sky, they made their way with the resigned expression of those who are condemned to hope forever.

Albert Camus's lucid Sisyphus might provide an interpretive model. In Baudelaire's fable, the wayfarers accept their servitude consciously and are thus spiritually free: "ils cheminaient avec la physionomie résignée de ceux qui sont condamnés à espérer toujours." This "hope" implies a grim energy that fights despair —forever.[13] They do not envisage any specific goal and do not surrender, since their incentive is part and parcel of their being. Like the disinterested mariners of "Le Voyage"—the final poem of the 1861 edition of *Les Fleurs du Mal*—they are "vrais voyageurs . . . qui partent / Pour partir" (true travelers . . . who leave for the sake of leaving [lines 17–18]).

This would be a fit morality, but the fable does not end here. These burdened men are *résignés* and *condamnés*. Could any positive faith justify their blind courage? Their stoicism may provide the perplexed observer with a reason to live. Indeed, the teller is more than a witness; his own odyssey reemerges as the collection's unifying plot, as he struggles to transform himself through identification. Curiosity about others is a necessary first step, yet at the end, after the attempted dialogue, he must overcome intellectual distance. But then, confronting his own existence, he succumbs to a portentous inhibition:

> And the procession passed by me and descended into the horizon's atmosphere, at that place where the planet's rounded surface hides from the curiosity of the human gaze.
>
> And for a few moments I persistently tried to understand this mystery. But soon insurmountable Indifference swooped down upon me, and I was more heavily oppressed than they were themselves by their overwhelming Chimeras.

The narrator cannot surpass his initial "curiosity," his intellectual drive, which, paradoxically, also insulates him from the others. But apathy marks his failure even to desire to understand. Repetitions underline this inhibition, to which the narrator will return, notably in "Vocations" (no. 31). The voyagers' strained expressions are "une chose curieuse à noter," and, in the penultimate paragraph, they disappear "à l'endroit où la surface arrondie de la planète se dérobe à la curiosité du regard humain." The observer experiences his mind's ultimate limits: "je m'obstinai à vouloir comprendre"; the construction expresses his desperate wish reinforced by a physical attempt to realize it.

Reason alone cannot instill in him their essential trust of existence. The narrator cannot imitate the stoical faith represented by the wayfarers' "Chimeras." First he must overcome the critical distance which has become absolute as "Indifference" (capitalized in the text). His passion for living is all too vulnerable, and so their hope, as absurd as it may be, remains inaccessible to him. His final response demonstrates that ennui is far more perilous than the endless anxiety of anticipation (Godfrey 1984), the burden of "ceux qui sont condamnés à espérer toujours." The narrator, at this point, cannot accept his condition, which "Le Voyage" (line 31) defines in similar words: "L'Homme, dont jamais l'espérance n'est lasse" (Mankind, whose hope never wearies). The fable ends as the observer's deadened will is again absorbed by "la coupole splénétique du ciel."

The four fables numbered 3–6 codify the collection's obvious thematic counterpoint, the strict disjunction between our inner and outer worlds. But self-awareness brings freedom. Although the compartments of our "double room" remain separate, sharp self-scrutiny might help us integrate them. Each fable also points to a more basic danger: lack of passion. The ending of "To Each His Chimera" asserts the strange, modestly heroic, tenacity of desire, confirming the famous introductory poem of *Les Fleurs du Mal*, "Au lecteur" (To the reader): "Il en est un plus laid, plus méchant, plus immonde! / . . . C'est l'Ennui! (The ugliest, most evil, filthiest vice is . . . Ennui [lines 33–37]). Without a passion for life there is no courage, no action—and certainly no art. The next series of fables explores the dynamics of this essentially artistic quest. People of imagination, overburdened with the Ideal, most fully realize mankind's limits and possibilities.

3

FABLES OF THE ARTISTIC QUEST

Sacrifices to the Absolute

T*he Parisian Prowler* completes its definition of artistic faith with three fables which also complete the *Presse* series of 26 August 1862. They all dramatize the fundamental paradox of the visionary who, unable to recreate perfection, nevertheless persists. The first two depict Beauty as utterly remote. "The Fool and the Venus" ("Le Fou et la Vénus," no. 7) is a tragic allegory in which a passionate worshiper is rebuffed by a cold and indifferent goddess, another avatar of the Idols of "The Double Room" and "La Beauté" (*FM*, no. 17). Its parodic doublet, "The Dog and the Scent Bottle" ("Le Chien et le flacon," no. 8), condemns superficial taste, just as "A Joker" had done. The third one is of major import: "The Bad Glazier" ("Le Mauvais Vitrier," no. 9) develops an ambiguous parable of esthetic idealism, completing the two preceding ones.

These "esthetic" fables parallel the primarily "ethical" series and add a profound narrative irony. Both "The Bad Glazier," which closes the first *Presse* sequence, and later "A Heroic Death" ("Une Mort héroïque," no. 27, first published in 1863), judge the conflict between art and morality to be irreconcilable. These two self-reflective masterpieces imply that art itself is not the problem—that is, the dialectic of ideal versus imperfection—but rather naive idealist conceptions as such. Baudelaire's irony continues the romantic traditions of Byron, Heine, Musset, Stendhal—and especially E. T. A. Hoffmann, whom he particularly admired. With a savage challenge to common sense, "The Bad Glazier"—featured in his sly dedication "To Arsène Houssaye"—allows "beauty" to trample common decency, forcing readers, in the manner of Socrates, to question its heroically tragic (or madly self-destructive) conclusions.

Most critics believe that Baudelaire most completely allegorizes himself as artist-clown. In an often-cited article, Jean Starobinski penetratingly analyzes how "A Heroic Death" and "The Old Acrobat" ("Le Vieux Saltimbanque," no. 14) develop "as an imaged *reflection* on the artist's existential (and social) failure, because of the radical lack of *being* associated with the illusory character of art" (Starobinski 1967, 409).[1] I agree with Starobinski that Baudelaire represents the artistic quest in a modern manner, one which juxtaposes normally exclusive alternatives. The narrator interiorizes these multiple identifications and endows them with symbolic meaning. Starobinski correctly identifies the author's conceptual polarities. However, I find that the tragic-clown image understates the narrator's self-awareness and its sophisticated expression as irony. These fables far surpass the romantic commonplaces of their manifest content. The larger context shows that Baudelaire's true portrait of the poet is the widow.

THE ARTIST'S TRAGIC DEVOTION

Each dualistic fable opens with an ecstatic landscape in which the self utopically overcomes its separateness—and in each a centrally located "pivotal sentence" destroys the dream.[2] The clown of "The Fool and the Venus" kneels at the pedestal of a gigantic statue which—like the Idol of "The Double Room"—represents the *idea* of perfect beauty. This allegorical tableau, evenly divided between idealization and disillusion, repeats the structure of "The Artist's *Confiteor*" and "The Double Room." Part 1 develops a pastoral reverie in a park, the urban equivalent of cosmic bliss:

> What an admirable day! The vast park swoons under the sun's blazing eye, like youth under Love's domination.
>
> The universal ecstasy of things declares itself without noise; the very waters seem to sleep. Quite unlike human celebrations, here is a silent orgy.

> An ever-increasing light seems to make objects increasingly sparkle. Aroused flowers burn with the desire to outdo the sky's azure by the energy of their colors, and the heat, turning scents visible, seems to make them rise to the stars like smoke.

A flow of intense sensations illustrates the premise: "Quelle admirable journée!" The park becomes an imaginative utopia, a "truly *spiritual* room" (no. 5) which produces *correspondances*. As in the poem of that name (*FM*, no. 4), the mind enters a fervent, though harmonious, space, "Ayant l'expansion des choses infinies, / . . . Qui chantent les transports de l'esprit et des sens" (Possessing the expansion of infinite things, . . . singing the ecstasies of the mind and the senses [lines 12–14]). A sort of pansexuality reigns in nature's "orgy" of smells, colors, feelings, and sights.

Then, as expected, one sentence suddenly destroys the idealization. A strategically placed brief paragraph interjects a discordant witness: "However, amidst this universal rapture, I noticed an afflicted creature" (*Cependant, au milieu de cette jouissance universelle, j'ai aperçu un être affligé*). Two crucial events: the narrator says "I" for the first time; and he introduces the allegorical court jester. The "jouissance universelle" is a sort of mental orgasm (*jouir* signifies a sexual climax) that lasts but an instant. Human finitude cannot sustain the union.

A Fool represents the artist's intermediate realm, which occupies a description of equal length (lines 16–30). While a statue (like the Idol of fable no. 5) parallels, but does not supersede, the natural (or supernaturalistic) reveries of part 1: "At the feet of a colossal Venus, one of those artificial fools, one of those voluntary buffoons assigned to make kings laugh when pursued by Remorse or Ennui, rigged out in a flashy and ridiculous costume, capped in horns and bells, all heaped against the pedestal, raises his tear-filled eyes toward the immortal Goddess." The "artificiel" artist is "volontaire" because he commits himself freely to his vision, transcending nature. His goal is spiritual, to reflect pure beauty, not merely to divert others from despair or guilt. But economic dependency enslaves him. Consumer's art, which masks anxiety, and Absolute art, judged by truth, appear to exclude one another.

The Fool is an emblem of the artist's duality. Like the burdened beasts and wanderers of previous fables, he is a servant. But this lesson is less compelling than the problem of interpretation. At the end, the narrator translates the allegory:

> And his eyes say, "I am the lowest and the most lonely of humans, deprived of love and of friendship, and for that reason quite inferior to the most incomplete animals. However I am made, I as well, to understand and to feel immortal Beauty! Oh Goddess! take pity on my sorrow and my madness!"
>
> But the implacable Venus looks into the distance at something or other with her eyes of marble.

Segregated from his ideal, the artist, nevertheless, feels dignified, worthy, superior, because he can *study* as well as perceive the Absolute, "comprendre et sentir l'immortelle Beauté!" The modern visionary is self-conscious and thus potentially free. At the same time, his self-awareness also creates an unbridgeable distance between himself and the world. Both inferior to beasts and above the herd, his energy derives from his lofty intuitions.

The infinite meets the finite in his consciousness. But if mankind is indeed a social race, as Aristotle proclaims, then the radical idealist cannot enjoy its consolations, for he possesses Beauty only in imagination, that "Queen of Faculties." Can he reconcile the "délire" of the Absolute (which isolates him) with the "tristesse" of finitude (which expresses his frailty)? His mixture of emotions represents an "indefinable amalgam" of spiritual and natural faculties (*Artificial Paradises, OC* 1:399; cf. Kierkegaard 1954 [*The Sickness Unto Death*], 162–75).

The next tableau reiterates the tragic impasse in a crude form —but it reinforces the solemn allegories. "The Dog and the Scent-Bottle" (no. 8) violently recasts "The Fool and the Venus" just as "A Joker" (no. 4) had caricatured "The Artist's *Confiteor*" (no. 3). Both sarcastic anecdotes (nos. 4 and 8) defend the artist's integrity, which the longer preceding ones (nos. 3 and 7) illustrate in a dignified manner. "The Dog and the Scent-Bottle" reiterates the moral judgment of "A Joker" as it unmasks the outraged judge behind the onlooker.

"The Dog and the Scent-Bottle" attacks mediocre art, which aims simply to excite. It takes literally the cliché of bad art as shit by opposing the "perfume" of studied beauty to the animal's gross instinctual titillation.[3] The *beau chien* is another avatar of the stupid *beau monsieur* of "A Joker" who typifies France's corrupted tastes. And like "The Artist's *Confiteor*" and "The Fool and the Venus," the story pivots upon a sentence in which the Ideal (represented by the "excellent perfume") is discarded in favor of trash: "And the dog . . . comes near and, curious, puts its wet nose on the unstoppered bottle. Then suddenly recoiling in terror, it barks at me, by way of reproach."

The "curious" public flees, panic-stricken, at the savor of too much truth or beauty. As the ending explains: "Because of this, you, unworthy companion of my dreary life, you resemble the public, which must never be offered delicate perfumes that exasperate them, but only meticulously selected garbage."[4] The narrator's rigorous standards, at this point in a sequential reading, exclude compromise. Not until "Loss of Halo" ("Perte d'auréole," no. 46), will he relax, and only in the final fable, "The Good Dogs" ("Les Bons Chiens," no. 50), does the narrator redeem this portrait of "bad" dogs.

IDOLATRY OF THE ESTHETIC

The famous story that follows, "The Bad Glazier" (no. 9), a favorite of anthologies, boldly challenges those who cannot fathom Baudelaire's Socratic masks. The cruel anecdote is a treasury of ironies, not the least of which is its title. Readers continue to be scandalized, bemused, or baffled by the narrator's tantalizing proclamation, at the end, that the pleasure of one instant is worth eternal damnation. This piece is largely responsible for the legend of the author as a satanic esthete and neurotic practical joker (Kopp, 209–12). No other fable depicts more sharply the putative ascendency of artifice over the ethical—the myth of Baudelaire the dandy.

It begins in the tradition of Christian moral philosophy. The first fifty lines (out of one hundred in the Kopp edition) explore the relationship between inwardness and action in a quasi-scientific style. The narrator introduces himself as an impartial student of a certain "artistic" temperament. The complex syntax stresses his initial detachment: "There exist characters, purely contemplative and completely unsuited for action, who, however, influenced by a mysterious and unknown impulse, sometimes act with a speed of which they would not have believed themselves capable."

Several examples in the following six paragraphs (lines 6–49) demonstrate how ennui can derail an imaginative person. The narrator identifies himself with these victims who "sometimes feel abruptly hurled into action by an irresistible force, like an arrow out of a bow. The moralist and the physician, who claim to know everything, cannot explain the cause of this crazy energy which hits these lazy and voluptuous souls so suddenly." These "âmes paresseuses et voluptueuses" recall "The Double Room" (no. 5) in which "the soul takes a bath of laziness" (*un bain de paresse* [line 4]). The narrator summarizes his psychological point: "It is the type of energy that springs from ennui and daydreaming; and those in whom it arises so unexpectedly are, generally, as I said, the most indolent and dreamiest of creatures." This fable will elaborate "The Artist's *Confiteor*" (no. 3), which stated that "the force of voluptuous pleasure [can provoke] uneasiness and concrete suffering."

The story's second half (lines 50–100) plays out the narrator's own confusion of true art with selfish pleasure, as he abandons his pose of objectivity and, typographically, puts himself at center stage—at the text's exact center (line 50): "More than once I have been victim of such attacks and outbursts, which justify our belief that some malicious Demons slip into us and, without our knowing it, make us carry out their most absurd wishes." Baudelaire's insistence upon the reality of satanic influences reflects his own troubled recognition that rationality can never completely rule the subconscious.

The problem of interpretation magnifies the fable's psychological import. Two central paragraphs make an ironic reading of the whole scenario inescapable. The first one emphasizes the narrator's irrationality, while the second proposes plausible diagnoses. However, the second paragraph, which consists of one complex sentence in parentheses, hardly clarifies the preceding one:

> One morning I had awakened sullen, sad, and worn out with idleness, and I felt impelled to do something great, a brilliant action. And I opened the window, alas!
>
> (Notice, if you please, that the spirit of mystification which, among certain persons, does not result from effort or scheming, but from a chance inspiration, if only because of the desire's fervor, has much in common with that humor, hysterical according to physicians, satanic according to those who think a little more lucidly than physicians, which drives us irresistibly toward a multitude of dangerous or improper actions.)

For the first time in the collection, the narrator addresses the reader directly. But we become more mystified than enlightened by his confidence. The pedantic digression separates the theological and scientific perspectives, now giving primacy to the former. He wants to interpret these "actes les plus absurdes et même les plus dangereux." Yet he appears to be unaware of contradicting himself—blaming "demons" while, at the same time, rationalizing the dynamics of free choice.

Does the fable itself promote "l'esprit de mystification"? "The Bad Glazier" becomes the first fable of modern life to elaborate an allegory of its own creation, anticipating the later "theoretical fables" (see chap. 7). The narrator performs a charade of the cliché "une action d'éclat" (a brilliant action); *éclat* has several meanings: glamour, radiance, vividness, fame, an outburst—or splintered, smashed material, especially glass. At the end, he will restate the verbal construct "action d'éclat" physically, in a strikingly ironic mode (pun intended).

This is the manifest content. An indolent writer becomes a satanic esthete for whom pleasure outweighs all virtue. His lethargy quickly turns into aggression when he hears the "piercing, discordant cry" of an ambulant windowpane peddler and invites him to his seventh-floor room. A savage glee excites the writer and we are shocked at his calculated cruelty. And yet we might sympathize with his gloominess, for he lives in a cheap, hard-to-reach, dismal half of his "double room."

The narrator accompanies his unconscionable mystification with an ironic verbal playfulness. He begins by denouncing the peddler for not transforming reality, reproaching his victim for not actualizing a variant of the cliché *voir la vie en rose* (to see the world through rose-colored glasses): "He finally appeared. Curiously I examined all his glass, and I told him, 'What? You have no colored panes? no pink panes, no red, no blue, no magic panes, no panes of paradise? You are shameless! You dare walk through poor neighborhoods, and you don't even have panes which make life beautiful!' [*qui fassent voir la vie en beau*]. And vigorously I pushed him to the stairs, where he staggered grumbling."

We finally understand why the glazier is "bad," according to the title's enigmatic hint. He does not help the narrator, or his neighbors, to remedy or disguise their poverty by creating illusions! Those who cannot afford an apartment on a lower floor, and in a nicer section of the city, must breathe "la lourde et sale atmosphère parisienne." The innocent worker who cannot provide "vitres de paradis" has adapted to reality.

The absurd situation, echoing the title's irony, and the vicious literalization of "to see the world through rose-colored glasses," all prepare the fable's "moral." The "artist" cannot embellish or transform his life, so he claims to create beauty through violence:

> I went to the balcony and I grabbed a little pot of flowers, and when the man reappeared at the door entrance, I let my engine of war drop down perpendicularly on the back edge of his pack. The shock knocked him over, and he ended by breaking his entire poor itinerant fortune under his back, which produced the brilliant sound [*le bruit éclatant*] of a crystal palace smashed by lightning.
>
> And, drunk with my madness, I shouted at him furiously, "Make life beautiful! Make life beautiful!" [*La vie en beau! la vie en beau!*]

This "beauty" yields multiple allegorical resonances. The flowers are of course real, but as instruments of anguish, their natural loveliness becomes an "engin de guerre"; the decorative pot turns into "flowers of evil." The narrative irony surfaces again in the awkward, quasi-scientific adverb *perpendiculairement*, and is reinforced by the sentence's geometrical precision. His insane repetition of the phrase *la vie en beau!* reiterates its hidden significance. The mad music of a crumbling palace is not art but its destruction. Here, finally, is the "action d'éclat" announced earlier (line 56).

The story has ended. The degenerate artist is intoxicated, "ivre de [sa] folie," not inspired. But again, an enigmatic coda tantalizes interpreters, raising more questions than it resolves. It defines an ethical challenge, for the joy it so defiantly vaunts is ephemeral, fragile as glass, while the transgression cannot be repaired: "Such neurotic pranks are not without peril, and one can often pay dearly for them. But what does an eternity of damnation matter to someone who has experienced for one second the infinity of delight?" The final rhetorical question, like Faust's damnation, suggests (but only suggests) that the pleasure principle can overrule all other values.[5] Would any rational person, consciously and so willfully, welcome endless torture simply to enjoy "une seconde" of sensory stimulation, even if it feels like "l'infini de la jouissance"?

The fable's "satanic" irony updates Socrates' challenge to *our* moral discernment. "The Fool and the Venus" (no. 7) depicted the negative counterpart of its "jouissance universelle," so "The Bad Glazier" takes a considerable risk by not explaining its meaning. In fact, over the years most readers have ignored its irony and maintained that the satanic poet ultimately surrenders to self-gratification.[6] True, the narrator does label his act a *plaisanterie nerveuse*, a demented impulse galvanized by an overly susceptible organism. And his repeated allusions to doctors of the church and of medicine should forestall a too facile answer to the concluding question. The narrator refuses to side with either Catholic or materialistic morality, forcing readers to reflect further.

Baudelaire's harsh parable avoids the moralistic clarity of his 1858 essay, "The Poem of Hashish," on the final page of which he raises the same question: "What kind of paradise is it that one buys at the price of one's eternal salvation?" (*OC* 1:441) The essay stages the same situation and in practically the same words. Only this time the Parisian gets up, as it were, on the right side of the bed:

> There are days when a person wakes up possessing a young and vigorous genius. His eyelids hardly relieved of the sleep which sealed them, the exterior world presents itself to him in powerful relief, a clarity of contour, a richness of admirable colors. The emotional world offers its vast perspectives, filled with new light. The person favored with that beatitude, unfortunately rare and fleeting, feels himself at once more of an artist and more just, more noble, to say it with one word. But what is most remarkable about that exceptional state of mind and senses, which without exaggeration I can call paradisiacal, if I compare it to the heavy darkness of common and daily existence, is that it has not been created by any cause quite visible and easy to define. (*OC* 1:401)

Baudelaire the essayist denounces the temptation to become God through magic, to "create Paradise with pharmaceutics, by fermented drinks"—the technology of a radical idealism which repudiates responsibility. Only "the daily exercise of the will" can free us. "The Bad Glazier" confronts this ethical imperative with an elusive irony by only sketching its contradictory guidelines.

"The Bad Glazier" is not a nihilistic mystification, but a double polemic directed against contrary standards: complacent didacticism or naive hedonism bereft of sensitivity. The modern fable would never repeat this eloquent admonition from "The Poem of Hashish": "There lies in that depravation of the sense of the infinite, as I see it, the cause of every guilty excess, from the writer's solitary and concentrated inebriation [*ivresse*] . . . to the most repulsive drunkenness [*l'ivrognerie*]" (*OC* 1:403). Its hazardous ambiguity subverts literature that serves bourgeois philanthropy, of which Houssaye's democratic idealization of a similar peddler is a countermodel: "Brotherhood had taken a glass with him" (*La fraternité avait trinqué avec lui*)—the refrain from "The Glazier's Song," which is bad writing, superficial sociology, and trivial ethics.

As a parable of *esthetic* experience, "The Bad Glazier" completes the first *Presse* series (26 August 1862) by reconfirming "The Artist's *Confiteor*" (no. 3) and its warning against loss of self. The depressed artist's "creation" (which is actually a demolition) did not demonstrate a true mastery over matter, but rather his displaced rage against life's unfairness. Nor is the crystal palace "music" true art. The narrator in despair has outlined the mortal dangers (in this case, a mortal sin) of confusing sensory stimulation with significant constructs. This is no substitute for the "stranger's" cloud reveries (at the end of fable no. 1), which bring no lasting solace. The value of conscience, although buried in mystification, nevertheless remains.

POLITICS AND THE TRAGIC CLOWN

Baudelaire's later fables are more self-reflective and exercise a more profound irony. "A Heroic Death" (no. 27) summarizes these relatively simple allegories by depicting the tragedy of a politically committed artist. It was first published in the 10 October 1863 issue of the *Revue Nationale et Étrangère* along with a brief allegory of self-sacrifice, "The Desire to Paint" ("Le Désir de peindre," no. 36). Its three main characters—a Prince, a Clown, and the narrator—act almost as one person attempting, unsuccessfully, to integrate the esthetic and the ethical. The narrator's portrait of the Prince, specifically condemns by implication artistic idealism confused with sensory excitement (Rubin 1985–86, 51–60; cf. Wing 1979; Swain 1982; Mehlman 1974, 7–13).

The irony of "A Heroic Death" is more akin to German romantic irony than to the pragmatic Socratic variety. Its multiple perspectives construct what Baudelaire defines, in "De l'essence du rire" (On the essence of laughter), as the "absolute comic"—a double consciousness in which one person (or his intellect) gloats over a victim.[7] This crucial essay, which champions E. T. A. Hoffmann's *Princess Brambilla* as a "catechism of high esthetics" (*OC* 2:538–43), parallels "A Heroic Death," which takes us to the heart of literature's meaning or self-subversion. For the narrator, who dominates both Fool and Prince intellectually, hovers over his text with the detachment of a writer who refuses to conclude.[8]

The pure artist of this fairy tale is the Prince's personal jester, Fancioulle, with whom the narrator deeply sympathizes. The Italian *fanciullo* means "child" and evokes Baudelaire's definition, a renewal of a romantic commonplace, that genius is "childhood recovered at will."[9] The opening paragraph sets the stage: "Fancioulle was an admirable buffoon, and almost one of the Prince's friends. But serious matters have a fatal attraction for people whose state destines them to the comical, and, although it might seem odd that the ideas of fatherland and freedom can despotically seize a playactor's brain, one day Fancioulle entered into a conspiracy formed by some disgruntled gentlemen."

The buffoon faces several impossible choices: (1) He is hired to divert the Prince, but he *almost* becomes his friend, thus transgressing the boundary between patron and servant. (2) The clown's political ideology violates his friendship, thus creating an ethical dilemma. (3) Most fundamental, perhaps, is the conflict between his social or genetic predisposition toward the comical ("voué par son état au comique" retains that ambiguity) and his "fatal" attraction to truth. (The words *état* and *fatal* will reappear in lethally ironic contexts.) Politics, which thrusts him into the world, threatens his art.

The story's allegorical import becomes more explicit when the outraged ruler uncovers the conspiracy and condemns everyone to death. The ruler's internal struggle betrays his competition with his buffoon; he may indeed be the aggravated narrator of "The Bad Glazier" (no. 9) promoted to the highest office of the land:

> His excessive sensitivity made him, in many instances, crueler and more despotic than all his peers. Passionately enamored of the fine arts, moreover an excellent connoisseur, he was truly insatiable for voluptuous pleasures. Himself a true artist, rather indifferent toward people and morality, he recognized but one dangerous enemy, Ennui, and the weird efforts he made to flee or to conquer that tyrant of the world would certainly have won him, from a severe historian, the epithet of "monster," had he been

> allowed to write anything whatever, on such matters, not exclusively associated with pleasure or astonishment, which is one of pleasure's most delicate forms.

The "historien sévère" condemns an esthetics of surprise, for he understands how the tyrant's creative personality had been distorted by an anxiety which his exaggerated need for *volupté* sought to suppress. Yet the observer remains neutral toward this demonic dandy who practices what the inebriated hashish eater proclaims: "For me, humanity has worked, become martyred, sacrificed,—to serve as fodder [*pâture*], as *pabulum*, to my implacable appetite for emotion, for knowledge and for beauty!" ("Le Poème du hachisch," *OC* 1:437).[10] The narrator of "Widows" ("Les Veuves," no. 13), also seeks "une pâture certaine" for his imagination.

The Prince's sadistic estheticism derives from what Kierkegaard calls "the despair of possibility," too much power—but not quite enough—to realize excessive desires (1954 [*The Sickness Unto Death*], 162–75). The final sentence of this long paragraph confirms the contradiction: "A heedless Providence had given this one [imaginative] faculties greater than his States" (*des facultés plus grandes que ses Etats*). He is another Melmoth, suffering the immense "disproportion between his marvelous faculties, instantly acquired in a satanic pact, and the milieu where, as a creature of God, he is condemned to live" (*OC* 1:438). Like Fancioulle, the Prince is "voué par son état," fatally predisposed, toward self-destruction; but unlike the buffoon, he becomes a dandy devoted to "l'étonnement, qui est une des formes les plus délicates du plaisir."[11]

The Prince stages a play-within-the-play, ordering the Clown to act a pantomime while his fellow conspirators, the nobles, just watch. The narrator ponders its psychological meaning but introduces a metatextual irony—more explicit than that of "The Bad Glazier"—through the italicized pun *capital* (meaning "death" or "of great import"): "But for those who, like myself, could probe more deeply into that curious and sick soul, it was infinitely more probable that the Prince intended to evaluate the theatrical talents of a man condemned to death. He wanted to profit from the opportunity of making a physiological experiment of *capital* interest, and to verify to what extent an artist's normal faculties can be changed or modified by his extraordinary situation." The multiple meanings of the word "curious" will also have lethal consequences.

Fancioulle's idealist art overwhelms the Prince's sensualism. The pantomime will transcend, for a moment, the actor's—and his spectators'—boundaries between fiction (or theater) and ontic truth. In addition, his acting is an extralinguistic commentary (recounted verbally, of course) defining this fable's own import:

> Seigneur Fancioulle particularly excelled in silent roles or ones burdened with few words, often the major roles in fairy dramas depicting symbolically the mystery of life. He came out onto the stage smoothly and perfectly at ease, which contributed to reinforcing, amongst the noble public, the *idea* of mildness and pardon.
>
> When it is said of an actor, "What a good actor," the expression implies that the actor can still be glimpsed beneath the character, that is to say, art, effort, will. Now, if an actor should succeed in being, relative to the character he is assigned to portray, what the best statues of antiquity, if miraculously animated, living, walking, seeing, might become relative to the general and vague *idea* of beauty, it would be, probably, a unique and completely unexpected event. The evening, Fancioulle was a perfect *idealization,* impossible not to *imagine* as living, possible, real. (Italics added)

The syntactically complex comparison of animated statues with mime makes a technical point: ideal (or mentally conceived) beauty only exceptionally finds adequate expression. Pure art strives toward "une parfaite idéalisation," so Fancioulle may already have entered the Venus-statue's transcendent domain (no. 7). Artistic illusion smothers the reality principle.

Then an even more extraordinary event occurs. At the fable's dramatic center (lines 88–105 out of 161), the narrator, penning these "recollections," falls victim to *his* sensitivity. His compassionate tears paralyze his writing. The just-cited paragraph ends thus:

> The buffoon went, came, laughed, wept, contorted himself, with an indestructible halo around his head, a halo invisible to everyone, but visible to me, and in which were blended, in a strange amalgam, the rays of Art and the glory of Martyrdom. By what special grace I know not, Fancioulle infused the divine and the supernatural, even into his most extravagant buffooneries. My pen trembles, and tears of a still-present emotion fill my eyes as I try to describe that unforgettable evening. Fancioulle proved to me, in a peremptory, irrefutable way, that the *intoxication* of Art is more apt than any other to *veil* the terrors of the abyss; that genius can play a part on the brink of death with a joy that keeps it from seeing the tomb, lost, as it is, in a paradise excluding any *idea* of tomb and destruction. (Italics added)

The writer's sudden paralysis unmasks his ever-present ethical standard. His empathy with the tortured actor disrupts the text itself. The terminology of inebriation (*l'ivresse de l'art*) suggests that Fancioulle's "spiritual room" will not outlast the earlier one (in no. 5), and the ending will prove it. Fancioulle's mime mixes Art (or imagined transcendence of death) with Martyrdom (or ethics) "dans un étrange amalgame." Genius can triumphantly *intoxicate* the weary, *veil* their anxiety—anesthetize "les terreurs du gouffre"—but only for a moment.

The next two paragraphs specify how those who consume art can also consume the artist, how material power can ultimately defeat spiritual autonomy. These observations reintroduce the dualistic clashes of the early fables, for, at the very moment of the actor's triumph, another strategic "However" shatters the dream. The ruler, fettered still within finitude, and inextricably so, will not capitulate to their delight:

> Everyone succumbed, without fear, to the multiplied voluptuous pleasures bestowed by the sight of a masterpiece of living art. Explosions of joy and admiration time and again shook the vaults of the edifice with the force of constant thunder. Even the Prince, intoxicated, mingled his applause with that of his court.

> However, for a discerning eye, his intoxication, his own, was not unmixed. Did he feel defeated in his despotic power? humiliated in his art of terrifying hearts and numbing minds? frustrated in his hopes and flouted in his predictions? Such assumptions, not exactly justified, but not absolutely unjustifiable, crossed my mind as I was contemplating the Prince's face, upon which a new pallor continuously increased his usual pallor, like snow added to snow.

The "historian" lucidly discerns the Prince's ambivalence, his internal battle between narcotizing joys versus reality. The repeated synonyms of *intoxication* and *ivresse* (lines 100, 114, 116) stress the fantastical foundation of these "voluptés multipliées" (line 110). Two types of "despotism" collide. The political despot, the Prince, a slave to his senses, must destroy "la toute-puissante domination de l'artiste" of the idealist mime, his former "favorite." The Prince cannot tolerate Fancioulle's own "pouvoir de despote"—an art that transcends all fear.

The story could very well end at the Prince's murder of Fancioulle, confirming the pessimism of "The Fool and the Venus" (no. 7). He tells a young page to blow a shrill whistle at the buffoon's climactic moment, so that his and the audience's illusions collapse: "Fancioulle, jolted, awakened from within his dream, first closed his eyes, then opened them almost immediately, enormously enlarged, then opened his mouth as though convulsively breathing, staggered a little forward, a little backward, and then fell stone dead upon the stage." This is indeed a tragic lesson of the artist as martyred hero succumbing to the ruler's power over bodies and Fate's superiority over individual will. The story has played out the dialectic of esthetic versus ethical, but it cannot satisfy the "severe historian."

The final paragraph destabilizes this noble parable of an artist's too "perfect idealization." This resolutely nondidactic closure subverts *his* interpretation with several, rather intricate, questions followed by another italicized pun:

> Had the whistle, swift as a sword, really thwarted the executioner? Had the Prince himself suspected the homicidal efficiency

> of his trick? There is ground to doubt it. Was he sorry about his dear and inimitable Fancioulle? It is sweet and legitimate to believe so.
>
> The guilty gentlemen had enjoyed a comic spectacle for the last time. That very night they were erased from life.
>
> Since then, several mimes, justly appreciated in different lands, have come to play for the court of ———; but none of them could duplicate the marvelous talents of Fancioulle, nor rise to the same *favor*.

The despot had fulfilled the letter but not the spirit of his experiment, "une expérience physiologique d'un intérêt *capital*." Now the fable's one other italicized word—at the very end—reinforces its moral ambiguity. No one can decide whether or not the Prince intended to kill—perhaps by de*capitation*—his artistic rival. Nor can we complacently admire the buffoon's religion of the Absolute.

The several, contradictory implications of the word *faveur* maintain the fable's openness. Did Fancioulle triumph because of his genius or because he was condemned to die? Was his ethical heroism congruent with or antithetical to his artistic gifts? He had been the Prince's "comédien favori" and had achieved his renown (his *faveur*), before the fateful conspiracy, enjoying the despot's *faveur*, a preference accorded to friends. The actor's triumph was a result of a special grace, a supernatural *faveur*, an advantage accorded by God. Finally, up until his last breath, Fancioulle held the *faveur* of the public, his power over spectators, including the Prince. And yet, the man was destroyed by this composite *faveur*.

IRONY OR COMMITMENT?

"A Heroic Death" demolishes heroism itself, and the metatextual irony of its italicized puns broadens the desperate sarcasm of "The Dog and the Scent-Bottle" and the reckless ambiguity of "The Bad Glazier," to cite two opposite examples. These final ironies introduce what Wayne Booth (1974) calls the "irony of infinite instabilities," the sense that behind this specific injustice there is no fundamental justice, even hidden, in the universe (esp. chap. 9). Toward the end of the collection, "Miss Scalpel" (no. 47, analyzed in chap. 8) expresses what I consider to be Baudelaire's most advanced intuition of cosmic injustice or meaninglessness.

The Fool and the Prince reenact the inevitable duel between nature and art, spirit and matter, to which the hero of "The Artist's *Confiteor*" confesses, proudly and courageously, in his rebellious profession of faith. But the narrator-writer refuses to conclude. The same teller, who introduces the second *Presse* series, attempts to jump the impasse through a movement of radical humility. See appendix 1.

4

POETRY VERSUS COMPASSION

Conversion to the Ethical?

The first thirteen fables of *The Parisian Prowler*, comprised of the two initial sequences published in *La Presse*, complete an itinerary from alienation to communion. "The Stranger" and "The Bad Glazier," which span the first issue, chart the "esthetic" extremes: excessive "spirituality," the infinite mobility of *reverie* (fable no. 1) versus excessive "materiality," violent stimulation of *senses* (fable no. 9), the immediate made absolute. The narrator, radically alone, appears unable to recast this oversimplified alternative: worship the Ideal or cherish others. In 1863 "A Heroic Death" literally reaches a deadend: Fancioulle cannot touch the Absolute while, at the same time, submitting to his "Prince," his patron and enemy. How can a "perfect idealization" live among others?

The second series published the next day (27 August 1862), through dramatic contrasts, achieves an authentic rapport with the everyday. For the first time in the sequence, the narrator identifies himself as a writer. Two adjacent fables, both set in contemporary (Second Empire) Paris, restore the value of dialogue —but through antiphrasis. "At One O'Clock in the Morning" and "The Wild Woman and the Affected Coquette" ("A Une Heure du matin," "La Femme sauvage et la petite maîtresse," nos. 10 and 11) reinforce the brutal defensiveness of "The Bad Glazier," which precedes them. A "man of letters" revels in his solitude, while a "poet" verbally assails his mistress for *her* insensitivity to the poor. These Socratically negative "messages" provoke disgust while their moral and theological vocabulary maintains a yearning for redemption.

THE POLARITY OF HUMILITY AND DESPAIR

The crucial transition piece, "At One O'Clock in the Morning," at first reading, appears to advertise the writer's alienation. He is a poet who locks himself in his room—with "a double turn in the lock"—and his space is only "spiritual" inasmuch as it seals out the world: "Finally! The tyranny of the human face has disappeared, and now only I myself will make me suffer. Finally! So I'm allowed to relax in a bath of darkness!" Protected from the Specter of his obligations, he plunges into "un bain de ténèbres," as he had when his "soul" drowsed in "un bain de paresse" (no. 5). But now he concentrates upon his ethical life and introduces, somewhat obliquely, the potential of humility.

The next, rather long, paragraph describes the disastrous result: "La tyrannie de la face humaine" contaminates his retreat.[1] Unable to resist a hostile system, he blames both, relentlessly prosecuting his dishonesty—with himself as with others. He lists several compromises which involve acquiescing to mediocre or stupid people who might contribute to his precarious livelihood: several other writers, a newspaper editor, and more.[2] He realizes how he allowed himself to be, in Kierkegaard's phrase, "defrauded by the other," absorbed into their triviality, but he cannot explain his persistent self-degradation: "Boasted (why?) of several bad deeds I never committed, and cravenly denied some other wrongs I carried out with joy, an offense of vainglory, a crime against human dignity," and so on.

The scene ends with an earnest confession of religious humility which almost neutralizes—almost—the prideful "Artist's *Confiteor*" (no. 3). The solitary poet in retreat petitions powers higher than himself—people he loved or wrote about, and finally God the Creator. This is the collection's first heartfelt prayer: "Annoyed with everyone and annoyed with myself, I long to redeem myself and to bolster my pride a bit in the silence and solitude of the night. Souls of those I have loved, souls of those I have sung, fortify me, sustain me, remove me from untruth and the world's corrupting fumes. And you, Lord my God! Grant me the grace to produce a few beautiful verses to prove to myself that I am not the lowest of men, and that I am not inferior to those I despise!"

This poignant outcry both contradicts and confirms Christian morality. The style is bereft of irony, as the poet seeks to "[se] racheter et [s']enorgueillir un peu," and especially to insulate himself from "le mensonge et les vapeurs corruptrices du monde." These theological terms translate his antisocial fortress into a monastic retreat. The soul straining to purify itself calls upon mediators as would a devout Catholic beseeching the Communion of Saints, kneeling before the Redeemer from whom his own powers flow. But, at the same time, he arrogantly rebels, "proving [his self worth] to *himself*" (not to God). [3]

The final clause is not ironic, but simply self-contradictory. His "mépris" violates both the letter and the spirit of his contrition with its contempt for his "inferiors." Every professional writer depends as much on journalists and critics as on lofty intuitions of the Ideal—and the narrator hates them for it! Embittered, he cannot purge himself, and his defensive rancor only sullies his modest wish to produce "quelques beaux vers" inspired by those he loved. This complex mixture of emotions hardly suggests a Socratic ploy to sidestep didacticism. The vulnerable artist still asserts his integrity but will not do so directly.

The next tale also contradicts itself. "The Wild Woman and the Affected Coquette" confirms the desperation and rage which the just-quoted prayer had not completely submerged. Its manifest theme is family love, but here the narrator—who, for the first time, explicitly labels himself a "poet"—assails his young mistress's egotism while professing his compassion (cf. Maclean 1988, 89–109). His violent sarcasm and offensive misogyny clash with the pained surrender of the preceding: " 'Really, my darling, you weary me beyond measure and without pity. Hearing you sighing, people would think you suffer more than sexagenarian bag ladies and the old beggar women who pick up crusts of bread at tavern doors.' "

Although, as the preceding, the narrator presents his story as "autobiography," we are not sure who does the telling, for the text is completely enclosed in quotation marks.[4] The story is patently allegorical. The man takes his mistress to a sideshow fair, where they examine a caged human female, crudely disguised in animal skins, who devours raw meat and makes a horrible ruckus when her "husband" (or keeper) beats her. The speaker's artificial, "precious" mistress parallels by contrast the excessively "natural" *femme sauvage* (although she is probably acting the part). The captive performer, degraded like the donkeys and the "damned" at the end of "The Double Room" (no. 5), arouses his pity, but his tone remains harsh.

This grotesque play-within-the-play about patriarchal marriage caricatures male brutality and the Napoleonic code (i.e., "the authorities") without taking sides. The speaker is sexist in its deepest sense, considering women as a separate and inferior race, the epitome of nature's intrinsic corruption.[5] That meaning emerges from the italicized adverb, now a fully recognizable sign of ironic distance:

> "Great God! That club is not a comedian's club, and did you hear her flesh reverberate, despite the fake hair? So her eyes now bulge from her head, and she howls *more naturally*. . . .
>
> "Such are the conjugal customs of these two descendents of Eve and of Adam, these works of your hands, O my God! . . . But in the world into which she has been flung, she could never believe that women deserve another destiny."

Only hinting at compassion, the speaker admits nevertheless that *le monde* (the world or society) keeps women unaware of their intrinsic dignity. But he chooses to ignore their suffering. He condemns male tyranny but prefers to focus upon his own isolation as a man without an ally. In fact, echoing the ending of the "*Confiteor*" (no. 3), he goes so far as to challenge his mistress to a duel: "Now, let's duel it out, dear precious one!" (*Maintenant, à nous deux, chère précieuse!*).

The conclusion, again displacing his frustration, attacks both women, for each type magnifies his irreconcilable worlds, as depicted in "The Fool and the Venus" (no. 7). The "petite-maîtresse" is *artificial,* like the joker, while the "femme sauvage," *natural* like the donkey (no. 4), is also depraved. As a poet he shares their symbolic duality: He too is a "delicate beauty, feet in the mire and eyes turned swooningly toward the sky." The italicized and repeated key terms summarize the allegory: " 'However much of a poet I am, I'm not as gullible as you would like to believe, and if you irk me too often with your *precious* whinings, I'll treat you like a *wild woman,* or I'll throw you out the window, like an empty bottle.' "

Instead of looking inward, into his own "bouteille vide," his own poetic responsibility, he will demolish his Muse. The *petite-maîtresse* is the modern equivalent of seventeenth-century *précieuses,* pretentious ladies of Louis XIV's court who eschewed ordinary language in favor of ornate and highly metaphorical circumlocutions. The duelist repudiates her "pretty hell" and "all those affectations learned from books." But *he* is another caged woman; though instead of expressing compassion, he projects his terror onto the woman who "howls like one of the damned."

THE ANTAGONISM OF POETRY AND COMPASSION

The final three fables of the second *Presse* series (nos. 12–14) depict poets who strain toward a harmony of ethics and art. I read them as a triptych because their complementary themes are confirmed by their prepublication history. "Crowds," "Widows," and "The Old Acrobat" ("Les Foules," "Les Veuves," "Le Vieux Saltimbanque") first appeared together in the *Revue Fantaisiste* on 1 November 1861, and then, in the same order, they concluded the second group published in *La Presse* on 27 August 1862. Their narrator is the same *flâneur* who explores his relationships with the populace and with lone individuals. The first and third fables are the best known: "Crowds" celebrates his imaginative communion with anonymous city dwellers while "The Old Acrobat" explicitly allegorizes the *poète maudit* whose *Fleurs du Mal* repelled official guardians of public virtue. These two prominent works have overshadowed "Widows" which, to my mind, surpasses them.

Baudelaire's most complete figuration of poetic creation emerges from this central panel of the triptych; together the three complete the narrator-poet's conversion from alienation to communion and from despair to love. "Crowds" devalues ethics for the sake of mental imperialism while "The Old Acrobat" seems to ratify the irremediable conflict between artist and public. "Widows," in this perspective, modifies its two pessimistic companions and demonstrates an exceptional ethical lyricism. Unlike the *flâneur* and the *saltimbanque*, the poet as widowed mother both loves and creates.

The narrator of "Crowds," at first glance, confirms the esthetic stereotype of Baudelaire.[6] He is a dreamer who, unlike the stranger (no. 1), seems to have prevailed over Parisian alienation. But his proclamation is riddled with contradictions. "Not everyone is capable of taking a bath of multitude: enjoying crowds is an art. And only he who can go on a binge of vitality, at the expense of the human species, is he into whom in his cradle a fairy breathed a craving for disguises and masks, hatred of home, and a passion for traveling." The stroller focuses only upon his inspiration, "une ribote de vitalité" as he takes an imaginary "bath," repeating another key phrase, "jouir de," which evokes intense inwardness. The next paragraph deliberately confuses fantasy with external reality: "*Multitude, solitude: equal and interchangeable terms for the active and fertile poet.* He who does not know how to populate his solitude, does not know either how to be alone in a busy crowd" (italics added).

Then, unwittingly contradicting himself, he claims that his art derives from true empathy. Implicitly but unmistakably he exposes the fallacy of imaginative "prostitution"—the power to leave oneself and dwell within another.[7] In point of fact, his freedom is entirely solipsistic: "The poet enjoys the incomparable privilege of being able, at will, to be himself and an other. Like those wandering souls seeking a body, he enters, when he wants, into everyone's character. For him alone, everything is empty. And if certain places seem to exclude him, it is because he considers them not worth the bother of being visited." This narcissistic "empathy" denies the autonomy of others, and, repeating the word *seul,* asserts a self-centered estheticism.[8] The "poet" does not really contact their personality, but rather their social role, "le personnage de chacun"; his putative identification is actually projection: "pour lui seul, tout est vacant." The stroller fills an empty space, the one within his own imagination.

The next two paragraphs glorify his ambulatory reveries with an enthusiasm that recalls "The Artist's *Confiteor,*" "The Double Room," and "The Fool and the Venus" (nos. 3, 5, 7). His "communion" is not a *transitive* empathy with separate persons who possess subjective depth but a *reflexive* mental drama:

> The solitary and thoughtful stroller draws a unique intoxication from this universal communion. He who easily espouses crowds knows feverish delights, of which the selfish will be eternally deprived, locked up like a chest, and the lazy, confined like a mollusk. He adopts as his every profession, every joy and every misery circumstances place before him.
>
> What people call love is awfully small, awfully restricted and awfully weak, compared with that ineffable orgy, that holy prostitution of the soul which gives itself totally, poetry and charity, to the unexpected which appears, to the unknown which passes by.

This is an urban writer's manifesto, replete with formulas and unshakable pride. Its key word is the ambiguous *enivrement* (intoxication). His mixture of religious and erotic terms—"ineffable orgie, sainte prostitution de l'âme"—elevates this inspiration far above his original claim to penetrate real people, but he seeks only his own internal pleasure. The "promeneur solitaire et pensif" strives only to become "actif et fertile."

The final paragraph—a sarcastic coda—unveils his realistic assessment, betraying the fragility of his "jouissances fiévreuses" (completing the original formula: *jouir de la foule est un art* [line 2]). He has not reconciled "poetry and charity," fantasy and authentic concern:

> It is sometimes right to teach the world's happy ones, if only to humiliate their stupid pride for an instant, that there are forms of

> happiness superior to theirs, more vast and more refined. Founders of colonies, shepherds of peoples, missionary priests exiled to the ends of the earth, probably know something of these mysterious intoxications. And, in the bosom of the vast family created by their genius, they must sometimes laugh at those who pity their fortunes so troubled and their lives so chaste.

The intellectual stroller feels compelled to denigrate "ce que les hommes nomment amour." Can we reconcile this acerbic denunciation of the "heureux de ce monde" with his claim to ascetic priesthood? Clearly the "poet" is as intent on mocking the bourgeoisie as he is on promoting ecstasy. Humility requires acceptance of others who may not measure up to your exacting standards. Here, the narrator's final, defensive assault against "le bonheur" (nineteenth-century code for complacency) seals his alienation.

The antagonism between "poetry" and "charity"—only implicit in "Crowds"—springs into relief in "The Old Acrobat," the triptych's second panel. "Crowds" demonstrated that sociology born of "empathy" is really invention. "The Old Acrobat," Baudelaire's most grim portrait of the writer, brings his ethical presuppositions to the surface.[9]

The narrative begins by evoking an "ineffable orgy" and "mysterious intoxication" similar to those evoked in "Crowds," "The Artist's *Confiteor*," and "A Joker." But an additional mixture of religious and profane terms undermines the validity of what the poet calls "one of those *solemn* occasions" (*solennel* retains its meaning of public ritual celebration): that is, a country fair. This time, the "steadfast solitary" (the expression comes from "A Joker," no. 4) "[has] difficulty escaping the influence of this plebeian *jubilee*." "An odor of frying which was like that festival's *incense*" (italics added) condenses its ambiguity.

The narrative pivots on the next two paragraphs, as the stroller —"a man of the world and a man engaged in spiritual works"— is moved by an afflicted man, "a pitiful acrobat, stooped over, obsolete, decrepit, a human ruin"—an aged counterpart of the Fool (no. 7). Stylistic repetitions juxtapose the collective delirium with the fallen artist, its victim: "Everywhere joy, profit, debauchery; everywhere the certainty of tomorrow's bread; everywhere the frenzied explosion of vitality. Here absolute wretchedness, wretchedness rigged out, most horrible, rigged out in comic rags, where necessity, much more than art, had introduced the contrast."

This antithesis reiterates all conflicts between art and economic distress, illustrating the fate of all dreamers, starting with the "stranger" and the "old woman" (nos. 1 and 2). Like the widows of the preceding fable, the "vieux saltimbanque" is bereft of consolations. But, unlike these women, he has surrendered: "He was mute and motionless. He had given up, he had abdicated. His destiny was done."

This pathetic lesson, however, is not the fable's true meaning. The narrator, quite exceptionally, attempts to act. Before he abstracts the *character* as a tragic exemplar, he responds concretely to the acrobat as *person* by deciphering his emotional turmoil:

> But what a deep, unforgettable look he cast over the crowd and the lights, whose moving waves stopped a few steps from his repulsive wretchedness! I felt my throat strangled by the dreadful hand of hysteria, and my sight seemed to be blocked by rebellious tears refusing to fall.
>
> What to do? Why ask the unfortunate man what curiosity, what marvel he had to display in that stinking darkness, behind his torn curtain? In fact, I did not dare; and, although the cause of my timidity might make you laugh, I admit that I was afraid of humiliating him.

As a first reaction, the observer can neither analyze nor cry, his compassion is too intense. So he remains "mute and immobile" like the old man himself. Their respective glances associate the two frail artists. The entertainer's "regard profond, inoubliable" evokes tragic memories and present failures.[10] The narrator's eyes betray his creative paralysis: "il me sembla que mes regards étaient offusqués par ces larmes rebelles qui ne veulent pas tomber." The writer's "hysteria" points to a conflict buried far within his consciousness.

Then a momentous change occurs; the stroller, for the first

time, ceases merely to observe and to reflect. But when he initiates an act of practical charity, he is again inhibited, this time —paradoxically—by his genuine sensitivity to the clown's personal dignity: "Je craignais de l'humilier." After he makes the move, the public's grossly material "ecstasy" drowns his generosity: "Finally, just as I had resolved to place some money in passing on part of his platform, hoping that he would guess my intention, a huge backflow of populace, caused by some unknown turmoil, swept me far from him." Ironically, the same "crowds" of fable number 12, a positive "bath of multitude," wash away this sensitive gesture.

A coda translates the allegory without resolving the problem of interpretation introduced in fable number 6, "To Each His Chimera" (e.g., "And for a few moments I persistently tried to understand this mystery"). "The Old Acrobat" formulates a similarly reflective moment: "And, turning around, obsessed by that vision, I tried to analyze my sudden sorrow." The lesson is moving but its obviousness arouses suspicion: "I have just seen the image of the old writer [*du vieil homme de lettres*] who has survived the generation whose brilliant entertainer he was; of the old poet without friends, without family, without children, debased by his wretchedness and the public's ingratitude, and whose booth the forgetful world no longer wants to enter!"

This formula sentimentally confirms the crowd's antagonism to kindness as well as to art, but it should not divert us from the fable's living center: the *young* writer's stubborn hope—which the *old* "acrobat" appears to refute—that creativity and community can coexist, and even reinforce each other. We wonder if all writers must inevitably finish their lives forgotten, solitary, and misunderstood.

The *explicit* translation of "The Old Acrobat" places all artists among the world's destitute. The old man's decay reiterates "The Old Woman's Despair" (no. 2) and "Widows," which directly precedes, presaging the narrator's own future as a childless, friendless bachelor who, like Kafka's "Hunger Artist," remains an entertainer without an audience, an artist-orphan. Baudelaire himself, in a remarkable letter to his mother (May 1861), makes suicidal threats in similar terms: "I am alone, without friends, without a mistress, without a dog and without a cat, to whom I might complain. I only have my father's portrait, which is always silent" (CPl 2:152; Mauron 1966, 43–60). The poet's fidelity to his mistress, the abusive and aging Jeanne Duval, testifies to his genuine identification.

"Crowds" and "The Old Acrobat," the two minor panels of the triptych, demonstrate that transcendence of the self through collective entertainment or self-projection into an empty Other are frail escapes from finitude and its sorrows. Yet, despite its convincing pathos, the clown allegory calls for more subtle interpretation, beyond the tidy exclusion of professional success and failure, and personal sterility and isolation. That is why I read the three fables as one hermeneutic entity. "Widows," the middle panel, highlights their positive implications. A process of bereavement allows the artist both to embrace finitude and to integrate his ideal.

THE COMPLETE POET AS WIDOWED MOTHER

The central tableau, "Widows," asserts the power of moral action while preserving the sanctity of solitary inwardness. Its ethical sensitivity completes the search for inspiration which unifies the completed collection. The *flâneur* undergoes a profound conversion; moved by his admiration for a majestic widow, the habitually detached observer becomes a "poet" before our very eyes. Until now, *woman* had confirmed a rigid duality, either perfect or depraved. Now the "widow" fosters his literary program (to write poetry) while touching his intimate yearnings, his search for a mother.

At the beginning, however, consistently with other fables, the narrator emphasizes the exploitive nature of his inquiry. He again chooses to study victims, such as the anguished friends in "The Bad Glazier" (no. 9), associating himself, in the opening allusion, to the eighteenth-century *moraliste* Vauvenargues. The postromantic observer combines the roles of "poet" (an artist) and "philosopher" (a sort of sociologist)—both of whom "feel irresistibly swept toward everything that is weak, ruined, saddened, orphaned." His studies of "those maimed by life" provide "a guaranteed fodder" for his machinelike mind: "A practiced eye is never wrong. In those rigid or dejected features, in those hollow and dull eyes, or eyes shining with the battle's final flares, in those deep and numerous wrinkles, in those so slow or so spasmodic gaits, it immediately deciphers innumerable legends of love deceived, of unrecognized devotion, of unrewarded efforts, of hunger and cold humbly, silently endured." Following standard literary practice, he translates "observed" physical traits into allegories of moral life. Like Balzac, he sharpens his ability immediately to invent *legends* (this key word will reappear in a decisive questioning of the esthetic in "Windows" ["Les Fenêtres," no. 35]).

From the beginning, he admits that his goal is not ethical, to touch persons, but to harvest stories. We cannot fathom the narrator's moral attitude. On one level, recognizing his craftsman's pride, we cannot help but pity the subjects of his contemplation. Is his expressed hardness of heart simply naive? We find no hint of irony, or compassion, tacit or direct, to reassure us. He addresses his readers, not to arouse our tenderness but, somewhat coldly, to sketch an intriguing contrast: "Have you sometimes noticed widows on those lonely benches, impoverished widows? Whether or not they are wearing mourning, they are easy to recognize. Besides, something is always missing in the poor's mourning clothes, an absence of harmony that makes them more heartbreaking. The poor are forced to skimp on their sorrow. The rich wear theirs in full force."

The analyst further contrasts the two types: "Which widow is the sadder, and the more saddening, the one who drags by the hand a little kid with whom she cannot share her reverie, or the one who is completely alone? I don't know..." He views their loneliness and grief in esthetic categories ("la plus attristante") as well as in ethical or inwardly empathic terms: she is also "la plus triste." Neither widow remarries and both remain spiritually pure. But the crucial difference is that one is a mother, while the other—the childless one—is utterly isolated. The widowed *mother* endures a more exquisite agony, since she can almost—but not quite—communicate her inner life, "partager sa rêverie."

The childless widow, who is a figure of the observer's own alienation, sterility—and desire—condenses all previous strangers: the old woman, strollers, rejected writers, clowns in despair, and of course narrators of previous fables. Still, she engages only his intellectual curiosity:

> I once happened to spend long hours following an old afflicted woman of that kind. Stiff, erect, wearing a worn-out little shawl, she maintained in her entire being a stoic pride.
>
> She was obviously condemned, by her absolute solitude, to an old bachelor's habits, and the masculine character of her behavior added a mysterious piquancy to their austerity.

The lone woman appears to be, as it were, a "bachelor-widow," almost bitterly ascetic, despite the urgency of her thirst for vitality: "she hunted through local papers [*gazettes*], with active eyes, once scalded by tears, for some news of intense and personal interest." Emotions enter her life, not through the conventional *journal* or *revue* (in French terms), but from sensationalistic *gazettes*.[11] At the same time, "le caractère masculin de ses moeurs" neutralizes any potential sexuality.

The bachelor-widow is a female counterpart of previous male attempts to overcome despair through sensory stimulation or reverie, self-engrossed fantasy. After reading, she will attend a public band concert, another equivalent of a fair (no. 14). But the crowd bestows no *bain de multitude*, no ecstatic release: "This was probably the little debauchery of that innocent old woman (or that purified old woman), a well-earned consolation for one of those oppressive days without friends, without chatting, without joy, without a confidant, which God allowed to fall on her three hundred sixty-five times a year, perhaps already for many years!" The bachelor-widow may be redeemed by her "innocence." Total loss has purified her in an ironically religious way, as if her chastity, enforced by her loved one's death, were a voluntary dedication to a sacred ideal. Her bereavement—underlined by the repeated *sans* (without)—consecrates her wretched devotion.

Popular music diverts this unrescued outcast abandoned to mute memories and vague wishes.

The narrator's curiosity quickly changes to admiration as the widowed mother—clearly the favorite—makes her glorious entrance: "On that particular day, across that populace dressed in overalls and calico dresses, I noticed a creature whose nobility stood in brilliant contrast to all the surrounding coarseness." The bachelor-widow is pathetic (like the old acrobat), but the mother is sublime. The story pivots on this paragraph (lines 84–93) which describes his conversion, echoing Pascal's *Pensée* 72 in which scientific ambition subsides into religious awe when faced with the two infinites. A double contrast underlines her superiority. Like the childless widow she attends a band concert, but she surmounts the proletarian mass—the "crowd of pariahs"—with which only her economic straits associate her.

The narrator excitedly repeats: which widow is the sadder, the one with, or the one without, a child? The mother is the paragon of beauty and she attracts heaps of positive adjectives:

> She was a tall, majestic woman, and so noble in her entire bearing, that I cannot recall having seen her peer in collections of aristocratic beauties of the past. A perfume of haughty virtue emanated from her entire person. Her face, sad and thinned, was in perfect accord with the formal mourning in which she was dressed. She, too, like the plebeians with whom she had mixed without seeing them, watched the luminous society with knowing eyes, and she listened while gently nodding her head.

The mother is admirable because of her self-awareness, her "pensiveness," her mental autonomy. The narrator is as much moved by her "knowing" gaze (*un oeil profond*) as he is by her graceful melancholy and mature loveliness. He evokes her physical harmony with the rare musical term *accordance*, while insisting on her integrity and her private thoughts: "elle écoutait en hochant doucement la tête."[12]

The narrator's decisive, though as yet imperceptible, conversion occurs in this third-from-the-last paragraph. He will switch from artistic judgment (informed by empathy) to intense but lucid identification. At this point, however, the majestic widow only arouses the philosopher's "admiration," and mere intellectual "curiosity" guides his attempts to explain this "Singulière vision!" He formulates another question that is both psychological and literary: "Then why does she remain voluntarily in surroundings where she creates such a brilliant contrast?"

The penultimate paragraph fulfills the philosophical goal of "To Each His Chimera" (no. 6): to understand heroism of the everyday. In "Widows" as well, the word "curiosity" signals the observer's vigilant though detached state of mind which camouflages a passionate desire to conquer despair. In "Widows" he succeeds: "But drawing nearer to her out of curiosity, I thought I guessed the reason. The tall widow was holding the hand of a child dressed in black like herself. However modest the admission, that price was perhaps enough to purchase one of the little creature's needs, better still, a superfluity, a toy." The poor child's true pleasure is not a glittering object (nor a rat!—see fable no. 19), but maternal devotion. Her tender regard rewards the observer as well.

The widowed mother finally cures the narrator's oft-repeated paralysis. Like himself, she is "without friends, without chatting, without joy, without a confidant," for her child is not an equal and mature companion. The regally sacrificial woman—and her child—are strangers like himself. Yet the mother is "majestueuse, et si noble dans tout son air," not because of her widowhood, her loss, but because she has been able freely to transcend heartache through active love. Her benevolent and modest heroism, combining self-involvement with solicitude for another person, reconciles her with the world. As Kierkegaard understood: "If one wants to make sure that love is completely unselfish, he eliminates every possibility of repayment. But precisely this is eliminated in the relationship to the one who is dead. If love nevertheless remains, it is in truth unselfish" (1962, 320). She is another Parisian prowler, but adequately fulfilled.

The widowed mother completes the writer's ethical conversion. "Crowds" had revealed the fallacy of projected empathy; "Widows" reenacts the genesis of poetry from self-transcending compassion, amalgamated in a "prose poem," as the final lines rhythmically attest: "And she probably walked home, meditating and dreaming, alone, forever alone. For a child is unruly, selfish, without gentleness and without patience; and he cannot even, like a mere animal, like a dog or a cat, serve as a confidant to lonely sorrows." A profound autobiographical pathos links Baudelaire the author with both mother and child—which textual analysis only confirms. The author has reconstituted his family! This widowed mother is a phantom of his own, left with a six-year-old Charles when her first husband, his beloved father, François Baudelaire, died. And imagine the poet's fierce ambivalence at the death of his feared stepfather, General Aupick, on 27 April 1857, barely two months before *Les Fleurs du Mal* first went on sale. The Oedipal poet-child had more than fantasized opportunities to make his mother available (Godfrey 1985).[13]

In the text, which needs no outside support, the widowed mother is a triumphal figure of the poet: exiled from her Ideal, her pain is redeemed by the lofty asceticism of motherhood. Death had removed her husband, and her isolation is only magnified by her little boy's appropriate egotism. But like the writer, she takes refuge in her inner world, "méditant et rêvant." And yet she also embellishes her son's life. The "little prose poem" (which the very end of the narrative becomes) embraces that dialectic of intimacy and distance shared by mother and child—and which characterizes all realistic relationships. Has the narrator accepted the necessary imperfection of reciprocal love?

"Widows" does not conclude simply with that wistful wisdom—the only meaning rendered by English translation. The closing sentences of "Widows" fold back upon themselves and change form. The sudden appearance of blank verse illustrates the genesis of poetry, thus completing the explicit account. The French original concretely imitates her emotions as the detached "philosopher" completes his metamorphosis into an "active and fertile poet." The narrator himself becomes, as it were, a poet–widowed mother—although socially, he remains a bachelor through bereavement.

The "prose poem" which closes the fable becomes a figure of

its creation. Alone among the collection of fifty, it ends with an alexandrine (twelve syllables) preceded by three clauses, each of which contains six syllables when pronounced normally, as it evokes the "selfish child":[14]

> et il ne peut mêm*e* pas,
> comm*e* le pur animal,
> comm*e* le chien et le chat,
> servir de confident aux douleurs solitaires.

This lyrical coda supplants the analytical narrative. Its harmony of form and content sings of the paradoxical seclusion and love shared by mother and child. Although they remain within the prose typographical format, the blank verse lines—reinforced by the alliteration *chien/chat* and the rhyme *pas/chat*—emerge rhythmically from that prose and point to the fable's *metatextual theme:* a textual reflection upon the text's own esthetic status. The widowed mother releases in the lone Parisian a mournful but magnificent music.

The true theme of "Widows"—and of the entire triptych—is the genesis of poetry through bereavement. The lyrical ending of "Widows" appears to dissolve the conflict between fantasy and compassion. The widowed mother reconciles her moral and introverted needs, and so her practical love inspires an ethical poetry. The narrator's identification with her resolves the frustrating closure of the *saltimbanque* allegory, in which the old man relinquishes hope and the observer cannot complete his charitable act.

Does Baudelaire the author become a widowed mother, incorporating her pain and joy, while at the same time engendering that "poetic prose, musical without rhythm and without rhyme, supple enough and choppy enough to fit the soul's lyrical movements, the undulations of reverie, the jolts of consciousness" ("To Arsène Houssaye," 1862)? The completed fable testifies to that possibility.

CONCLUSIONS ARE PROVISIONAL

The poet's emulation of the widowed mother reflects his self-figuration as an estranged, bereaved, but essentially loving and productive person. The conflicting perspectives of what I call the "Widows Triptych" encompass this profound coherence. When the alienated bachelor becomes a "fertile poet," his divided selves commune. Two sets of oppositions are, at least theoretically, harmonized: (1) solipsistic projection versus systematic observation of real persons, in "Crowds" and "Widows"; (2) "empathy" experienced within oneself versus transitive concern for another individual, in "The Old Acrobat" and "Widows." The first is the dialectic within "poetry": realism versus reverie; the second, the dialectic within "charity" (or practical caring): imagined identification versus action. Our heuristic distinction between "the ethical" and "the esthetic" collapses.

But can we honestly conclude? As convinced as I was that Baudelaire reached his most advanced integration of poetry and tenderness, my evolving reflection faced me with what appears to be an unresolvable contradiction between my optimism and the skepticism represented by Paul de Man. My initial article, "Baudelaire's Portrait of the Poet as Widow" (Kaplan 1980), had defended the triptych's implicit ethic against the view that allegory proves ultimately incapable of reflecting personal presence or the Absolute.

Barbara Johnson's response (in a personal communication, 27 February 1981) placed my denial of de Man's "negativity" into a balanced perspective: "The existence of poetic energy, which you take as compensation for the loss of immediacy or possession, can be read positively (as you do, as creative maternity) or negatively (as the confirmation of inescapable loss by the very language that seeks to overcome it, as I think Paul de Man does). De Man's apparent belief in the fallacies of identification and your apparent belief in the saving action of empathy are probably irreducibly divided."

This dialogue of scholars shows how Baudelaire's practice surpasses our theories. A critical view is just that—a perspective (more or less) justified by the primary texts. I remain convinced, of course, that the real integrity of Baudelaire's writings lies in the author's thrust toward some sort of insight into reality and his sometimes anguished attempts to communicate those insights during an unfriendly cultural moment.[15] The critical aporia defined by deconstruction did not stymie the poet; it inspired him to inaugurate a literature which relentlessly delves beneath all good intentions, challenging norms defended by me or anyone else. Just as in chapter 1 we noted that the poet of "Le Masque" was "intoxicated" (*enivré*) by the suffering woman, so now we might suspect that his empathy with the widowed mother might serve primarily to induce his verbal productions.

In fact, Baudelaire was not naive; he was acutely aware that moral emotions can become confused with self-gratification. In "The Poem of Hashish" (1858), he describes how the two, in practice, despite any theoretical distinction, remain inseparable for the poet: "The craving for protection, a feeling of devoted and fervent paternity can become mixed with a culpable sensuality that can not always be explained or forgiven by hashish" (*OC* 1:434). The moving poem from "Tableaux parisiens," "Les Petites Vieilles" (Little old women, *FM*, added in 1861 as no. 91), which typifies the new ethical poetry, also points to its inherent estheticism:

> Mais moi, moi qui de loin tendrement vous surveille,
> L'oeil inquiet, fixé sur vos pas incertains,
> Tout comme si j'étais votre père, ô merveille!
> *Je goûte à votre insu des plaisirs clandestins*
>
> (Lines 73–76, italics added)

(But I, I who tenderly observe you from a distance, as if I were your father, O miracle! *I enjoy clandestine pleasures without you knowing it*)

The seamless compassion of this triptych—which completes the narrator's idealist struggles—will give way to irony, confirming the essayist's self-scrutiny. Further fables accept inescapable clashes between two valid, but logically irreconcilable, perspectives. In that sense, Baudelaire becomes our first deconstructionist poet; his often devastating irony, however, maintains as its counterpoint a reverence for ordinary people. Today's theories are only beginning to fathom the new genre which emerged from this "critical poetry." What we have abstracted as the ethical and the esthetic are—quite separately and within themselves—inherently flawed.

5

THE MODERN FABLE IS BORN

The Esthetic and Its Ontological Fallacy

Baudelaire's memorandum of 1865 established the definitive order of *The Parisian Prowler*, thus preserving as its foundation the ensemble of twenty-six pieces printed, in four sets, for *La Presse*. The prepublication history of the latter two (the third series appeared on 24 September 1862 and the fourth was composed in proof for the 27 September issue but never published) demonstrates the gestation and birth of the mature genre. The process began in 1855. By 1862, Baudelaire had fully reconceived his initial experiments—"Twilight" and "Solitude" ("Le Crépuscule du soir," "La Solitude")—for *La Presse*, eventually placing them at the center of his future collection (nos. 22 and 23). In ten years the poet had inaugurated his "absolute beginning."

Two historical stages mark the process by which "prose poems" became "fables of modern life." First, Baudelaire revised the earliest texts: two verse poems, "Le Soir" and "Le Matin" (Evening, Morning) which had accompanied two rhythmic prose pieces, "Le Crépuscule du soir" and "La Solitude," in the 1855 *Hommage à C. F. Denecourt*. These original melodic prose pieces were intended to complement the verse "models." These truly "prose poems" were still formal experiments. Then Baudelaire revised them and included them in a larger sequence: "Plans," "The Clock," "Tresses," and "Invitation to the Voyage" ("Les projets," "L'Horloge," "La Chevelure" [the original title which later was changed to "Un Hémisphère dans une chevelure"], "L'Invitation au Voyage"). He labeled these six pieces which appeared in *Le Présent* the same year as *Les Fleurs du Mal*, in 1857, "nocturnal poems." Self-reflective irony and analysis, not lyrical prose, now became their hallmark.

The second stage introduces a more sophisticated theme: the struggle between lyricism and worldly responsibilities, and a new name: "prose poems." Their principal subject becomes the poet's vocation in relation to other people. In February 1861 the second edition of *Les Fleurs du Mal*, which has remained definitive, went on sale. Baudelaire revised his six "nocturnal poems" of 1857 and, in November 1861, the *Revue Fantaisiste* published his series of nine *poèmes en prose*—so named for the first time—adding three very significant fables to the earlier sequence: "Crowds," "Widows," and "The Old Acrobat."

Next, he transported this "*Revue Fantaisiste* triptych" to close the second series published on 27 August 1862 in *La Presse*. He had thus split the *Revue Fantaisiste* series into two "triptychs." He added "The Cake" ("Le Gâteau," no. 15) to introduce the third *Presse* series. To the 1862 proofs of the fourth *Presse* series he added "The Temptations, or Eros, Plutus, and Fame" ("Les Tentations, ou Eros, Plutus et la Gloire," no. 21) at the head, and a revised sequence of three at the end: "Twilight," "Solitude," and "Plans" ("Les Projets," nos. 22–24); the original versions of the first two, we recall, had appeared in 1855 as the most primitive "prose poems."[1] Baudelaire had successfully completed his battle with the idealist first edition of *Les Fleurs du Mal* and consolidated his modern fables.

"The Cake" and "Temptations" (nos. 15 and 21) are critical guides to the two sets of "esthetic fables" which follow them. These two long narratives introduce a crisis of self-awareness and establish the subversive irony which characterizes the later pieces. (The two pairs of "ethical fables" which follow each "esthetic" grouping will be examined in the next chapter.) Now his philosophical judgment comes to the fore and recenters the stories. The initial dialectical conflicts ripen into an ontological questioning of imagination as such. Fantasy no longer appears to be superior to the "exterior life" (no. 24).

A FRATRICIDAL WAR

The sequence of six in the *Presse* series 3 juxtaposes masterful dreams with equally impressive fables of self-consciousness that highlight their frailty. This double perspective within the esthetic extends "The Artist's *Confiteor*" (no. 3) which had defined the "uneasiness and concrete suffering" produced by intense reverie (or voluptuous pleasure). The "truly *spiritual* room," after all, had retained its twilight alloy, "perfumed with regret and desire" (no. 5). Now these contradictions inherent to autonomous imagination threaten the narrator as much as the world's demands.

"The Cake" begins the cycle by demolishing utopian euphoria. Its irony follows from two contradictory perceptions of the object *gâteau:* common bread, or "cake," food transformed by starvation into an aristocratic delight, recalling Marie Antoinette's vicious quip, "Let them eat cake!" The italicized title word provides metatextual irony as it juxtaposes the narrator's comfort and the desperation of two wretched boys. The adventure transpires within the familiar "supernaturalist" landscape, introduced in the first and longest paragraph (33 lines out of 81).[2] A traveler's reverie expands while, at the same time, he observes and evaluates his mental processes.

Earth and heaven "correspond" with themselves and with the self's plenitude, as in "The Artist's *Confiteor*," "The Fool and the Venus" (nos. 3, 7), and the famous poems "Elévation" and "Correspondances" (*FM*, nos. 3 and 4). The dreamer's inner and outer worlds meld into each other and flow into his "soul": "Vulgar passions, such as hatred and worldly love, now felt as distant as the clouds parading deeply in the abysses beneath my feet; my soul seemed as vast and as pure as the sky's dome which enveloped me." But the analyst within him senses danger: "And I remember that this rare and solemn sensation, caused by a grand and perfectly silent movement, filled me with a joy mingled with fear."

This prologue describes how "beatitude" briefly suspends the nagging evidence of original sin—mankind's inborn impulse to do evil—which Baudelaire militantly defended against his liberal contemporaries.[3] Personal anxieties also disappear:

> In short, I felt myself to be in perfect peace with myself and with the universe, thanks to the impassioning beauty encircling me. I even believe that, in my perfect beatitude and in total forgetfulness of all earthly evil, I had arrived at the idea of no longer finding so ridiculous the newspapers which claim that people are born good—until incorrigible matter renewed its demands. Then I began to think about relieving the fatigue and alleviating the hunger caused by such a long ascent. I took from my pocket a big piece of bread, a leather cup and a flask of a certain elixir that pharmacists sell these days to tourists to be mixed when needed with melted snow.

The dreamer's trance almost neutralizes his post-1848 cynicism, and he almost espouses the current ideology of infinite progress, Enlightenment faith imported into romantic natural religion. He "forgets" his body until hunger and weariness remind him of food and drugs. His "elixir" could very well be another "vial of laudanum," "fertile in caresses and betrayals" (no. 5) which could not magically transform his tawdry life.

The next paragraphs display the disastrous results of generosity, such as the narrator of "The Old Acrobat," in the preceding fable, could not realize. The famished hiker offers his bread to a poverty-stricken urchin; his own affliction makes him sensitive to another's needs. Then the fable's title reappears, now italicized to introduce the irony: "A little ragged creature stood before me, black, dishevelled, whose hollow eyes, wild and as if beseeching, were devouring the piece of bread. And I heard him, in a low, hoarse voice, moan the word: '*cake!*'"

The tourist's idyllic peace vanishes when another starving "savage" intrudes and both immediately begin to tear each other, and their nourishment, apart. The elegant, precise style reinforces the irony as it emphasizes the mechanical gestures of these "twins." The brutally graphic description of their "hideous struggle" (which I omit entirely) dramatizes the futility of ethics: "the piece of bread had disappeared, and its crumbs were scattered like the grains of sand with which it was mixed."

A self-reflective coda interprets the parable by contrasting the traveler's initial delight with his disillusion. The text's rigorously dialectic structure reinforces the absolute separation of the dreamer's two worlds: "That performance obscured the landscape for me, and the calm joy gladdening my soul before I saw those little men had completely disappeared. I remained saddened for quite a while, and I incessantly repeated to myself: 'So there exists a magnificent land where bread is called *cake*, a delicacy so rare that it suffices to beget a perfectly fratricidal war!' " His naive joy mixed with fear matures into what Paul Ricoeur calls "the sadness of finitude," the recognition and acceptance of mortality and our fallible nature (1965, 123–24; Kaplan 1979). But does his grief reconcile him with reality through a process of mourning? The sarcastic conclusion about "un pays superbe où le pain s'appelle du *gâteau*"—reinforced by the repeated italics—suggests that he despairs of resolving the battle between dreamed freedom and physical hunger, undermining both "poetry *and* charity." All that remains is a vigorous distrust of all subjectivity.

LYRICISM IN QUESTION

By way of contrast, the three following "esthetic" pieces celebrate the powers of fantasy. "The Clock," "A Hemisphere in Tresses," and "Invitation to the Voyage" (nos. 16–18), truly lyrical prose poems forming the primitive genre, remained together as a sequence from *Le Présent* (1857) to the 1861 *Revue Fantaisiste* to the 1869 posthumous edition. Their rhetoric and imagery indeed recall seductive love cycles of "Spleen et Idéal" such as "Parfum exotique" and "La Chevelure" (Exotic perfume, Tresses [*FM*, nos. 22–23]), "Le Beau navire" and "L'Invitation au voyage" (The beautiful ship, Invitation to the voyage [*FM*, nos. 52–53]).[4] "The Cake"—introduced only in *La Presse*—reinforces their self-critical potential.

"The Clock" as a straightforward allegory of timelessness parallels the subverted supernaturalism of the preceding adventure. Its imagery is conventionally exotic: China as an ideal world and the cat as a female. But the humorous tone immediately alerts us to the presence of irony. A missionary in the "outskirts of Nankin" asks "a kid from the Celestial Empire" what time it is. The latter looks into the eyes of his "very fat cat" (*un fort gros chat*) and answers: "it is not yet quite noon." Translating the anecdote, the narrator looks into his mistress's eyes and sees "Eternity!" What could be more congenially "poetic"?

She appears to liberate his imagination. And her eyes are not the "terrifying *peepers*" of the Idol (no. 5) which betray, nor those of the Venus (no. 7) staring into the beyond. One long, rhythmical sentence weaves a poem of fragrances, boundless reveries, and we are lulled by its florid style:

> As for me, if I turn toward beautiful Felina, so well named, who is at once the honor of her sex, my heart's pride and my mind's perfume, whether it be night, whether it be day, in full light or dark shadow, I always see the time clearly, in the depths of her adorable eyes, a vast, solemn time, always the same, huge as space, without divisions into minutes nor seconds—an immobile time not marked on clocks, and yet light as a sigh, swift as a glance.

But the final paragraph deflates this swell. A coda addresses an anonymous muse for whom the poet had presumably written his song. It is a flippant *envoi* which parodies its own artifice:[5] "Now is this not, Madam, a truly praiseworthy madrigal, and as exaggerated as yourself? In fact, I took such delight in elaborating this pretentious romance, that I will ask nothing of you in exchange." What he calls *cette prétentieuse galanterie* and the term *emphatique* apply equally to text and mistress, recalling the *emphase* of cleverness or pretense vehemently denounced in "A Joker" and "The Wild Woman and the Affected Coquette" (nos. 4, 11). The cat's eyes open to a treacherous paradise, and the "poem" they inspire is a deceptive "exchange" for love. Another animal tale, "The Good Dogs" (no. 50), will complete the collection with a decisively nonironic exchange of art for friendship (see chap. 9).

The justly famous "A Hemisphere in Tresses" fulfills the author's ambition to perfect "a poetic prose, musical without rhyme and without rhythm"—but it also subverts its own lyricism. It is one of *the only three* in the collection of fifty that are conventionally "poetic" (the others are "Invitation to the Voyage" and

"Twilight," nos. 18, 22). Barbara Johnson sensitively details the ways in which the prose poem "ironizes" its verse counterpart, unraveling the metaphorical equivalences and analogies implicit in the lyric.[6] "A Hemisphere in Tresses," in its own right as well, pinpoints its own artifice.

Rhythmical repetitions structure the seven brief paragraphs as stanzas. The narrator becomes a visionary who, like the poet of "La Chevelure" (*FM*, no. 23, added in 1861), generates scenes of sensuality and repose from smelling a woman's head of hair (Bersani 1977, 31–35). Memories appear to stimulate these voluptuous idealizations:

> Let me inhale ever so long, ever so long, the odor of your hair, plunge my whole face into it, like a thirsting man into the water of a spring, and wave it with my hand like a fragrant handkerchief, stirring memories into the air.
>
> If only you could know everything I see! everything I feel! everything I hear in your hair! My soul travels on aromas like other men's souls on music.

This is the "Baudelaire" cherished by posterity. A pulsing synesthesia flows from a provocative aroma. Departure shapes the seemingly limitless mental energy of which the "tresses" are but a sensuous pretext: "Your hair holds an entire dream, filled with sails and rigging," and so on. The rhapsodic prose elaborates this hypnotic process with virtuosity.

Three paragraphs construct a cosmos, each one launching its profusion of enchanting pictures with the same expression: "In the ocean of your tresses," "In the strokings of your tresses," "In the fiery hearth of your tresses." Familiar images evoke physical joys: a teeming port, "an immense sky where basks the eternal heat," rocking motions of boats, "the odor of tobacco mixed with opium and sugar"—summarized in "the infinity of the tropical azure." A confluence of essences representing sexual arousal, traveling, and relaxation completes the inward paradise: "on the downy shores of your tresses I become intoxicated with the mingled smells of tar, musk, and coconut oil." At last the sign of critical self-awareness: "enivré" (intoxicated).

The concluding "stanza" repeats and resolves the prelude, while the final refrain echoes the end of the first paragraph. First the dreamer had "stirred memories in the air" as if he were on a departing boat, waving at loved ones remaining on shore. His voyage now ends with a shocking literalism: "Let me bite ever so long into your tresses heavy and black. When I nibble at your elastic and unruly hair, I seem to be eating memories."

For the first time in this melodic prose, the narrator questions the authenticity of his productions: "*il me semble* que je mange des souvenirs." Were his previous images fictions or actual recollections of experience? Does reverie awaken memories or alienate him further from the world by creating fantasies which then became memories, dreamed traces of desire? Now it is clear that the ontological confusion was immanent from the very beginning, when he had explained: "Your hair holds an entire dream." Baudelaire's "prose poem" has deconstructed its own "poetic" world.

This internal skepticism parallels important poems Baudelaire added to the 1861 edition of *Les Fleurs du Mal*. The "second revolution," which Barbara Johnson attributes to the prose poems, actually derives from his revised masterwork. In chapter 1, we examined the transformed "Beauty Cycle" of the first section, "Spleen et Idéal." A sequence of at least seven poems, from "La Beauté" (*FM*, no. 17) through "La Chevelure" (*FM*, no. 23), juxtaposes poems which indulge in reverie naively with pieces doubting the viability of such transcendence. "Parfum exotique" (*FM*, no. 22 of both editions) celebrates synesthesia, while "La Chevelure" (added in 1861) ends its intoxicating utopia with a question (lines 34–35):

> N'es-tu pas l'oasis où je rêve, et la gourde
> Où je hume à long traits le vin du souvenir?

(Are you not the oasis where I dream, and the gourd from which
I inhale deeply the wine of memory?)

It is true, as Barbara Johnson writes, that the prose poem, in which the dreamer "mange des souvenirs," "bares the arbitrarily *linguistic*, discontinuous character of the rhetorical transfer in the verse: The figure 'to eat memories' thus becomes a figure of the factuality of the poetic figure 'to drink the wine of memory' that it literalizes and metonymizes" (1979, 53). The verse, as well, anatomizes the dynamics of autonomous imagination; the final question simultaneously justifies idealization while posing a fundamental extraliterary question: Is it real?

"Invitation to the Voyage" that directly follows, usually appreciated as a poetic rhapsody, in fact perfects this self-analysis. It completes the sequence with a similar combination of intense symbolic experience and "critical distance"—also brilliantly analyzed by Barbara Johnson (1980, 23–48). Its 1857, 1861, and 1862 versions are essentially the same, as they orchestrate a reverie of eleven strophic paragraphs. Toward the middle (lines 55–57 out of 92), after magnificent developments, the narrator detaches himself from the metaphorical flow when he describes his ideal world as a "remarkable land, superior to others, as Art is to Nature, where dream refashions Nature, where it is corrected, embellished, recast."

He then explains that his female companion symbolizes the landscape which itself symbolizes the poet's mental state: "Would you not be framed by your analogy there, and could you not mirror yourself, as the mystics say, in your own *correspondence?*" She is an "incomparable flower, retrieved tulip, allegorical dahlia." These internal translations, reinforced by the rhetorical question, counterbalance the captivating rhythms. Our intelligence supplants the vague verbal figments.

All four fables (nos. 15–18)—within each text and as a group—defend "the possible." (The two "ethical fables" that complete the third *Presse* sequence—"The Poor Boy's Toy" and "The Fairies' Gifts"—will be examined in the next chapter.) The ending of "Invitation to the Voyage" systematically recapitulates the entire adventure while translating—or demystifying—its origin as desire. The penultimate paragraph formulates the ontological question of literature's unreality:

> Dreams! always dreams! And the more ambitious and delicate the soul, the more dreams remove it from the possible. Each of us carries within a dose of natural opium, ceaselessly secreted

> and renewed; and, from birth to death, how many hours can we count filled with concrete delight, with well-executed and resolute action? Will we ever live, will we ever enter that picture painted by my mind, that painting which resembles you?

"Invitation to the Voyage" bares the art of extended metaphor and image association. And the narrator remains skeptical about the possibility of "la jouissance positive . . . l'action réussie et décidée." Obviously, no one can "passer dans ce tableau qu'a peint mon esprit." Objectivity inhibits our powerful urge to replace reality with pictures.

TEMPTATIONS TO PERSONAL INTEGRITY

The unpublished fourth—and final—*Presse* sequence opens with a parallel grouping of four which further specifies that all esthetic choices lead nowhere. "The Temptations, or Eros, Plutus, and Fame" introduces three shorter pieces, "Twilight," "Solitude," and "Plans" (nos. 21–24), which anatomize the process. This parody of a Faustian fable, despite its tongue-in-cheek tone, staunchly maintains the narrator's independence against the "sulfurous splendor that emanated from these three characters" who represent the three main areas of his artistic aspirations.

Eros condenses all the preceding esthetic fables. A synesthesia, with which we are quite familiar, joins color, touch, smell, and sound, and transports the imagination. Odors mix with heat to produce "visible perfumes," as in "The Fool and the Venus" (no. 7), "hothouse sensations" and narcotizing reveries of "The Double Room" (no. 5), summarizing all inspiration derived from the senses and artificially induced visions: "and each time he sighed, musky insects, flitting about, would light up in his burning breath." But his allegorical accoutrements condemn their demonic potential: a purple, regal tunic, compromised by a living belt in the form of a langorous, fire-eyed serpent, bottles filled with "sinister liquors," "shiny knives," and surgical instruments. Eros's effete vanity is revealed by the broken gold chain on his "delicate ankles."

This first temptation promises the power to create forms which may rival divine creation (as in "The Artist's *Confiteor*," no. 3): " 'If you want, if you want, I will make you the lord of souls, and you will be the master of living matter, even more than the sculptor masters clay. And you will experience the pleasure, ceaselessly reborn, of leaving yourself so as to forget yourself in others, and of attracting other souls until you absorb them into yours.' " But, firmly resisting this "insidious intoxication," the *flâneur* of "Crowds" now redeems his "holy prostitution of the soul" (no. 12) and refuses to confuse fantasy with power over others. He defends moral self-awareness and seems to welcome reality, the "Specter" of "the double room" (no. 5), as he now responds defiantly: "I remember!"

Plutus is less subtle than the esthete "of an ambiguous sex"; he represents the collusion between money, power, and love. Its moral horror, "the myriad forms of universal wretchedness," are tatooed on the hide of this "huge man, with a fat eyeless face, whose massive potbelly sagged down over his hips." The narrator easily "turns away in disgust" and secures his compassion against this counterfeit equivalence of might and right: " 'I do not need anyone's wretchedness for my delight [*jouissance*].' " He forgoes financial despotism in favor of justice.

Yet the female Satan changes his attitude to lively interest. "La Gloire" (Fame) is an attractive middle-aged woman, spiced with marks of mortality, like many females to whom he feels especially drawn, like the old woman (no. 2) and the majestic widow (no. 13). Her "weird charm" touches his deepest yearnings for a submissive but nurturing mother: "To define that charm, I could compare it to nothing better than to that of quite beautiful women past their prime [*des très-belles femmes sur le retour*], who have stopped aging however, and whose beauty preserves the penetrating magic of ruins." Other "quite beautiful" older women will reconfirm the narrator's authentic compassion, but this one only aggravates his ambivalence and sense of danger.

The female Devil of "The Temptations" unmasks the erotic lust which the poet was able *relatively* to repress toward these literary stand-ins for his mother.[7] A lessening of sexual anxiety, so threatening when associated with young women, usually allows

Baudelaire to cherish them more freely, as this album notation, dated 26 August 1851, proves: "The irresistible sympathy I feel toward old women, those creatures who have suffered greatly through their lovers, their husbands, their children, and also through their own fault, is not mixed with any sexual appetite" (*OC* 2:37).

Returning to our fable, we see for the first and only time in the collection, the narrator using the word "paradoxical" to characterize Beauty's repeatedly expressed contradictory powers. "The false goddess with her charming and paradoxical voice" offers public recognition: "And then she placed her lips on a gigantic trumpet, beribboned, like a reed pipe, with headlines from every newspaper in the universe, and, through that trumpet she shouted my name, which thus crossed the spaces with the noise of a hundred thousand thunderbolts, and returned to me reverberating with an echo from the most distant planet." But her "hoarse sound of brass brought to [his] ears some obscure memory of a prostituted trumpet," and, "with his entire disdain," the narrator —for the third and final time—reasserts himself: "'Get away! I'm not the type to marry the mistress of certain people I don't care to name.'" Publicity demands constant compromises, typified by the flatteries the writer of "At One O'Clock in the Morning" (no. 10) had lavished on narrow-minded editors, mediocre authors, and the like. Any surrender of one's autonomy is "prostitution." Even the "holy prostitution of the soul" in "Crowds" (no. 12) proved to be an illusory "empathy" with an empty other.[8]

But the fable's two-paragraph epilogue contradicts this arduous, though sound morality—confirming the ironic distance set up by the stilted prologue. It reintroduces the opening scene, a sleeping man who dreams. The ending's first version, found in the unpublished proofs of the fourth *Presse* series, is crudely opportunistic: "For sure, I had the right to be proud of such courageous self-denial. But unfortunately I woke up, and all my strength abandoned me. 'Really,' I said to myself, 'I must've been quite deeply asleep to display such scruples. Ah! If only they could come back while I'm awake.'" The fully conscious writer appears to repudiate his dreamed rectitude. But his moralistic tone may hide a dangerously subtle irony, dangerous because we run the risk, as in interpreting "The Bad Glazier" (no. 9), of taking him at his word. Is his "unfortunately" in earnest? Should he have stayed asleep?

The longer, definitive closure, which first appeared in the *Revue Nationale* (1864), and then in the 1869 posthumous edition, adds a full paragraph. This final revision completes and exaggerates the original regrets:

> "Ah! If only they could come back while I'm awake, I wouldn't be so fussy!"
>
> And I appealed out loud, entreating them to forgive me, offering to dishonor myself as often as necessary to earn their favors. But I had probably offended them quite badly, for they never returned.

Interpreters can reconstruct the narrator's irony but not his final decision. Is the alert man of letters so corruptible? We might sympathize with his "temptation" to retaliate against obtuse readers and publishers—we too, ambitious academics, sometimes share his Faustian wish for "fame." But there is nothing to confirm his proposal to trade his honor for the Demons' *faveurs*. The unyielding ambiguity signifies an impossible choice: either surrender our soul or compromise our drive to succeed.

FROM MELANCHOLY TO MOURNING

The 1862 *Presse* ensemble solidifies a paramount intuition: grief and mourning can integrate utopian fantasy and everyday demands. The early, dialectical fables had derived their energy from the tensions between them. Baudelaire's later fables surpass these binary exclusions by recognizing that vision is engendered from loss itself, and consequently from reality. The self-reflective narrator imitates, as it were, the widowed mother, who preserves both inwardness and her involvement in the world.

The first two paragraphs of "Twilight" (no. 22; only the second truly "poetic" narrative) explore "Paris spleen," or urban depression, evoking the conflicts lurking in our subconscious. The narrator begins as a detached observer who listens to the effects of "Daylight falls" (the opening line) from a "mountaintop," one of Paris's many hills. The fable is structured as systematically as the sonnet "Recueillement" (Meditation; published in 1861 but not included in *FM* [for a detailed analysis see Kaplan 1987–88]), which also contrasts emotional states: first, relaxation and peace experienced by those "pitiable minds wearied by the day's toil"; second, irritation produced by "a multitude of discordant shouts . . . transformed by the space into a dismal harmony."

The "friends" he evokes, as in "The Bad Glazier" (no. 9), amplify twilight's negative vibrations. The first one "would neglect all friendly and polite ties, and abuse the first comer like a savage." He "died insane, unable to recognize his wife and child." The second one, "wounded in his ambition, as the daylight faded, would become more bitter, gloomier, more pestering." He did not go crazy, however, like his married friend, but remained prey to "the anxiety of a perpetual disquiet" (*l'inquiétude d'un malaise perpétuel*), which also pursues the narrator—and which will not be placated by "every honor republics and princes can confer." Fame, here, receives her definitive defeat.

The narrator then takes center stage. Another "pivotal sentence" distinguishes him from these angry victims of delusion: "Night, which puts its darkness into their minds, illumines mine." As in "La Fin de la journée" (The day's end, *FM*, no. 124; the antepenultimate poem, added in 1861) the urban poet withdraws into his room. The fable brings the romantic's cosmic inspiration down to earth, elaborating a cityscape lit by the recently installed gas lamps: "O night! O refreshing darkness! For me you signal an inward celebration, you are the liberation from anguish! In the solitude of the plains, amidst the stony labyrinths of a capital, sparkling with stars, explosion of street lamps, you are the fireworks of the goddess Liberty!"

The Baudelairean fable of modern consciousness is born. The rhythmic prose jumps out of the narrative which it completes. At the same time, a process of poetic abstraction interprets the sunset as symbolic of great transitional moments. Such lyrical meditation transcends suffering when it successfully finds verbal form.

The two final paragraphs maintain the excitement while formulating the symbolism of nocturnal solitude. Brief exclamations give way to a long, pictorial sentence which analyzes, through imagery itself, the poetics of dusk: "Twilight, how gentle and tender you are! The pink glows still lingering on the horizon like the day dying under its night's victorious subjugation, the fires of candelabra forming spots of opaque red on the sunset's final glories, the heavy draperies drawn by an invisible hand from the depths of the East, imitate all the complicated feelings struggling in a person's heart during life's solemn hours." The thickly wadded clouds, like an intimate boudoir, cloak an unworldly presence brooding over hearth and home. Those harmonies, however, retain their alloy of dread, "tous les sentiments compliqués qui luttent dans le coeur de l'homme aux heures solennelles de la vie." As in the equally musical "Recueillement," the poet appears to have achieved wisdom: accept inevitable death, the march of time, with equanimity.

The "prose poem" might finish here—if its purpose were simply to interpret urban reveries. It has reached thematic closure: the sunset as both a natural and conventional metaphor of human tribulations, bringing madness to some (lines 21–42 out of 69); to others, as the narrator, repose (lines 42–69). But the final paragraph adds metaphor to metaphor, leading us from a soothing meditation to suggest how we might—in life as well as in reading—integrate anguish into an embracing confidence. This self-reflective supplement defines the therapeutic operation of lyric poetry:

> Or it appears like a strange dancing dress, whose transparent and dark gauze reveals a glimpse of the muted splendors of a brilliant skirt, just as the delectable past might pierce through the gloomy present. While the trembling gold and silver stars, sprinkled over it, represent those fires of fantasy which ignite well only under the deep mourning of the Night.

Sixty years later, Sigmund Freud's pioneering paper "Mourning and Melancholia" (1917) would explain how healthy grief, which accepts loss, "le délicieux passé," can work through the unconscious ambivalences of depression, "le noir présent."[9] The two madmen with whom the narrator contrasts himself had destructively raged against themselves as against others. The Parisian poet, whom the dusk inspires, interprets it. The sunset "imitates," it "represents" struggles within himself.

Baudelaire's fables import a remarkable self-awareness into the lyrical process that transforms its enslaving naïveté. Their complex beauty arises from the masterful confluence of analysis and profound symbolic experience. Reverie may alleviate anguish, but only lucid hope might "cure" life. The narrator does not fixate upon guilt or regret. He can retrieve past joys, "ces feux de la fantaisie" which shine through the "gaze transparente et sombre" of his dreary present. Insight penetrates the deceptively opaque fabric of consciousness. The personified "deuil profond de la Nuit" is another majestic widowed mother (no. 13) who had inspired the "curious" prowler to love and to write.

SOLIPSISM AND FREEDOM

Successful mourning can generate, in addition to nostalgia, an ironic perspective on wishful thinking. The two fables that complete this cycle—"Solitude" and "Plans"—defend the benefits of fantasy while pointing to the existential anxiety it can never entirely quell. A glance at their changes in the course of several prepublications reinforces our internal analysis of their evolved skepticism. Both were revised in 1862 for the fourth *Presse* series. The original "Solitude" appeared in 1855, 1857, and 1861, whereas the original "Plans" appeared first in 1857 and then in 1861. The definitive versions introduce the absolute consequence of reverie: philosophical solipsism. When the cosmos inside the mind becomes the sole reality, a dreamer might alleviate his despair but, in the process, he would lose the world.

"Solitude" (which followed "Plans" in *La Presse*, but became no. 23 in the PE) denounces democratic preachers. Yet there is self-irony in the narrator's attacks. Its primitive versions (printed directly after "Twilight" in 1855, 1857, and 1861) continue observations about his "second friend," the one driven by "l'inquiétude d'un malaise perpétuel." Its definitive version (1862, in the corrected proofs of the fourth *Presse* series and the 1869 PE) polemically refutes a "philanthropic journalist [who] tells me that solitude is bad for people; and to support his thesis, like all unbelievers, he cites sayings of the Church Fathers."

The fable is less concerned with the ideology of social equality than with the bad faith (or self-deception) of activists. The narrator deplores solipsism transported into politics. The verbal productions of "our jabbering races" (*nos races jacassières*) are delusory, as was Fancioulle's "perfect idealization" which enraptured his spectators and "veiled for a moment the terrors of the abyss" (no. 27). Politicians too "would accept the supreme torture less reluctantly, if they were allowed to deliver a copious harangue from the scaffold's heights." These "democrats" do not, as they claim, "share [their] delights" (*jouissances*), and all self-intoxicated hypocrites arouse his wrath: "I do not pity them, because I suspect that their oratorical outpourings gain them voluptuous pleasures equal to those which others derive from silence and meditation. But I despise them."

Yet "Solitude" also expresses solidarity with anyone pursued by anxiety—which *equally* pursues philanthropists and poets. The narrator's expressed hostility contradicts his sympathy, the sincerity of which is reinforced by his respectful allusions to seventeenth-century *moralistes* who recognize, as he does, that those who shun solitude cannot relax. He cites La Bruyère's plea for privacy which "shames everyone who rushes into crowds to forget themselves, probably afraid they couldn't tolerate themselves." And he summarizes his view with Pascal's famous dictum: "Almost all our woes come from not being capable of remaining in our rooms."

The real crime of democratic preachers is that they deny their own affliction. The fable confutes complacency of any kind, and the narrator's sarcasm, at the end, shatters philanthropists' finest intentions, as he attacks "all the panic-stricken who seek happiness in movement and in a prostitution I would call *fraternitary*, if I would agree to speak the lovely tongue of my century." Their *bonheur* implies a lack of self-scrutiny and indifference to the laboring or indigent classes.[10] The italicized neologism *fra-*

ternitaire has a double target: to repudiate any egalitarianism, patronizing or otherwise, and to champion the individual, the "single-one" in Kierkegaard's terms. Yet the peevish tone should warn us, as did the defensive endings of "At One O'Clock in the Morning" and "Crowds" (nos. 10, 12), that only a vulnerable stranger feels compelled to insult the "stupid pride" (no. 12) of the "happy" whom he chronically "despises" (no. 10).

The ending of the original version of "Solitude" dwells more directly upon anxiety, subordinating the political polemic to a defense of imaginative autonomy. An elevated mental act conquers the world and endows the observer with an "unalienable individual property." The conclusion explicitly disavows the ideals of 1789 and 1848 in favor of contemplation: " 'As for delights [*la jouissance*],—the most beautiful fraternal agapes, the most magnificent meetings of men electrified by a common pleasure, will never produce ones comparable to those experienced by the Solitary, who, with one glance, has embraced and understood the entire sublimity of a landscape.' "[11]

The two stages of "Plans" also exhibit a deliberate ironic development in the final version. Its initial forms (1857, 1861) highlight the irremediable unhappiness which stimulates imagination. Fantasy might help us "appease" but never "drown the *Beast*" of despair. Its original ending embraces the "esthetic"—not as pure liberation, but as self-destructive escape:

> . . . . . Dreams! Dreams! always accursed dreams! —They kill action and devour time! —Dreams momentarily appease the voracious beast stirring within us. It is a poison that appeases, but which nourishes it.
>
> So where can one find a cup deep enough and a poison thick enough to drown the *Beast!*[12]

The definitive version of "Plans" (no. 24), in its definitive place *after* "Solitude," submerges this judgment as it savors a solipsistic journey. The stroller daydreams while "walking in a large solitary park," much like the narrator of "The Fool and the Venus" (no. 7), whose ecstasy also began in "a vast park [which] swoons under the sun's burning eye." Its conclusion repeats the esthetic paradox of "Invitation to the Voyage," which glorified mankind's inherited "dose of natural opium" while, at the same time, questioning its viability: "Will we ever live, will we ever enter the picture painted by my mind, that painting which resembles you?" (no. 18). "Plans" elaborates similar travel images and also concludes ambiguously by juxtaposing action and dream. [13]

"Plans" anatomizes the solipsistic fallacy while broadcasting its privileges. The third-person narrative, and the strategically placed reflexive verbs, convey an autistic dialogue: "He was saying to himself" (the first words), "He stopped [*il s'arrêta*] . . . said to himself" (second paragraph), "he continued mentally" (third paragraph), "he said to himself" (fourth paragraph), and again in the last, "he said to himself." The stroller's "plans" recapitulate other paradises: first, in the park, he dreams of adorning a woman, "for she has the natural bearing of a princess"; an engraved tropical scene he discovers at a print shop provokes reveries akin to "Invitation": "*here* is where we must dwell to cultivate the dream of my life." The details then unfold into a tropical scenario: "At the seashore, a lovely wood cabin, . . . in the atmosphere, an intoxicating, undefinable fragrance, . . . the bedroom . . . where she would rest so calm, so well fanned, smoking slightly opiated tobacco"; then a country inn whose fireplace, crockery, food, wine, and rustic bedsheets summarize all these "banal" images of "pleasure and happiness."

The concluding paragraph reevaluates these invocations. The familiar analytic coda juxtaposes reality and imagination so as to undermine the authority of solipsism. Quite significantly, the germinal theme of homelessness subtly returns but with unmistakable strength: "And returning home alone, at that hour when Wisdom's advice is no longer stifled by the buzzings of the exterior life, he said to himself, 'Today, in dream, I had three domiciles where I found equal pleasure. Why force my body to change location, when my soul voyages so nimbly? And what good is it to carry out plans, since planning itself is a sufficient delight?' " The rhetorical questions are equivocal. Is the "Wisdom" exterior to his mind necessarily deceitful? Is his companionless return to a vague "home" (*en rentrant seul chez lui*) truly redeemed by his invented "trois domiciles"? This bluff does not entirely conceal an ethical standard, for he implicitly points to unresolved but thoroughly normal yearnings.

The stroller does indeed seek a *domicile.* From the Latin *domus*, it is the judicial equivalent of security, stability, shelter, protection, family—everything the "stranger" of the first fable presumably forgets. The *flâneur* of "Crowds" no longer vindicates his "craving for disguise and masks, the hatred of home, and a passion for traveling" (no. 12). Perhaps he has become the widowed mother who "walked home, meditating and dreaming, alone, forever alone" (no. 13), an emblem of the observer's interpersonal as well as poetic compassion?

These contradictions collapse his vaunted storybook castles. His idolatry of mental constructs, his disingenuous "plans," are impoverished, flourishing solely in his brain. Could anyone believe that "le projet est en lui-même une jouissance suffisante"? The word *jouissance*, with its consistent ambiguities (the word appears fourteen times throughout the collection: see Cargo 1971), undermines this flouted solipsism. Its autistic pleasure is too good to be true. And that is the point. It is not true.

Revising both his poetic monument and his poetics, about 1860, Baudelaire relinquished the protective solitude of the unreal, confirming that "those fires of fantasy ignite well only under the deep mourning of the Night" (no. 22). The ironic distance within even these "esthetic" fables also delimits a challenge greater than that of irretrievable loss. Our present sensitivity to the ontology of Literature (portentiously capitalized) clarifies their true modernity: writing as such, by its inherent arbitrariness, and compelling illusion, unendingly undermines itself. Baudelaire did not despair of literature. He had enough common sense, and post-romantic self-knowledge, to accept the truism that language cannot change reality. Yet the narrator's simultaneous movements of escape from, and return to, literature generate the fables' boldest developments.[14]

6

THE ETHICAL AND UNIVERSAL ABSURDITY

A Drive Toward Dialogue

The "ethical fables" depict existential binds analogous to despotic idealism. Two parallel pairs complete the two cycles of four "esthetic" fables just examined and straightforwardly allegorize life's "logic of absurdity" (no. 20).[1] The 1869 posthumous edition preserves these original sequences: (1) From the third *Presse* series, "The Pauper's Toy" and "The Fairies' Gifts" ("Le Joujou du pauvre," "Les Dons des fées," nos. 19–20) complete the first group of five introduced by "The Cake"; (2) From the fourth *Presse* series, "Beautiful Dorothy" and "The Eyes of the Poor" ("La Belle Dorothée," "Les Yeux des pauvres," nos. 25–26) complete the second group of five headed by "The Temptations."

Our historical correlative of the collection's internal coherence changes (see appendix 2). After the third *Presse* sequence appeared and the fourth was suppressed, Baudelaire no longer had a regular outlet for this project. The following year he placed nine pieces in three different periodicals. The *Revue Nationale* (of 10 June 1863) included "The Temptations" and "Beautiful Dorothy"—retrieved from the proofs Houssaye had refused to publish. The year 1864 was more successful: *Le Figaro* of 7 and 14 February took six pieces, all but one unpublished (nos. 22, 29, 30, 31, 33, 39 of the PE), and the *Revue de Paris* of December also took six, only two unpublished (nos. 23, 24, 26, 28, 40, 41). Baudelaire's 1865 table of contents retained practically the same order and placed them so as to effect a transition from esthetic or ethical conflicts to the threat of universal meaninglessness.[2]

LIFE'S ARBITRARY INJUSTICES

These ethical fables originate in Baudelaire's systematic switch of emphasis from hedonism to value judgments. "The Pauper's Toy" (no. 19), in fact, emerged from an anecdote included in his 1853 essay, "Morale du joujou" (The morality of the toy), which had focused upon "the spirituality of childhood in its artistic ideas" (*OC* 1:583).[3] Nine years later, the fable recasts it as an ethical experiment: "I want to present an idea about innocent entertainment. For so few diversions are not wicked!"

The fable contrasts two boys on either side of "symbolic bars separating two worlds," a rich one and a poor one. The clean and well-dressed wealthy child, the "enfant beau et frais," faces "another child, dirty, puny, grimy, one of those pariah-brats whose beauty an impartial eye might discover, if it could wipe away his repulsive patina of privation, just as a connoisseur's eye detects an ideal painting beneath the coachmaker's varnish." Only the precipient narrator understands that loveliness can flourish under the surface of this "marmot-pariah," an unblossomed flower of affliction.

The two brief final paragraphs depict a cruel surprise. The rich child was admiring the urchin's toy as he might "a rare and unknown object." What is this delight? "A living rat! His parents, probably to save money, had extracted the toy from life itself." What repulses the bourgeois observer gratifies both children. Equality of need and spirit—of life itself—unites those economic antagonists. Their innocent companionship gratifies "un oeil impartial."

But "The Pauper's Toy" does not preach democratic tolerance, and its ironic coda is more significant than its manifest "morality." The narrator presupposes the sanctity of every person, but he refuses directly to assert the principle. The final one-line paragraph lifts this social evil to a higher theoretical level:

> And the two children laughed together fraternally, with teeth of *equal* whiteness.

The closure does not take sides in a class war. The grotesque irony of the rat and the teeth is brutally objective, undermining any reassuring lesson. The boys' transient "equality" is a figment of desire, as is the "beauty" of the rat entertaining them. Their tastes, their joy, their natural endowments (e.g., their teeth) are the same—but not their condition, their true opportunities: the italicized *equal*, echoing *cake* of fable no. 15, which heads the series, reconfirms the impotence of good will. It prepares one for "Solitude" (no. 23, analyzed in the previous chapter), which further attacks socialistic delusions, "a prostitution I would call *fraternitary*" (also italicized by Baudelaire).

"The Fairies' Gifts" (no. 20), closes the third *Presse* series with another existential parody. It traces our unjust condition to a mythical "intermediary world, placed between man and God, subject like ours to the terrifying law of Time." Fairies give the boys unequal gifts, as they hand out potentialities, "like prizes at a graduation," to recently born infants. These unearned rewards represent life's contingency and are "able to decide [their] fate and become just as easily the source of [their] misfortune as of [their] happiness." To underline this moral absurdity, repetitions of "just" add up to "unjust": "If there is some haste and chance in supernatural justice, don't be surprised that human justice is sometimes similar. We ourselves would be, in that case, unjust judges."

These multiple ironies undermine "those all too common rationalizers (*raisonneurs*), unable to elevate themselves to the logic of the Absurd." Talents of particular interest to the narrator (and to the author), out of several, typify life's perverse unfairness: "So a love for Beauty and Poetic Power were given to the son of a sullen pauper, quarryman by trade, who could not, in any way, assist the faculties, nor alleviate the needs of his pitiable progeny." The last one, the "*Gift of Pleasing*" (italicized in the text), does not satisfy the narrow-minded father whose son had been left with nothing. This "little shopkeeper," who cannot appreciate its immense value, represents the fable's obtuse readers.

This *boutiquier* (in nineteenth-century parlance, a bigoted, petit bourgeois mentality) also introduces the standard of humility. He is thoughtless and obstinate, confined by naive preestablished ideas. The Fairy voices the narrator's judgment: " 'What do you think of that vain little Frenchman, who wants to understand everything, and who, having acquired the best share for his son, still dares to question and to dispute the indisputable?' " How might we absorb an unmotivated injustice? Challenge proudly, "interroger et discuter l'indiscutable?" "Ce petit Français vaniteux" completely misunderstands his good luck, believing that his son's "gift of pleasing" is the least valuable, since it was the last to be bestowed. His indignation ironically reconfirms "the very essence of France's wit" ("The Joker," no. 4), an arrogant stupidity unaware of any rationale beyond its ken.

COUNTERFEIT GRACE

The fourth *Presse* sequence ends with two major parables of ethical blindness, "Beautiful Dorothy" and "The Eyes of the Poor" (nos. 25–26); the first takes place on an exotic island, the second in the "renewed" Paris of Napoleon III, which favored luxury, redesigning the city and removing the poor and the working classes to the outskirts (Clark 1984; 3–22). Both refute the second Demon of "The Temptations" (no. 21), which heads the group. To Plutus, who promises, "I can give you that which . . . replaces everything," the narrator will amplify the stranger's response: "I hate gold as you hate God" (fable no. 1).

On the surface, the heroine of "Beautiful Dorothy" symbolizes the seductive ambiguity of "The Temptations," "Twilight," "Solitude," and "Plans," which directly precede it. But "Dorothy" reinforces "The Pauper's Toy" in making the issue of moral discernment even more explicit. Its key word is "beauty," established in the title and repeated at crucial moments in the narrative, and, like "The Artist's *Confiteor*," "The Double Room," "The Fool and the Venus" (nos. 3, 5, 7), it opens with a sensuous passivity: "The sun overwhelms the city with its direct and fearsome light; the sand is dazzling and the sea shimmers. Stunned people slackly collapse and take a siesta, a siesta which is a sort of delectable death where the sleeper, half-awake, relishes the voluptuous pleasures of his annihilation."

After a pivotal "However," Dorothy herself appears and introduces a vigorous contrast. Her self-involvement counterpoises the suicidal introversion around her. She is erotic, described in the manner of a striptease: "Her dress of clinging silk, light-colored and pink, vividly stands out against her skin's darkness and molds her tall figure, her furrowed back and pointed breasts exactly." Censors at the *Revue Nationale* substituted the euphemistic "the forms of her body" for those details, but the author fought for the integrity of his text (*OC* 1:1333; CPl 2:307). His black Venus preserves her enticement.

Her alluring poses prepare a surprise. Dorothy's loveliness both excites and menaces men because her self-sufficiency borders on the fatuous. But we do not dwell on this equivocation, as one sentence introduces her *ethical* dilemma. We ourselves have almost become engulfed in the "esthetic." This pivotal sentence reminds readers that pleasure is never final: "Since Dorothy is so prodigiously attractive, her pleasure at being admired prevails over her pride at being a freed slave, and, although she is free, she walks shoeless." She is a former slave! The dramatic contradiction between her evocative (or "poetic") power versus her servitude magnifies the world's injustice. Life's various realms are inseparable—as are the conflicting themes of Baudelaire's fables. We, the spectators—not Dorothy—have forgotten that she suffers. Beauty now becomes a person.

The final paragraph clarifies this implicit "lesson" as it expands upon the surprise. As we have learned to expect, the insights emerge fitfully through several ironies. A striking disequilibrium pits the initial extravaganza (lines 1–57) against the ethical impasse at the end (lines 57–64). An "if clause," by its understatement, explodes the utopia: "Dorothy is admired and pampered by everyone, and she would be perfectly happy if she were not duty bound to save up piastre by piastre in order to ransom her little sister who is indeed eleven years old, and already ripe, and so beautiful! She will probably succeed, good Dorothy. The child's master is so miserly, too miserly to understand any beauty other than that of cash!" This ending redeems her "perfect happiness"—or self-absorption. The Idol is transformed, by the epithets, from "lazy and beautiful Dorothy" (lines 37–38), "famous Dorothy" (line 51), to "good Dorothy" (line 62). She is indeed her sister's keeper. There is even a final irony: the slave master's greed, which blinds him to beauty, enslaves the liberated Dorothy to her "goodness."

"The Eyes of the Poor" (no. 26) completes the fourth *Presse* series with another ethical judgment; only this time the "good" and "bad" roles are reversed (cf. Monroe 1987: 93–127; Friedman 1989). The narrator begins by denouncing self-centeredness, confirming the reconstructed irony of "A Joker" and "The Wild Woman and the Affected Coquette" (nos. 4, 11). But his premise is far from compassionate:

> Ah, you want to know why I hate you today! It will probably be less easy for you to understand why than for me to explain; for you are, I believe, the most beautiful example of feminine impermeability anyone can meet.
>
> . . . We had indeed promised each other that all our thoughts would be shared with each other, and that our two souls would henceforth form but one.—Anyway, there is nothing original about this dream, except that, dreamed by everyone, no one has realized it.

The collection's most abused word—"beautiful"—condenses the latent contradictions almost hidden by his misogynistic indignation. The narrator appears to reprove chimerical desires, as noble as their goal of loving communication might be. Then why does he "hate" his mistress, if her "imperméabilité" is universal? Why blame her for the objective fact of sexual *difference?* Why lash out against the fantasy of perfect understanding?

He faces a number of incompatible perceptions of value, further developing "The Pauper's Toy" and "Beautiful Dorothy" (nos. 19 and 25). Everyone's *eyes* represent moral and esthetic taste, or the lack thereof. Here, in the street, an indigent father with a small boy and an infant admire the garish emporium before which the narrator and his mistress are enjoying a drink: "Those three faces were extraordinarily serious, and those six eyes fixedly contemplated the brand-new café with equal admiration, but variously nuanced by their ages." The word "equal," echoing fables 19, 20, and 25, and the sentence's mathematical precision, mimic their pathetically mechanical, economically conditioned enthrallment. This covert social criticism both magnifies and trivializes their inappropriate joy before the "café tout neuf" and its conspicuous waste, its "modern," sumptuous corruption.

The narrator, however, falls victim to an equally naive denial of reality, for he expects his sweetheart to mirror his own pity. When she violently disillusions him, he disguises his self-criticism with a pessimistic adage:

> I turned my gaze toward yours, dear love, in order to read *my* thought there. As I was plunging into your eyes so beautiful and so weirdly soft, into your green eyes, the abode of Caprice and inspired by the Moon, you said, "I can't stand those people with their eyes wide open like entrance gates! Can't you ask the headwaiter to send them away?"
>
> How difficult it is to understand one another, my dear angel, and how uncommunicable thought is, even among people who love each other!

The narrator's frustration is justifiable, but not its stated cause. He attacks his "cher amour," his "cher ange," although he is an equally appropriate target. For her callous remark reminds him of the shameful contrast between his self-indulgence and the derelict family (headed by a man about his age, forty years old). The "eyes of the poor" cannot see *his* contemptuous hedonism as they remain oblivious to their repressed outrage against their poverty. The narrator complains that he cannot "read *my* thought" (the text's only italicized word) in his lover's eyes—but who can? Is he not blind as well to his delusion that she automatically shares his (unstated) feelings?

"The Eyes of the Poor" records everybody's exile from shared truth. Yet Baudelaire, unable to accept compromise, experienced the normal differences between man and woman (or two separate beings of either sex) as absolute: "In love as in almost all human affairs, the peaceful agreement [*l'entente cordiale*] is the result of misunderstanding. . . . —The unbridgeable abyss, which creates uncommunicability, remains unbridged" (*Mon coeur mis à nu, OC* 1:695–96; cf. *JI*, 379). Neurotically he displaces metaphysical otherness, as well, onto females, certainly reflecting his self-defeating love relations, starting—and ending—with his mother. She is a chasm, a "horrifying and uncommunicable being like God (with the difference that the infinite does not communicate itself because it would blind and crush the finite, whereas the creature we speak about [woman] is perhaps uncommunicable because it has nothing to communicate)" (*OC* 2:713). Fortunately for posterity, the fable is more lucid than Mme Aupick's misunderstood son.

BLINDNESS IS UNIVERSAL

The Parisian Prowler's central section is framed by two crucial parables of injustice and fate—"A Heroic Death" (no. 27, analyzed in Chapter 3) and "Vocations" (no. 31, analyzed in the next). Five major fables (nos. 27–31)—probably written after the 1862 *Presse* series—depict an absurdity more devastating than arbitrary injustice. These middle groupings feature postromantic parables which almost reach the complexity and length of short stories. After the July Monarchy and the repressions of 1848, the search for faith (religious or political) was not completely obsolete, but Baudelaire's contemporaries recognized its futility. "A Heroic Death" (161 lines long), "The Counterfeit Coin" ("La Fausse Monnaie," 61 lines), "The Generous Gambler" ("Le Joueur généreux," 135 lines), "The Rope" ("La Corde," 145 lines), and "Vocations" ("Les Vocations," 147 lines) establish the narrator's skepticism. Although irony again disguises his position, he unflinchingly depicts life with no rational foundation despite attempts to maintain a just order. Yet, these stories also speak to our struggle to differentiate benevolence from evil, to alleviate our travails, and perhaps also to remedy the affliction of others. As a response to their pessimism, the narrator ultimately defies meaninglessness and anticipates a recovery of meaning.

"A Heroic Death" (first published with "The Desire to Paint" ["Le Désir de peindre," no. 36] on 10 October 1863), confirms the lethal risks of artistic transcendence. The first recounts the tragedy of a court clown and disqualifies even a "perfect idealization" which can only "*veil* the terrors of the abyss"; it diverts only momentarily the "*idea* of tomb or destruction" (italics added). "The Desire to Paint," placed later in the collection, reiterates the dilemma: "Unhappy perhaps is the man, but happy is the artist shattered by desire!" The visionary may preserve his spiritual "power," as in "The Fool and the Venus" (no. 7), or he may surrender by embracing "the desire to die slowly under her gaze" (no. 36).

The cycle as a whole emphasizes ethical predicaments. The narrator of "The Counterfeit Coin" (no. 28, first published in 1864 and placed after "A Heroic Death" in the PE) finds charity to be impossible. This ironic parable, like "The Pauper's Toy," emerges from one of Baudelaire's earliest essays, "The Pagan School of Poetry," which warns against a formalist's hardness of heart (*OC* 2:49; cf. Lemaître, 122–23). A Parisian who resembles the narrator of "A Joker" (no. 4) sees his friend give a fake coin to a beggar. But instead of protesting against it, he speculates upon his friend's motivation:

> My friend's offering was much more substantial than mine, and I told him, "You're right. After the pleasure of being astonished, there's none greater than making a surprise."
>
> "That was the counterfeit coin," he replied calmly, as if to defend his prodigality.

This scurrilous deception contrasts two ways of thinking about right and wrong: one corrupt, that of the companion who trades truth for cruel amusement; the other, represented by the compassionate observer. Yet the latter, who is "always busy finding complications," might excuse the other's crime were he "curious" to see how the worthless cash would affect the poor man's destiny. But his friend merely sought immediate stimulation.

The final paragraph explores the paradox of unconsciously perpetrated evil. The "charitable" swindler, like the female companion of "The Eyes of the Poor," misses the moral point. The narrator at first respects his "incontestable candor," his stated belief that the beggar's surprise at the *appearance* of wealth was more beneficial than gain. But then he grasped the cynical calculation: "I understood clearly that he had tried at one and the same time to accomplish an act of charity and a good deal; to earn forty pennies and God's heart; to carry off paradise economically; finally to snatch gratis his certificate as a charitable man." The counterfeiter's logic, like his coin, is false: it is inconceivable to "earn [both] forty pennies and God's heart."

The narrator now removes his Socratic mask as he condemns the trickster, who after all had deliberately sorted his change. The analytical observer now judges according to a higher morality:

> I might almost have forgiven his desire for the criminal delight [*criminelle jouissance*] of which I had just assumed him capable. I might have found it curious, unique, that he would enjoy compromising poor people; but I will never forgive him for the incompetence of his calculation.
>
> It is never excusable to be mean, but there is some merit in knowing that you are; and the most irreparable of vices is to do evil through stupidity.

This conclusion defends the value of self-awareness. Obtuseness is less tolerable than an instinctive selfishness; often we cannot help doing harm (*être méchant* is almost an inherent disposition). And yet, might not these maxims also be ironic? Would he have sponsored a subtler theory of deceptive charity?

Satan himself tests the moralizer in "The Generous Gambler" (no. 29, first published 7 February 1864). This mock mystery play, like "The Temptations" (no. 21), offers the prowler all the utopias he had previously desired. The Devil himself appears on a Parisian boulevard and invites him into his infernal den, where the damned souls reflect his own stubborn resistance to alienation: "never have I seen eyes shining more forcefully with a dread of ennui and an immortal desire to feel themselves live."

His jovial conversation with Satan unveils his own nihilism. While drinking and smoking, they debunk the basic articles of contemporary faith: "The great idea of the century, that is, of progress and perfectibility," "the absurdity of different philosophies," the corruption of academies, and so on. The narrator gambles his soul away; but the other, "generous," gambler rewards him with everything proffered by the three Temptations, and more:

> "So, to compensate the irremediable loss of your soul, I give you the stake you would have won if fate was on your side, namely the possibility of alleviating and conquering, for your entire life, that weird ailment Ennui, the source of all your ills and all your wretched progress. Never will you form a desire I will not help you to fulfill. You will rule over your vulgar peers. You will be provided with flattery and even adoration. . . . You will change fatherland and region as often as your fancy dictates. You will carouse in voluptuous pleasures, without weariness, in enchanting lands [etc.]."

This total imaginative mastery would realize the dreams of "Plans" (no. 24) so that the "unlucky" gambler could indeed "live in the picture painted by [his] mind." But just before agreeing to believe in nothing, he resists. What holds him back? Not his principles, nor will power, but some sort of fear.

The ambiguous ending, like that of "The Temptations," resists interpretation, forestalling any reassuring morality. The narrator is not cowardly, nor does he defend his integrity up to the point of a heroic death. We cannot decide whether his refusal is a cynical compromise or a pitiful defeat: "But after I left him, incurable distrust gradually returned to my bosom. I no longer dared to believe in such prodigious good fortune, and, going to bed, still saying my prayers as part of an idiotic habit, I repeated, half-asleep, " 'My God! Lord, my God! Make the devil keep his promise!' " This "prière [qu'il fait] par un reste d'habitude imbécile" would contradict the earnest outcry which concluded "Solitude" (no. 23), were it not for the latter's alloy of resentment. Here, more so, we cannot reconstruct a stable position. He asserts only a lax opportunism. Is this the radical esthete of "The Bad Glazier" (no. 9) who would sacrifice his salvation for tinted glass? His "incurable défiance," his chronic inability to take a stand, mirrors our frustrated desire for definite meaning.

LETHAL ILLUSIONS

"The Rope" (no. 30; first published in the same issue of *Le Figaro* as "The Generous Gambler"), is Baudelaire's most brutally skeptical fable of modern life, suspending the certainty at the foundation of all ethics: maternal love.[4] The entire narrative is quoted from a painter, an innocently egotistical artist (perhaps Edouard Manet to whom the piece was dedicated), and demonstrates "how he was remarkably duped by the most natural illusion," that one can "ascribe to motherly love all a mother's actions and words, relative to her child." The self-deceiving painter's expressed kindness ironically contradicts its dreadful results (Hiddleston 1987, 9–11; 50–51).

The fable begins as the artist notices an appealing boy in his neighborhood and asks the destitute parents "if they would agree to hand him over" (*de vouloir bien me le céder*) to live with him, run errands, clean brushes, pose for paintings, and the like. The lad moves in, but soon, moody and depressed, gorging himself on candies and liquors, he begins to steal. One day, after the painter threatens to send the thief back to his parents, he returns to find that the boy has hanged himself: "his eyes, wide open in a frightful stare, at first produced the illusion of life."

The painter's final disillusion dominates the story's second half (lines 71–145). Everyone—doctors, neighbors, the police—all found the situation "suspicious" (*louche*), except the bereaved parents: " 'But, to my great astonishment, the mother was indifferent, not one tear oozed from the corner of her eye. I attributed that strangeness to the very horror she must be feeling, and I remembered the well-known saying: "The deepest griefs are silent." As for the father, he was content to say in a half-stupefied, half-dreamy manner, "After all, it's probably better this way; he still would've come to a bad end!" ' " The painter collaborates with the family's callousness by resisting several facts. First, he imagines that the parents' pain was too intense to express. Their impassiveness reinforces his avoidance of guilt for the suicide he had, in part, provoked. Like the listless father, he invokes a pessimistic cliché, "la sentence connue," to sidestep his shared responsibility.

The mother's visit to the scene, the artist's studio, resolves the prologue's statement about maternal love. All misunderstandings are summarized in the discrepancy between the mother's and the observer's interpretations of "the rope": " 'The poor woman grabbed my arm and said with an irresistible voice: "Oh Sir! Let me have that! Please! I beg you!" Probably, it seemed to me, that her despair had so crazed her that she was now tenderly enamored of what had been the instrument of her son's death, and she wanted to keep it as a horrible and cherished relic. — So she seized the nail and the string.' " The teller's uncertainties (e.g., "sans doute, me paraît-il") increase the reader's, while the still-silent narrator expresses nothing. No one, in fact, betrays any hint of revulsion. The painter returns to his work "still more vigorously than usual, so as to gradually drive away the little corpse haunting the folds of [his] brain." He is no longer upset and simply continues to puzzle over the mother's motivations.

The ambiguous final paragraph destabilizes all judgments. The speaker's aloofness turns to "curiosity" when a stack of letters arrives the next day, some deceitful, others ignorantly shameless and "badly spelled"—all of which attempt "to obtain from me a piece of the deadly and beatific rope" (*la funeste et béatifique corde*): " 'And then, suddenly, a light went on in my brain, and I understood why the mother was so eager to grab the string from me and by what sort of trade [*commerce*] she meant to console herself.' "

His intellect was stimulated by the insight that she would sell the item that had killed her boy! (Hanged person's rope is supposed to bring good luck.) Motherly love, indeed! presumably the most natural, and the least corruptible impulse, had been dominated by money. Neither painter nor narrator (who has silently listened) denounces her spiritual treason. Only the adjective "beatific" (recalling Rabelais's "Prologue" to *Gargantua*) alerts us to a covert moral judgment.

This provocatively neutral closure reinforces the fable's irreducible irony. Readers wonder at the painter's indifference and cerebral pride. Only in the second publication of "The Rope" in *L'Artiste* (1 November 1864) did Baudelaire add the narrator's retort, which only accentuates the ambiguity:[5] " 'My God!' —I answered my friend, '—a meter of a hanged person's rope, at one hundred francs the decimeter, all in all, each paying according to his means, that makes a thousand francs, a real, an effective relief [*un réel, un efficace soulagement*] for that pitiful mother!' " Baudelaire never explained why he added and later suppressed this commentary. The first and final versions (*Le Figaro*, February 1864; *L'Evénement*, June 1866, and the PE) end with the painter's complacent illumination about the mother's self-interest. He did not judge whether or not it was habitually vicious, or, like the trick in "The Counterfeit Coin" (no. 28), stupidly opportunistic. Yet both understatements explode the myth that all mothers cherish their progeny. The second version, perhaps acquiescing to censors (also replacing the ironic "funeste et béatifique corde" with the safer, moralistic "funeste corde"), expresses an odd compassion for "cette pauvre mère" and condemns only by antiphrasis her expedient trading of eternal values.

SOLIPSISM IS NO SOLUTION

"Vocations" (no. 31), which appeared the following week in *Le Figaro*, one of the most elaborated narratives, recapitulates the preceding thirty.[6] This strategically placed summary unifies *The Parisian Prowler* and speculates about "the stranger" (in fable no. 1) who repudiates family, friends, national identity, and wealth to abandon himself to mobile fantasies, and to a hypothetical ideal of beauty.

Each of the four young characters represents basic areas of the narrator's competing needs. Charles Mauron, the most perspicuous analyst of Baudelaire, has summarized the author's self-projections in three of them: "A. My mother takes me to the theatre; some actors make me desire to do as they (associations: mother—actors—I who want to be admired); B. I see God on marvelous clouds which *flee* in the sky (associations: omnipotent ecstasy—father—clouds at sunset—I who want to be God); C. I sleep with my maid, I caress her arms and I plunge my face into her hair (associations: Mariette and her mane—first genital arousal)" (Mauron 1966, 86; cf. Kopp, 306–10, for details). The fourth child, we shall see, is closest to the narrator.

It is significant that "Vocations," unlike the two Devil stories, or "The Rope" (nos. 21, 29, 30), is not ironic. The story is set in an allegorical sanctuary where everything is bathed in aspiration as "four beautiful children" (*quatre beaux enfants*) talk in "a beautiful garden" (*un beau jardin*). Like "The Temptations," to which it also responds, the text is rigorously structured by a prologue and an epilogue, a sunset evoking a solemn and introspective mood. The allurement of imaginative escape is represented by the first boy who, like Fancioulle (and the young Baudelaire) loses himself in theater (*OC* 1:682, 702–703): "'Ah! it is so beautiful! The women are much more beautiful and much taller than those who visit us at home, and, although their large hollow eyes and blazing cheeks make them look terrifying, you can't help loving them. You're frightened, you want to cry, and yet you're happy...'" He treasures this double utopia, for theater is already an idealization of life. This hyperbolic world of fictitious relationships absorbs him, as did the widowed mother's pensiveness (no. 13), and the "fatal beauty" of the damned (no. 29). The symmetrical contrasts stress the superiority of melodrama over daily life: "grand" (repeated in lines 7, 16, 18) evokes its sublime magnification.

We can only guess why the excited spectator avoids crossing the ramp. Is he repelled by their inner sadness underlined by the parallels: "palais grands et tristes" / "des hommes et des femmes, sérieux et tristes aussi"? Perhaps he dreads the intimacy and violence churning within himself? Or he senses the fragility of art which can only *veil* his ennui. He might consume his old age as a clown or an acrobat (as in fables 3, 7, 14, 27) or die like the desperate model of "The Rope" (no. 30)—all victims of Art's double-edged "favors."

The second boy, a "religious" dreamer, interrupts his comrade's "speech" (*discours*) with a vision. He reinstates the stranger's inchoate reverie as "God." But his intimations of cosmic anthropopathy quickly vanish, for "God" too is a traveler. Cloud fantasies are just another mental excursion with no spiritual stability, and so the boy is left with "an inexpressible expression of ecstasy and regret," like the narcotized dreams of "The Double Room," "perfumed with regret and desire" (no. 5).

"Vocations" covertly denounces the solipsism of these theatrical and "supernatural" visions. The narrative analyzes how they begin in the concrete (a play; reflections of sunset on floating clouds) and then drift into an uncritical identification, a sort of *participation mystique*.[7] The first boy imagines himself as a hero (or heroine) and the second probably wants to become God (or at least his favored Son). Both lose their capacity rationally to differentiate reverie from perception. They compensate for their loss only through an idealized recollection.

The third boy, whose "entire little person gave off a remarkable vivaciousness and vitality," brutally rejects his companion's immaterial pleasures: " 'That guy is really stupid, with his dear Lord only he can see!' " He then recounts a family trip during which he had shared a bed with his maid: " 'Since I couldn't sleep, I entertained myself, while she was sleeping, by running my hand over her arms, her neck and her shoulders. Her arms and neck are much bigger than any other woman's, and the skin so soft, so soft, it seems like writing paper or tissue paper.' " The analogy of female flesh with paper has rich connotations. For this stupendous erotic opportunity provides more stimulation to the boy's mind than to his genitals—as would be expected at his age. The maid's corpulence activates an abundance of images, perhaps because the "relationship" remains invented: he strokes only while she cannot respond.

The third boy, like his theatrical counterpart, resists navigating from thought into action. Something more perilous than disapproval inhibits his touching—while also impelling him to dream more powerfully: " 'I enjoyed it so much that I would've continued for a long time, if I hadn't become frightened, afraid first of awakening her, and then even more of I don't know what. Then I shoved my head into the hair hanging down her back, thick as a mane, and it smelled as good, I assure you, as garden flowers, right now. When you can, try it too, like me, and you'll see!' " Poetry provides limitless freedom for mental lust. The boy's association of thick female hair with animal fur (*épais comme une crinière*) and a perfumed garden recalls "A Hemisphere in Tresses" and "Invitation to the Voyage" (nos. 17–18) and sensuous rhapsodies from *Les Fleurs du Mal*. But here, in this analytical fable, he stops. Perhaps, as in "The Artist's *Confiteor*" (no. 3), his arousal becomes too energetic for his young nerves to endure. Perhaps he simply dreads otherness, the woman's own desires and free will. The narrator does not explain what the boy labels as "je ne sais quoi." Quite clearly, this incipient poet prefers to dream.

How appropriate that the narrator sympathetically teases the third boy, choosing this semblance of love, another "sort of stupefaction," over the others' illusions: "It was easy to guess that he would not waste his life looking for the Divinity in clouds, and that he would frequently find it elsewhere." Baudelaire, in fact, traced his own vocation to the child's enthrallment with his mother's body: "Precocious taste for women. I confused the odor of fur with the woman's odor. I remember... Finally, I loved my mother for her elegance. I was thus a precocious dandy" (*Fusées*, *OC* 1:661).[8] His prepsychoanalytic insight illustrates the profound cooperation of sexual desire, anxiety, suppressed action, and imagination which might have protected the "unruly" boy from his incestuous designs. Baudelaire's suspension points can easily be filled in.

A BROTHERHOOD OF DISSATISFACTION

The narrator then forecasts his own redemption through friendship as he poignantly identifies with the fourth boy whose story is the longest and most detailed. This play-within-the-play further specifies their common urge to escape: " 'I've often thought that my pleasure would be to travel continuously straight ahead, without knowing where, without anyone bothering about it, and always to see new lands. I'm never at ease anywhere, and I always believe I'd feel better anywhere else than where I am.' " He embraces the Unknown as he follows three itinerant musicians, gypsies who embody the esthetic life (see *Mon coeur mis à nu:* "Glorify vagabondage and what can be called Bohemianism, cult of multiplied sensations, expressed by music. Refer to Liszt" [*OC* 1:701]).[9] Their liberated consciousness, in fact, produces " 'a music so surprising that sometimes it makes you want to dance, other times to cry, or to do both at once, and you might almost go crazy if you listened to them too long.' "

Yet, when the fourth boy tries to join them, like the others, he is inhibited: " 'But I didn't dare, probably because it's always quite hard to make any decision, and also because I was afraid I'd be caught before getting out of France.' " He cannot relinquish his French identity and become a gypsy without a domicile.

But now the narrator realizes a momentous breakthrough. Moved to compassion, in the penultimate paragraph, he professes his solidarity with all exiles. The conclusion of "Vocations" confirms "To Each His Chimera" (no. 6), and especially "Widows" and "The Old Acrobat" (nos. 13–14), which demonstrate his identity with all people marked by malevolent fate, *le guignon*. The fourth boy, to whom the others do not listen, calls forth the narrator's deepest consent: "The uninterested attitude of the three other friends made me reflect that this little one was already one of the *misunderstood*. I examined him carefully. There was something or other precociously fatal in his eyes and on his brow which generally repels sympathy, and which, I don't know why, aroused mine, so that for an instant I had the weird thought that I might have a brother to me unknown."

For the first time in *The Parisian Prowler*, we glimpse a portrait of the author—such as the famous 1861–62 photograph by Carjat, in which Baudelaire's tightened lips, bitterly sad eyes, and large forehead convey an unsettling mixture of hostility and anguish (Pichois and Ruchon 1961, no. 35.) He shares the boy's lack of "the gift of pleasing" (no. 20) and recalls Baudelaire's portrait of Edgar Poe: "On his brow sat enthroned, with calm pride, the feeling for ideality and absolute beauty, the esthetic sense par excellence. In spite of all those qualities, the head did not present a pleasant and harmonious unity. Seen straight on, it struck and commanded attention by the forehead's dominating and inquisitorial expression, but the profile unveiled a certain lack" (*OC* 2:269). He *has* found a brother.

This extraordinary affirmation transcends cosmic injustice and confirms the narrator's existential faith. Placed conspicuously in the middle of *The Parisian Prowler*, "Vocations" summarizes all those "ethical fables" which presuppose the uncertainty of human meaning without rationalizing it. The final paragraph resolves the prologue with a "poetic" closure which accepts the frailty of free will: "The sun had set. Solemn night had established itself. The children separated, each one going along, unaware, depending on circumstances and chance, to ripen his destiny, to scandalize his peers and gravitate toward fame or toward dishonor." These boys have surrendered their innocence and now face the world. Each one—the narrator in potential—will "mûrir sa destinée," at once assertive and accepting, "unaware" (*à son insu*), cured of the delusion of complete control. For one precious moment, the anguished observer defies absurdity and transcends his own essential solitude by loving "un frère à [lui] inconnu."

THE PRECARITY OF MEANING

These existential fables appear to be nihilistic and their ironies imply what Wayne Booth has termed the "conviction that 'there is more here than meets the eye' and the suspicion that there is less" (1974, 178). The poor and the rich boys are not true brothers, despite their "teeth of *equal* whiteness." The italicized word obliquely asserts that neither charity nor revolution can erase economic disparities. The eyes of the poor are as blind as those of the narrator's lover—as is the narrator himself to his consuming narcissism. Dorothy is beautiful and self-sufficient, but, even as a freed person, she remains enslaved to her blood obligations, like her sister to her master's blindness to beauty. Even a mother might sell her dead son's relics to the highest bidder.

Baudelaire's modern fables preserve this appropriate precarity of meaning. The most explicit existential parable insists that the

Fairies' gifts are quite arbitrary. The "vain little Frenchman" will not accept his limits and so the narrator's proxy, the Fairy, unable to explain, can only turn away in disgust. Likewise, many fables provocatively rub our noses in the dirt. Only the remarkable ending of "Vocations" anticipates a resolution, as the narrator recognizes a brother.

Baudelaire (and his narrator) may indeed have succumbed, to echo Paul de Man's disenchanted view, to "the temptation to move outside art, its nostalgia for immediacy, the facticity of entities that are in contact with the present" (de Man 1983, 158–59). Baudelaire's "temptation" is indeed the ethical. But so far, his characters touch but the threshold of dialogue, while the narrator still addresses readers indirectly. And yet, and yet—these fables thrust us into the world, still striving, patiently (as in "To Each His Chimera"), "condemned to hope forever."

7

THEORETICAL FABLES OF REALITY

The Ontological Paradox of Literature

Baudelaire's self-reflective "theoretical fables" allegorize their own mechanics and subvert their own meaning.[1] Some at first glance appear to be unfinished, sketchy, crudely symbolic, their bare style conveying emptiness and incompletion. This reading and some knowledge of the author's encroaching syphilis have led some critics to surmise that he had realized the prediction of 23 January 1862 when he felt "brushed by *the wingbeats of idiocy*" (*OC* 1:668, already cited; cf. Bernard 1959, 113). Quite the contrary, I find that these late fables fulfill the author's ambitions far beyond the intimations expressed—albeit ironically—in his 1862 dedication "To Arsène Houssaye." The narrator not only confronts the contradictions of modern consciousness; he faces the fragility of the literary artifacts which capture them.

The prepublication history reconfirms the coherence of even these last fables (nos. 32–50). Baudelaire, in his waning days, placed two earlier sequences, of different character, at the end of his table of contents. The first was a series of three, first published in the 10 December 1863 *Revue Nationale:* "The Thyrsus" (dedicated to Franz Liszt), "Windows," and "Already!" ("Les Fenêtres," "Déjà!," nos. 32, 35, 34 of the PE), to which he added "Get High" ("Enivrez-vous," no. 33). These fables formulate a theory of their own form and state the ultimate value of what I call "the question of reality."

The second sequence, the "Julien Lemer Packet," eleven pieces (three previously published) retrieved from the editorial offices of the *Revue Nationale* after Baudelaire's death, contains his most radical conceptions. The author, ailing and depressed, in a letter from Brussels dated 15 February 1865, announced a list of eleven titles (CPl 2:464; *OC* 2:1306 for the list; Kopp, 415–16).[2] After Lemer's maddening refusal to publish them, Baudelaire's autograph table of contents, probably written a few weeks later, reverses that sequence exactly. This rearranged order displaces the emphasis from demolished illusions to realistic possibilities.

The definitive ordering can be divided into four distinct hermeneutic entities. The first four titles, "Loss of Halo," "Miss Scalpel," "N'Importe où hors du monde. Any where out of the world," and "Let's Beat Up the Poor!" ("Perte d'auréole," "Mademoiselle Bistouri," "Assommons les pauvres!"), became nos. 46–49 in the posthumous edition; they question the universal order and consecrate the poet-narrator's modernity. The second group, "The Moon's Benefits" and "Which Is the True One?" ("Les Bienfaits de la lune," "Laquelle est la vraie?"), became nos. 37–38; they are unified by images of women who are either ideal or disgustingly commonplace. These stereotypes of polarity are synthesized in "A Thoroughbred" ("Un Cheval de race," no. 39). A middle-aged woman again symbolizes the reconciliation of esthetic and ethical and, again, generates a rich pathos.

AN AMALGAM OF GENIUS

"The Thyrsus" (no. 32), the intricate metacritical conceit studied in chapter 1, guides our interpretation of the cycle which demystifies the tyranny of solipsistic imagination. The group as a whole (nos. 32–35), by consolidating the boundaries between everyday life and theory, presents an ironic counterpoint to the tragic fables "A Heroic Death" and "The Desire to Paint," originally published two months earlier. "The Thyrsus" best defines the Baudelairean "prose poem" and emulates Franz Liszt, to whom the piece is quite enthusiastically dedicated:

> Dear Liszt, through the mists, beyond the rivers, above the cities where pianos celebrate your fame, where printing presses

> translate your wisdom, in whatever place you may be, in the eternal city's splendors or the mists of the dreamy lands consoled by Gambrinus, improvising songs of delight or of ineffable sorrow, or confiding your abstruse meditations to writing, singer of Voluptuous Pleasure and Anguish eternal, philosopher, poet and artist, I honor you in immortality!

Liszt might typify the fourth boy of "Vocations" now full grown, inspired by gypsies, many of whom are also Hungarian. Baudelaire's diverse works should likewise reconcile lyricism and theory, art and ethics, imagination and knowledge. Germany (the country of Gambrinus, reputed inventor of beer) and Italy capture the two stereotypical poles of the European imagination, fantasy (mist) and lucid light. "The Thyrsus," as verbal artifact, unlike "The Clock" (no. 16), a "pretentious romance," represents the Frenchman's sincere monument of friendship—anticipating "The Good Dogs" (no. 50), the collection's true conclusion.

Baudelaire's essays translate "thyrsus" as "amalgam" to surpass dualistic thinking. His mature reflections on "artificial paradises" conceive of truth in terms of mixture, not as a distilled perfection. When he judges Thomas De Quincey's thought as "essentially digressive," he compares it to a "mere staff that takes all its character and its charm from the complicated leaves enveloping it" (*OC* 1:444; ibid., 514–15). These images reappear in Baudelaire's ill-received 1864 Brussels lectures on the opium eater: "I made such an amalgam that I could not recognize the part that comes from me, which, moreover, could only be quite small" (ibid., 519). His rhetorical modesty appears to reflect his personal calamities—his debts, ill health, and despair—but also a sense that his isolated self is not ultimate.

By contrast, the following piece, "Get High" (no. 33), asserts a provocative rebellion. This celebrated escapist manifesto, first published in *Le Figaro* of 7 February 1864, was added to the group of three which had appeared in the 10 December 1863 *Revue Nationale:* "The Thyrsus," "Already," and "Windows" (published in that order). These nineteen intense lines promote any sort of ecstasy, yet they fit into a sequence, arranged after its initial journal publication, which stresses a disenchanted realism. This reading of "Get High" as ironic confirms Baudelaire's perspicuous reproach of Jean-Jacques Rousseau, thrilled by his own virtuous appearance, for becoming "intoxicated without hashish."[3]

The first two paragraphs proclaim the metaphorical equivalence of all pleasures, expanding "The Thyrsus," which celebrates music and writing. Lyrical repetitions in the opening dramatize mental freedom while, at the same time, they stress a tragic awareness, recalling the courageous "slaves of Time" and the burdened travelers of "The Double Room" and "To Each His Chimera" (nos. 5 and 6). Although this one unabashedly serves the "active and fertile poet" who vindicates his "holy prostitution of the soul which gives itself entirely, poetry and charity, to the unexpected" ("Crowds," no. 12), it also highlights the ambivalence of imagination: "You must always be high. Everything depends on it: it is the only question. So as not to feel the horrible burden of Time wrecking your back and bending you to the ground, you must get high without respite."

Art and ethics are absorbed into a mind-altering ecstasy: "[Get high] on wine, on poetry or on virtue, whatever you like. But get high," it repeats. This commitment to altered consciousness differs from the lucid defiance of, say, Albert Camus's Sisyphus. The "poet" in potential outlines a facile alternative: surrender to Time or narcotize our consciousness of the real. "Get High," admired for its radical estheticism, when read ironically, confirms the judgment that "charity" (as well as "poetry") is a barely disguised narcissism.

The third and final paragraph reinforces this contextual irony. Longer, rhythmical, and more specific, it contrasts a number of poetic pretexts—stars, waves, birds, clocks, and again, "wine, poetry or virtue"—with the dreamer's actual life: "on the green grass of a ditch, in your room's gloomy solitude." And that is the point. Although intoxication may intensify exterior perception, despair is its premise, as the final peroration—repeating the prologue—insists: "'It is time to get high! So as not to be the martyred slaves of Time, get high; get high constantly! On wine, on poetry or on virtue, as you wish.'"

The next two theoretical fables point to a nuanced realism. "Already!" and "Windows" (nos. 34 and 35), first published in reverse order (with "The Thyrsus") in the *Revue Nationale* (December 1863), distinguish truth from fantasy with remarkable precision—while debunking the idealism of "Get High"; both serve as skeptical counterpoints to "A Heroic Death" and "The Desire to Paint" (nos. 27, 36). The self no longer struggles simply (though painfully) to distinguish rationality from illusion; it now admits the ontological paradox that fiction feels truer than fact.

"Already!" is longer (51 lines long) and more discursive than "Get High" and it amalgamates opposites as defined in "The Thyrsus." The narrator of "Already!" relishes a sea journey which represents autonomous imagination, while the brash philistines accompanying him prefer to "digest in an immobile armchair." The redundant adjective "immobile" underlines the contrast between his volatile desire and their coarse materialism. The "poet" is excited by the "immense vat of the sea whose shores you could hardly distinguish," while the literalistic others yearn for prosaic "meat that isn't salted like the vile element carrying [them]."

"Already!" reconciles these antagonistic perceptions. Somehow, the traveler will welcome certain bourgeois desires. But first—and somewhat defensively—he depreciates their social and familial stability: "Some of them brooded about their homes, missing their unfaithful and sullen wives, and their screeching progeny." But as the voyage ends, even this *canaille* can appreciate the lush coast, which he evokes in mellifluous prose: "Life's musics seemed to emerge from it in an indistinct murmur, and its shores, abounding with all varieties of greenery, exuded a delicious odor of flowers and fruits, as far as several leagues."

An abyss still separates the dreamer and his impatient companions who do not mourn the loss of cosmic harmony. But as a poet he manages to accept what is by translating his grief into a symbol, as he had at the end of "Twilight" (no. 22). His lyrical allegory recovers a realistic beauty which boundless desire had denied:

> I alone was sad, inconceivably sad. Like the priest whose divinity is snatched away, I could not separate myself, without heartbreaking bitterness, from that so monstrously seductive sea, from that sea so infinitely varied in its terrifying simplicity, and which seemed to contain within itself and to represent by its play, its appearances, its angers and its smiles, the moods, the agonies, and the ecstasies of every soul who has lived, who lives and will live!

The voyager painfully acknowledges the transiency of his delight but does not rage against disillusion, as he had in "A Joker," "The Dog and the Scent-Bottle," "The Bad Glazier," "The Wild Woman and the Affected Coquette" (nos. 4, 8, 9, 11), among others. His mourning is realistic; it begins with "une navrante amertume" but concludes by integrating the contradictory sensations of nostalgia and anticipation.

The unusual narrative structure of "Already!" highlights this matured perception. This fable is not divided into two relatively equal parts, dialectical opposites, as were the early ones. The pivotal contradiction has passed from the middle, as in "The Old Woman's Despair," "The Artist's *Confiteor*," "The Double Room," "The Fool and the Venus" (nos. 2, 3, 5, 7), to the final paragraph, where the polarities, no longer absolute, harmoniously play.

"Already!" completes this cycle of four with a nuanced conception of existence. The depressed dreamer, who pronounces (and italicizes) the title "*Déjà!*" for the only time, condenses two contrary, but equally valid, points of view. The penultimate paragraph summarizes its "prose," while the final one orchestrates its "poetry":

> Saying farewell to that incomparable beauty, I felt depressed unto death. And that is why, when each of my companions said, "Finally!" I could only shout, "*Already!*"
>
> Yet it was land, the land with its sounds, its passions, its con-

> veniences, its festivities. It was a rich and magnificent earth, full of promises, sending us a mysterious aroma of rose and musk, with life's musics reaching us in an amorous murmur.

The passionately recovered "terre"—with its troubles and trials—realizes the mixture theorized in "The Thyrsus," which introduces the sequence. Even "ses commodités et ses fêtes," repudiated in "A Joker" and "The Old Acrobat" (nos. 4, 14), find their rightful place. The "mystérieux parfum de rose et de musc"—of inwardness and instinctual mating—produce "un amoureux murmure." The poet, like Constantin Guys, "has successfully concentrated in his [writings] the bitter or heady savor of the wine of Life" (*OC* 2:724, final sentence).

SOLIPSISM OR TRUTH?

The following fables hoist this reconciliation with reality to an even higher level of theoretical self-awareness. "Windows" can be read, as Sima Godfrey has incisively done, as "the quintessential celebration of the poet-*flâneur*, observer of *Tableaux parisiens*" (1982, 90). Our overall analysis supports her conclusion: "The tension the modern poet feels, between the personal need to confront the real temporal world of contingency and the poetic need to frame it in art, parallels the double gesture of the *flâneur-voyeur-artiste* who plunges into the crowded streets of Paris only to extract from them an estheticized vision of modern life" (ibid., 83). Interpreted within the sequence, however, "Windows" deliberately subordinates the esthetic. And it formulates the writer's dilemma more explicitly than any other theoretical fable: Can an artist reconcile invention and truth? Does imagination by necessity stultify his capacity to love?

"Windows" begins, as did "Get High," by applauding artistic privilege, in this case, voyeurism as a source of inspiration. Like "Crowds" (no. 12), which it extends, this manifesto is also fervently dogmatic. The writer stops prowling to frame life behind a closed window. The open window represents infinite reverie which had threatened to disperse the self; now he focuses upon people:

> He who looks outside through a window open never sees as much as he who looks at a window closed. No deeper, more mysterious, more fertile, more obscure, more dazzling object exists than a window lit by a candle. What you can see in sunlight is always less interesting than what transpires behind a windowpane.
>
> Life lives, life dreams, life suffers in that black or luminous hole.

The observer professes the realism of "looking," but he contradicts himself. His enthusiasm betrays the selfish delight he feels in projecting his imagination onto an "*objet* plus profond, plus mystérieux, plus fertile" (italics added). He conceives of Life in the abstract and then attaches personal verbs to it; but only individuals can "live, dream, and suffer." What the "candle," that humble metonymy of intimacy, rouses in his mind is more dramatic.[4] His closed windows are really mirrors.

The two middle paragraphs admit the "observer's" exclusively literary aims. He plumbs the depths of his sympathy for lonely and impoverished old women, such as those in "The Old Woman's Despair" (no. 2), "Widows" (no. 13), "A Thoroughbred" (no. 39), and "Les Petites Vieilles" (The little old women) of the section "Tableaux parisiens" (*FM*, no. 91, added in 1861). In the present case, his impulses toward "charity" clearly serve literature:

> Beyond the billowing rooftops, I notice a mature woman, already wrinkled, poor, always bent over something, and who never goes out. With her face, her clothing, her gestures, with almost nothing, I have refashioned that woman's history, or rather her legend, and sometimes I tell it to myself weeping.
>
> If it had been a poor old man, I would have just as easily refashioned his as well.

The narrator's inscribed hesitations arouse suspicion. Why does he rectify "history" for "legend" ("j'ai refait son histoire, ou plutôt sa légende")? *Histoire* lays claims to truth (through interpretation, of course), whereas *légende* denotes a mythic or imaginative tradition.[5] That he "refashions" (*refaire*) it and then weeps obscures the meaning of his tears.

The artist who drowns in tears appears to be stirred by the woman's furrowed face, her marks of mortality and suffering endured. But what of his boast that "un pauvre vieux homme" would inspire him "tout aussi aisément"? An internal conversation, a mirrored monologue as it were, not even a "legend" of an imagined woman, excites his pity. His verbs are reflexive, not transitive: "je me la raconte à moi-même en pleurant." The ambiguity of the antecedent of "la"—confusing "history" and "legend"—further undermines his authority. His "relationship" remains solely within his fantasy.

Then, at the end, an unprecedented dialogue with an incredulous reader externalizes the narrator's self-critical stance. For the first time in the collection, an interpreter intervenes, confirming the (ironically) defensive function of the narrator's boast at being able to invent an old man's *legend.* Marie Maclean takes less seriously than I do the narrator's respect for his "implied bourgeois audience with the bourgeois preoccupation with veracity and reality" (1988, 53). This self-questioning in the two final paragraphs is deliberate and specifies the instability of all literature:

> And I go to bed, proud of having lived and suffered in others than myself.
>
> Perhaps you will ask, "Are you sure that legend is the true one?" Does it matter what the reality located outside of me might be, if it has helped me to live, to feel that I am and *what* I am?[6]

For the alienated Parisian who looks—and loves—from a distance, a "closed window" is more "open" to compassion than direct contact. His "empathy" for the old woman is, in fact, projection exploited in the service of fiction. Does he consider his story, formed out of "presque rien," to be *histoire* or *légende?* After all, his fabricated tale, not the woman's domestic toil, provoked his tears.

We even question the literary result. What did he finally produce, since that story remained in his head? Literally solipsistic, the legend inspired from looking into windows also remained unwritten, unpublished, unread by others, and unspoken, recited (silently or out loud?) only to himself. What the observer has "lived" and "suffered" is *not* "the true [ontic reality]" of what he invents.

As impressive as this "dialogue" appears, it is another faulty claim, a conversation only in potential. The observer and his implied reader do not communicate reciprocally. Like the interviewer of "The Stranger" (no. 1), I challenge him: "Es-tu sûr que cette légende soit la vraie?" while he answers me with the formal *vous*, as did the alienated dreamer. The writer's final question is at once honest, humble, and futile. Fiction allows him to exist both as a person (*sentir que je suis*) and as a writer (*ce que je suis*). The writer-narrator challenges interpreters to evaluate the paradox that his substance as a person in the world—*what* he is, that is, a writer—derives from untruth.

VARIETIES OF FEMALE AMBIVALENCE

Baudelaire's drastic change in "poetic philosophy" between 1857 and 1861 fulfills his earliest essays which openly resist idealist dualisms. The final section of his "Salon of 1846," entitled "Of the Heroism of Modern Life," formulates a principle which has become a commonplace: "All forms of beauty contain, as do all possible phenomena, something eternal and something transitory—something absolute and something specific. Absolute and eternal beauty does not exist, or rather it is only an abstraction skimmed from the general surface of diverse forms of beauty" (*OC* 2:493).[7] Contemporary art *mixes* classical and realistic elements, and original works strive to "represent the present" (quoted by de Man 1983, 156–57), that is, evoke concrete reality without submitting to abstract or conventional models.

Such is the modernity of *The Parisian Prowler*, to realize that synthesis of abstract and concrete; the "Lemer Packet" fables most fully conceptualize its categories. In particular, the next cycle, devoted to women, completes a consistent development (cf. Bassim 1974, 211–23). Brief, almost crude allegories of feminine beauty—"The Desire to Paint," "The Moon's Benefits," "Which Is the True One?" and "A Thoroughbred" (nos. 36–39) —all project the narrator's anguished struggle with his own internal contradictions onto the model of a capricious, "moon-like" woman. The transcendent Idols of "The Double Room" and "The Fool and the Venus" (nos. 5, 7) had metamorphosed into the hermaphroditic Eros or seductive Fame of fable number 21, the teasingly beautiful Dorothy (no. 25), and finally the "goddess Liberty" of "Twilight" and "Solitude" (nos. 22–23). These late fables, and poems added to the 1861 edition of *Les Fleurs du Mal*, realize a livable amalgam.

"The Desire to Paint" and "The Moon's Benefits" draw the extremist battle lines by depicting a man facing a bewitching woman. "The Desire to Paint" summarizes the "surprising beauty" of modernity, its powerful ambivalence, as the "sinister and intoxicating moon" of our unconscious. Her eyes are "an explosion in the darkness. I might compare her to a black sun, if you could imagine a black star pouring forth light and happiness." Her face displays violence—"stubborn will and love of prey"—and her tenacious vitality inspires him, as would a delicate flower asserting herself against destruction. But why does the artist surrender? He will *not* seek "to defeat and take full pleasure from her." His willful "desire to paint" translates into a lazy suicide, "dying slowly under her gaze."

"The Moon's Benefits," which follows, defines this thrust toward perfection as "madness" (or lunacy). The fable's title anticipates its ironic favors, for her "bienfaits" are as much a curse as a blessing. The protagonist of this almost childish fable is "caprice itself," the poet's inspiration, a wish or craving—in the nineteenth century, automatically associated with females. These musical lines recapitulate the most captivating "esthetic" images and sensations: "'You will love what I love and what loves me: water, clouds, silence, and night; the sea limitless and green; water shapeless and multiform; places where you will not be; lovers you will not understand; monstrous flowers; aromas that give you delusions; cats fainting on pianos and moaning like women, in a husky and gentle voice.'"

"The Artist's *Confiteor*" (no. 3) had established the confusion of perception and dream: "in the grandeur of reverie, the *self* is quickly lost!" "The Double Room" (no. 5) had introduced ambivalent "perfumes of regret and desire," the inborn and not-so-natural opium that momentarily stops Time. "The Fool and the Venus" (no. 7) had defined "the universal ecstasy of things" as silence, still waters, and excited flowers which struggle to "make perfumes visible." The solitary "bath of darkness" in "At One O'Clock in the Morning" (no. 10) did not protect the writer from females he did not understand—and who did not understand him ("The Wild Woman and the Affected Coquette," no. 11). The fourth boy of "Vocations" (no. 31) yearned to fulfill the dreams of "The Cake" (no. 15), "A Hemisphere in Tresses," "Invitation to the Voyage" (nos. 17 and 18), "Plans" (no. 24), "Already!" (no. 34), "The Harbor" (no. 41), and especially "Any where out of the world" (no. 48)—which all sought happiness "there where [the narrator was] not."

But "The Moon's Benefits," more than any other theoretical fable, combines seduction and irony. It broadcasts the enticing poetic rituals of *Les Fleurs du Mal* while it anatomizes their despotism.[8] Its bare allegorical format fosters a critical distance which outlines dream's dangers. The penultimate paragraph, which rhythmically repeats these images in slightly different words, celebrates a corrupt cult: "sinister flowers resembling censers of an unknown religion, aromas that disturb the will, and wild and voluptuous animals which are the emblems of their madness!" The italicized epithet *lunatique* leaves undecided whether or not the narrator ultimately repudiates or rebelliously defends esthetic transcendence.

"Which Is the True One?" and "A Thoroughbred" (respectively 26 and 29 lines long) answer the preceding one ("The Moon's Benefits," no. 37) by defending the ultimate value of temporality. Both depict complex women who are both ugly and beautiful—women who demonstrate that such idealist polarities are too abstract for the world in which we live. These theoretical fables, in fact, parody binary exclusions as such. Theory can conceive of absolutes, but the ethical facts of human frailty, and tenderness, dwell somewhere beyond. These fables begin with a loss of the

Ideal; the narrator's ensuing grief leads in two directions, one protesting against and the other relishing mortality.

The narrator ratifies his commitment to the world at this crucial point in the collection, and a title change confirms his advanced theoretical choice. Baudelaire first published "Which Is the True One?" (so named) in *Le Boulevard*, on 14 June 1863.[9] After its initial publication, "Which Is the True One?" entered the "Lemer Packet" and was republished as "The Ideal and the Real" ("L'Idéal et le réel") one week after the author's death, in the 7 September 1867 issue of the *Revue Nationale*. The 1869 posthumous edition restored the original title—replacing the banal opposition with a profound ontological question. This suspiciously transparent allegory begins thus:

> I met a certain Benedicta, who filled the atmosphere with the ideal, and whose eyes spread the desire for grandeur, beauty, fame, and everything which makes us believe in immortality.
>
> But that miraculous girl was too beautiful to live a long time. So she died a few days after I had made her acquaintance, and it is I myself who buried her, one day when spring was shaking its censer even into the cemeteries.

Her name if taken literally signifies Blessed—like esthetic beatitude. Or, if we follow the poem by Edgar Allan Poe (entitled "Benedicta") that it reflects, she represents literature itself, *le Bien dit*, as total idealization (Johnson 1979, 75–76). Her "incense" might even banish melancholy from the idea of death, "veil the terrors of the abyss" (no. 27).

But another allegorical female replaces Benedicta. In the next paragraph, the bereaved idealist faces a gross caricature of disillusion, "a little person who remarkably resembled the deceased." Mad herself, this one mocks the dreamer's lunacy: " 'It is I, the true Benedicta! It is I, a first-class riffraff! And to punish your madness and your blindness, you will love me as I am!' "

This is the old story. Fantasy must inevitably return to trivial reality. The demystified Benedicta is "une fameuse canaille!" This expression echoes previous ironies such as the *fameux* book of Aloysius Bertrand, somewhat deceitfully praised in the 1862 dedication to Houssaye; while "canaille" (derived from the Latin, *canis*, dog) recalls the obtuse public repulsed by the exquisite scent-bottle (no. 8) and anticipates its positive brethren in "The Good Dogs" (no. 50), which closes the collection.

The narrator answers the "true" Benedicta forcefully, but ambiguously. He grieves his loss of the Ideal, "trop belle pour vivre longtemps." A nonironic reading supports his rejection of the real, yet the translation is as deceptive as the ending of "The Old Acrobat" (no. 14). This simplistic allegory caricatures the very notion of binary opposition (Johnson 1979, 82): "But I was furious, and answered, 'No! No! No!' And to emphasize my refusal more, I stamped the ground so violently that my leg sank up to the knee in the recent burial place, and so, like a trapped wolf, I remain fettered, perhaps forever, to the grave of the ideal."

The fable destroys all stable meaning. After all, its title is a question that echoes the skeptic of "Windows" (no. 35), who asks: "Are you sure that legend is the true one [*la vraie*]?" Barbara Johnson astutely notes that Baudelaire "did not cease burying his poetry of the ideal," but in this and other fables "it is the very *meaning* of his mourning that is put into question. 'Which Is the True One?' becomes the allegory of the loss of meaning of a poetry of loss. No longer able to distinguish between the ideal and the rabble, the subject no longer knows what he is condemned to mourn for" (ibid., 76). The narrator does not tell us "laquelle est la vraie?"

These unanswered questions undermine the narrator's naive dualistic presuppositions. Benedicta is actually one person with a double identity—ugly *and* beautiful—as well as none. The crucial "pour toujours peut-être" in the final clause suggests that neither Benedicta is the true one! The ugly little monster is no more authoritative than the "fille miraculeuse" she replaced so deftly. Both are figments of the beholder's subjectivity.

In "A Thoroughbred" (no. 39), the narrator relishes the positive counterpart of this paradoxically beautiful-ugly woman, defining the "vague, but eternal charm" of a mature heroine of the everyday. Published in *Le Figaro* with "Vocations" (14 February 1864) and then included in the "Lemer Packet," it presents a very positive judgment of the person (Bassim 1974, 219–23). For the first time in *The Parisian Prowler,* the narrator has found a female he can love. This authentic Benedicta is a genuine human being, reborn from the grave of the Ideal:

> She is quite ugly. She is delectable however!
>
> Time and Love have branded her with their claws and have cruelly taught her what each minute and each kiss subtract from youth and luster.

The narrator had already demonstrated his superior discernment in "The Pauper's Toy" (no. 19), when his "connoisseur's eye detect[ed] an ideal painting beneath the coachmaker's varnish." Baudelaire's "true ideal" is afflicted but strong, like the introspective widowed mother (no. 13): "Deteriorated perhaps, but not wearied, and still heroic, she reminds you of those horses of pure breed recognized by a true connoisseur's eye, even when hitched to a hired coach or a heavy wagon" (no. 39). On the outside she looks like "a spider" or "a skeleton"; to the penetrating glance she becomes a work of art, an "armature," the sculptural frame.

The narrator's delectation in the middle-aged is not just a psychological soft spot for these beautiful though blemished, and only slightly grotesque, women tempered by time. He identifies with their persistent passion. In the final paragraph she supplants all the aggressive or coldly indifferent goddesses, the young virgins, of earlier fables: "And besides she is so gentle and so fervent! She loves as one loves in autumn. Winter's approach seems to light a new fire in her heart, and never is the servility of her tenderness in any way irksome." This mature woman realizes his ethics and esthetics of finitude: "Les approches de l'hiver allument dans son coeur un feu nouveau." Still some irony, naggingly impossible to reconstruct, clings to his ambiguous praise for "la servilité de sa tendresse [qui] n'a jamais rien de fatigant." Considering her as a person, how does her submissiveness serve the "fire" in *her* heart?

"A Thoroughbred" formulates the narrator's definitive ethical breakthrough, although its laconic format and its selfishly male-oriented closure compromise its stated goal of reciprocal affection. Yet he has indeed ratified the autonomy of another person's inner life. As a woman at life's autumn, she is an allegory of his cherished older women, from the "kind decrepit woman" (no. 2) to the "women quite mature" in the concluding fable, "The Good Dogs." She reconfirms his sympathy for all courageous subjects of time in "Widows," "The Old Acrobat" (nos. 13–14), and "Windows" (no. 35), reinforcing the ethical assertions of "A Joker," "The Double Room," "To Each His Chimera" (nos. 4, 5, 6).

Baudelaire readily identifies with people who, like himself, nurse the "painful secret" of mortality (see "La Vie antérieure" [The previous life, *FM*, no. 12 of both editions, lines 13–14]). Women "*touched with pensiveness*," to use the poignant phrase he quotes in English, and italicizes, from Thomas De Quincey, inspire him with their agitated subjectivity. Like the widowed mother "gently nodding her head" (no. 13), they all betray "a brain prematurely cultivated by a fertilizing pain—a brain marked by fatal reveries" (*OC* 2:444; Baudelaire repeats the phrase in his review of Asselineau, *La Double Vie*, *OC* 2:87). Baudelaire finds this meditative turmoil most graphically present in Delacroix's afflicted women: "Their eyes seem to bear a painful secret, impossible to bury in the depths of pretense. Their palor is like the revelation of internal battles" (*OC* 2:594).[10]

Later fables (nos. 42–45), as well, confirm Baudelaire's most subtle definition of modern beauty. His meditation upon the head of a similar woman arouses an essentially moral pathos: "It makes one dream at one and the same time—but in a vague mixture—of voluptuous pleasure and of sadness; that includes an idea of melancholy, of weariness, even of satiety—or an opposite idea, that is a fervor, a desire to live, associated with a reflux of bitterness, as coming from privation or hopelessness" (*Fusées*, *OC* 1:657). This brilliant notation digresses to Milton's Satan and other esthetic mixtures, but its origin in shared finitude prevails. Transcending his misogyny, Baudelaire the theorist of modernity chooses the impassioned mortal behind Art's "mask."

TRANSITIONS TOWARD EXTREMISM

Two brief pieces effect a transition between two cycles of fundamental importance. "The Mirror" and "The Harbor" ("Le

Miroir," "Le Port," nos. 40 and 41)—*not* included in the "Lemer Packet," but published in the 25 December 1864 issue of the *Revue de Paris*—provide a resting place between fables that thrive on ambivalence (nos. 32–39, just studied) and the radically anti-idealist fables (nos. 42–46) which demolish absolutes. [11]

"The Mirror" is a humorous paradox which caricatures ideology. We again question the dogma of human equality (see "The Cake" and "The Pauper's Toy," nos. 15, 19). The failures of 1789, Napoleon's fall, and the brutal repressions of 1848 provide ample evidence of its fallibility. The narrator asks an ugly man why he admires himself in a mirror:

> The frightful man replies, "Sir, according to the immortal principles of '89, all men are by right equal. Thus I possess the right to see my reflection; with pleasure or displeasure, that only concerns my conscience."
>
> According to common sense, I was probably right; but, from the legal viewpoint, he was not wrong.

The wry coda is a legalistic conundrum, anticipating the Socratic irony of the next-to-final fable, "Let's Beat Up the Poor!" ("Assommons les pauvres!" no. 49), which "demonstrates" a harsher democratic dictum. Such theories can be correct and wrong at the same time.

"The Harbor" combines melodic stanzas with an analysis of poetic reverie. The opening line is a "kernal phrase" or verbal formula which engenders the text (Riffaterre 1978; Hiddleston 1985, 563–70): "A harbor is an enchanting abode for souls wearied by life's struggles. The sky's fullness, the mobile architecture of the clouds, the sea's shimmering colorations, the sparkling of lighthouses," stimulate fantasies and justify their compensatory mission: "And then, especially, there is a sort of mysterious and aristocratic pleasure for someone no longer curious or ambitious enough to contemplate, lying in the belvedere or leaning on the pier, all the movements of those who depart and of those who return, of those who still have the strength to will, the desire to travel or to grow rich."

Consoling enchantments—from "The Stranger" (no. 1), "Invitation to the Voyage" (no. 18), to "Any where out of the world" (no. 48)—lull anxiety, providing havens of "regularity and symmetry," which Baudelaire considers to be "one of the primordial needs of the human mind" (*Fusées, OC* 1:663–64; cf. ibid., 655). The dreamer submits to fate, although he imagines that he can negotiate the world as a reasonably free agent. "The Harbor" points to an eventual harmony, but its contradictions remain unresolved.

8

FINAL EXECUTIONS OF IDEALISM

The Esthetic, the Ethical, and the Religious

The last fables shatter the binary dialectics which structure the narrator's journey. "Portraits of Mistresses," "The Gallant Marksman," "The Soup and the Clouds," and "The Shooting Range and the Cemetery" ("Portraits de maîtresses," "Le Galant Tireur," "La Soupe et les nuages," "Le Tir et le cimetière," nos. 42–45) conclude *The Parisian Prowler* by demolishing idealism with varying degrees of allegory or directness. Each depicts the dangers of dogmatic abstractions (or ideologies) and deconstructs, through figurative self-analyses, literature's redemptive claims.

It is fittingly ironic that these hard-nosed theoretical fables—whose linguistic mayhem so appeals these days—repudiate theory uncriticized, reconfirming the author's recognition that "a system is a kind of damnation which forces us to a perpetual recantation" (*OC* 2:577–78; cited in my preface). At the same time, these extremist adventures buttress the narrator's "impeccable naïveté" as they prepare their antithesis, the endearingly modest manifesto, "Loss of Halo" ("Perte d'auréole," no. 46), which consecrates the unpretentious "poet of modern life." At the threshold of a conclusion, this deliberately contemporary fable permanently seals the narrator's two conversions: a transition from conventional dualisms to an understanding of experience as impure, mixed; a historical exchange of the sanctimonious "halo," which had glorified the French poet from the Renaissance through the 1848 revolution, for the droll, low-life humility of a Second Empire intellectual dissident.

The four, very substantial, concluding fables—"Miss Scalpel,"

"Any where out of the world," "Let's Beat Up the Poor!" and "The Good Dogs" (nos. 47–50)—recapitulate the journey and map out its boldest consequences. Two of them (nos. 47 and 49) were in fact rejected by the editors of the *Revue Nationale* (Kopp, lxix). The most probing, in my opinion, is "Miss Scalpel," which summarizes the strand of "ethical" fables. Contemporary readers seem to have considered its implication that no divine order exists to be blasphemous (Prévost 1953, 100), and posterity has favored the next one, "Any where out of the world" (no. 48), which summarizes the fables of esthetic stimulation and permanent flight. "Miss Scalpel"—which closes this chapter—most sharply juxtaposes the esthetic and the ethical—and that which transcends them while including both, the religious.

DECONSTRUCTION OF NARCISSISM

The collection's longest fable, "Portraits of Mistresses" (181 lines in the Kopp edition), accomplishes the idealist artist's ultimate revenge. (The next longest, "A Heroic Death," 161 lines, symmetrically acts out the *artist's* execution *by* the Ideal.) The four middle-aged males of "Portraits," representing the poet-narrator's disenchanted maturity, seem to be the four boys of "Vocations" (the third longest, 147 lines) grown up: "they bore that unmistakable quality of veterans of joy, an indescribable something, a cold and mocking sadness." Detached, yes, but their "sadness" points to tenacious desires, despite fate's tenacious hostility, and they still excitedly discuss what they "can love or respect" (cf. Maclean 1988, 125–40; Wing 1986, 28–29).

Each claims to seek reciprocal affection, although the mistress of each magnifies his particular brand of narcissism. After describing four degrees of love, the first reproaches his lover "who always wanted to play the man's part" by criticizing his numerous failings, especially his lack of knowledge and his powerlessness.[1] Oddly enough, this female thinker committed the least cerebral of infidelities: "One day I found that Minerva, starved for intellectual power [*affamée de force idéale*], face to face with my servant." The second fellow is tormented by the opposite, his lover's lack of initiative: "Recently, fate accorded me the enjoyment [*jouissance*] of a woman who was indeed the gentlest, the most submissive and most devoted of creatures, and always available! and without enthusiasm!" Her aloofness infuriated him: "After one year of living together, she confessed to me that she had never enjoyed sex [*elle n'avait jamais connu le plaisir:* literally, never had an orgasm]. I got fed up with that *unequal duel* [italics added], and the incomparable girl got married." The third was involved in a ridiculous relationship with a "polyphagous monster" who constantly gorged herself. What kind of "duel," or loving dialogue, might satisfy these self-centered gentlemen?

The fourth speaker—who recalls the fourth boy of "Vocations" (no. 31)—introduces one of the great moments in a sequential reading of the collection. His grave, somewhat acerbic tone, and his dignified austerity, reinforce the impression that the author himself addresses us directly. For the first time we see and feel Baudelaire's bodily as well as emotional presence, as he distinguishes himself from his companions:

> "As for me," said the fourth, "I have endured atrocious sufferings from the opposite of what we usually blame selfish females for. I find you to be in a bad position, you all-too-fortunate mortals, to complain about the imperfections of your mistresses!"
>
> That was spoken in a quite serious tone, by a man of gentle and poised appearance, with an almost clerical physiognomy, unhappily lit by light gray eyes, the sort of eyes whose gaze says, "*I want!*" or "*You must!*" or again, "*I never forgive!*"[2]

We are reminded of photographs of Baudelaire by Carjat and Neyt about 1864–66, of which Théophile Gautier's introduction to the 1868 edition of *Les Fleurs du Mal* provides a verbal counterpart: "Thin, long silky hair, already sparse and almost completely gray, accompanied that face at once so aged and youthful and lent it an almost sacerdotal appearance" (Pichois and Ruchon 1961, 64; photographs numbered 57–59). We face the ailing poet, dressed in black, whose gaze radiates uncompromising integrity, tenderness, and rage: his unconquerable will (*Je veux!*); his *amor fati*, heroic embrace of Fate (*Il faut!*); and his righteous, or embittered, repudiation of mendacity (*Je ne pardonne jamais!*).[3] This maladjusted hero, who cannot accept the world, is too rigorous for anyone to imitate.

Now the "perfect" artist faces the "perfect" female, not in a duel between more or less equals, but in an apparent triumph of the man's desire. This flawless female allegorically represents (i.e., figures) the man's absolutely free will; another ego, she is a "room of paradise" (no. 5) utterly responsive to his presence: "'Imagine [*Figurez-vous*] a person unable to commit an error of feeling or of calculation. Imagine a devastating serenity of character; devotion without playacting or exaggeration; gentleness without weakness; power without violence.'" Paradoxically, she mirrors both his *narcissism* and his inescapable *submission* to the consciousness of an Other.[4] There remains no boundary between wish and fulfillment, as the "Generous Gambler" (no. 29) had promised. She becomes "'a surface pure and polished like a mirror, breathtakingly monotonous, which would reflect all my feelings and gestures with the ironic precision of my own conscience.'" But the beneficiary loses his autonomy: "'So much that I couldn't yield to an unreasonable gesture or feeling without immediately noticing the silent reproach of my inseparable specter. Love seemed like a guardianship.'"

"Portraits of Mistresses" brutally unmasks the ironic privileges of untrammeled narcissism. The search for perfection of any kind is self-defeating, for the "ideal," by definition, lives only in the mind, as a concept, an idea (if understood rationally), or as an illusion (if taken literally). This "perfect love"—in reality, the ego judging itself through another person—seems to fulfill the narrator's expectation, in "The Eyes of the Poor" (no. 26), to "read [*his*] thoughts" in his mistress's eyes. But he is not the ugly man of "The Mirror" (no. 40) who manipulates his civil rights. His "reflexiveness," in Kierkegaard's terms, his constant self-scrutiny, destroys his spontaneity and ability to love another person. His specular mate is an "*ironic* conscience"—a sort of castrating superego—which indicts his freedom.[5] Absolute love, without otherness, translates into no love at all.

The ending of "Portraits of Mistresses" figuratively and literally executes the idealist categories that motivated the original search: "'Conquer or die, as Politics states, fate forced this choice upon me!'" So he killed her: "'What could you expect me to do,'" he asked, "'*since she was perfect?*'" (italics in the text). The "three other companions implicitly admit" their inability to follow such "a rigorous action, although otherwise sufficiently justified." The *theory* is logical, but they possess neither the principle nor the heart to carry it out.

Absolute desire becomes an enslavement which isolates me from the world. Midas is "the saddest of alchemists" ("Alchimie de la douleur" [Alchemy of pain], *FM*, no. 71). Baudelaire's alter ego in "Portraits of Mistresses" confirms his *Artificial Paradises* which denounces this subjective imperialism. Hallucinations produced by drugs or intense reverie make the mind's products seem more real than the world outside. An opium addict habitually confuses dream, fantasy, and waking consciousness: "Midas changed everything he touched into gold, and felt martyred by that ironic privilege. So the opium eater transforms into inevitable realities all the objects of his dreams" (*OC* 1:480). The mind absorbs the world and, in the process, loses it.

FINAL EXECUTIONS

This murder introduces four theoretical fables that similarly demolish idealistic thinking. The italicized verb "*to kill*" of "The Gallant Marksman" (no. 43) is a metatextual conceit which unifies this sequence typographically. These brief, schematic parables, reduced to the bare minimum, ironically mirror the more discursive preceding ones. "The Gallant Marksman" parodies "Portraits of Mistresses" just as "A Joker" (no. 4) caricatures "The Artist's *Confiteor*" (no. 3); and as "The Dog and the Scent-Bottle" (no. 8) vulgarizes "The Fool and the Venus" (no. 7). The quoted dialogue of "Mistresses" ends as the narrator describes how the men order wine in order to "kill Time which has such resistant life, and to speed up Life which flows so slowly."[6]

"The Gallant Marksman" consumates the duel between mind and reality, repeating the fourth man's murder of the Ideal in the preceding fable. I quote it in full, for it both typifies the narrator's Socratic irony—an outrageous pose meant to challenge common sense—and adds verbal signs of irony which question literature itself. Here the narrator becomes a "marksman" who literalizes the cliché—the "dead metaphor"—to "kill Time." I agree generally with Barbara Johnson that the fable develops as an infinite play of metaphors of metaphor and linguistic figuration, but I do not accept her notion of undecidability (Johnson 1979, 83–100; Johnson 1987, 100–15). The fable does indeed parody linguistic figuration, but, interpreted within the collection, it also challenges a brand of formalism which ignores literature's ethical content.

This dreadful parable repeats the fourth man's quarrel with his censorious lover with grim humor. To begin with the title, *galant* means both (1) flirtatious and (2) polite to the opposite sex—both of which this narrator, as usual, is not. He will soon abuse the female object of his affection. The opening paragraph establishes the wordplay:

> As the carriage was crossing the woods, he had it stop in the vicinity of a shooting range, saying that it would be enjoyable for him to shoot a few bullets to *kill* Time. Kill that monster, isn't that everyone's most usual and most legitimate pastime? —So he gallantly offered his hand to his dear, delectable, and execrable wife, to that mysterious woman to whom he owes so many pleasures, so many woes, and perhaps also a large part of his genius.

The terms "sa chère, délicieuse et exécrable femme" and "galamment" prepare his displaced rage against his muse. Time as either a psychological or metaphysical entity does not really count here, if I may say so. A linguistic structure, not a moral principle, generates the story which itself literalizes a cliché—thus anticipating the Saussurian insight into the independence of language from its referential function, and illustrated from Hugo, Rimbaud, Lautréamont, Mallarmé, through the surrealists to present-day semiotics.[7]

Literature's figurative functions become the second paragraph's target. When the man takes his shots, one might say, with Barbara Johnson, that, paradoxically, "the dead figure [*to kill Time*] is resurrected." Italicized words again bare the mechanics of literary figuration:

> Several bullets hit far from the intended target [*le but proposé*]; one of them even sank into the ceiling. And since the charming creature was laughing madly, mocking her spouse's bad aim [*maladresse*], he abruptly turned toward her, and said, "Observe that doll, over there, on the right, sticking its nose in the air and with such a haughty expression. Well dear angel! *I imagine that it is you.*" [*Je me figure que c'est vous,* italicized in the text]. And he shut his eyes and released the trigger. The doll was cleanly decapitated.

This acting out of "tuer le Temps" reinforces the satanic literalization of the cliché "to see life through rose-colored glasses" (*voir la vie en beau*) in "The Bad Glazier" (no. 9). The marksman's aggression becomes even more metatextually ironic as he decapitates (or figuratively "kills") the doll which is, itself, a *figure*—of a muse, and, at that instant, of the man's wife. A trope, a substitution, makes of the doll a substitute woman, just as the couple's "exchange" (hardly two-sided) is a *figure* of a moral—or immoral—lesson about the artist and his inspiration. The italicized statement "*je me figure que c'est vous*" realizes the lethal ambiguities of colloquial rhetoric.

Obviously, the story is not a realistic, psychologically motivated battle, but a charade. The third and final paragraph, completing this syllogism of absurd logic, scoffs at the complacency of allegorical translation itself. The symmetrical contrast between the narrator's initial "bad aim," or clumsiness (*maladresse*), and his inspired "good aim," or skill (*adresse*), completes this verbal joke: "Then bowing to his dear, his delectable, his execrable wife, his inescapable and ruthless Muse, and respectfully kissing her hand, he added, 'Ah my dear angel! How I thank you for my aim!' [*Je vous remercie de mon adresse!* not italicized]."

Literature itself is "the intended target" of this theoretical fable. Although the poet decapitates only his muse's figural counterpart, not the person herself, the puns cannot entirely distance us from the disgusting action. A woman once again receives a blow which the narrator himself might more appropriately deserve. The figurative assassin bows to his victim as the "joker" (no. 4) had obsequiously bowed to the zealous beast.

The signs of metatextual self-parody appear less prominent in the following two fables, "The Soup and the Clouds" and "The Shooting Range and the Cemetery" (nos. 44–45). These almost skeletal anecdotes recycle the initial dialectical fables that oppose Ideal and Real, Ambition and Mortality. And they reintroduce images and expressions, now easily recognizable, from the narrator's ironic lexicon. They tersely undermine the esthetic idealism we have learned to suspect.

Another hostile mate, in "The Soup and the Clouds," rejects fantasy (clouds) for bodily comfort (soup). The narrator is dreaming next to an open window and, with inflated oratory, he almost flippantly evokes pleasurable reveries which so many times before he had solemnly relished: "My little crazy beloved was serving me dinner, and through the dining room's open window I was contemplating the moving architectures that God fashions from vapors, the marvellous constructions of the impalpable." His wife is another ugly Benedicta (of no. 38) crudely hostile to solipsistic freedom. Like the male "Specter" of "The Double Room" (no. 5), she clouts the poet and yells: " 'Will you ever eat your soup, you goddamn cloud peddler?' " She diminishes the visionary to what he is, socially and economically, a "sacré bougre de marchand de nuages"—a creator prostituted by economic penury to tasteless consumers. [8]

"The Shooting Range and the Cemetery" returns to the allegorical graveyard of "Which Is the True One?" The ending translates the familiar lesson that one cannot "kill Time" with entertainment or esthetic narcotism: " 'Cursed be your targets and your rifles, unruly living ones, who take such little heed of the deceased and their divine repose! Cursed be your ambitions, cursed be your calculations, impatient mortals [etc.].' " No one can escape practical responsibilities.

These radically skeptical fables clearly avoid what Baudelaire considered to be "the great poetic *heresy of modern times* . . .

the idea of direct usefulness" (*Edgar Allan Poe, sa vie et ses ouvrages*, 1852, *OC* 2:263). Their gallows humor and dearth of narrative detail maintain a dispassionate violence which continues to disguise the narrator's position. Consistently refusing to lift his mask, he replaces tenderness with ambiguity, sententiousness with Socratic provocation: "Art's supreme accomplishment is to remain glacial and closed, and to leave all the merit of the indignation to the reader" (*OC* 2:186). The ethical ironist forces us to respond.

A POET OF MODERN LIFE

The narrator then achieves, for the first time in *The Parisian Prowler*, an "impeccable naïveté." This cycle ends with "Loss of Halo" (no. 46), which "The Painter of Modern Life," written before 1860, helps us to interpret. Out of the numerous expressions and ideas the essay shares with several fables, the most relevant is the quest for presentness, a paradoxical, inconceivable, attempt to convey through art the immediacy of life outside (de Man 1983, 156–65; *OC* 2:696). "Loss of Halo" fulfills Baudelaire's earliest ambition to capture "the transitory, the ephemeral, the contingent, that half of art, whose other half is the eternal and the immutable" (*OC* 2:695).

The self-deprecatory humor of this strategically placed parable is drastically new, revising the pathos of "A Heroic Death" and the other tragic clown stories. The modern poet no longer wears, like Fancioulle, "an indestructible halo . . . which blended, in a strange amalgam, the rays of Art and the glory of Martyrdom" (no. 27). The anecdote appears to illustrate the preceding "Shooting Range and the Cemetery," which grimly assumes that our inevitable mortality—and not eternity or perfection—is the "Goal [*le But*, also "target"], the only true goal of detestable life!" In fact, "Loss of Halo" and "The Gallant Marksman" both originate in brief scenarios in *Fusées* (*OC* 1:660, 659, respectively). Now bitterness and irony have all but disappeared. The Parisian absorbs these simple facts and "descends" into fellowship.[9]

Napoleon III's renovated capital provides the site of this happy fall from paradise in which the poet-prophet dethrones himself before our very eyes. The understated story quite significantly takes the form of a dialogue. Another proxy of the reader, a friend, is surprised to see "the poet" in a degraded setting (not necessarily a brothel, just a generalized *mauvais lieu*): " 'Hey what! You here, my dear fellow? You, in a house of ill fame! You, the drinker of quintessences! You, the ambrosia eater!' " The "mauvais lieu" accomplishes the "desecration with a vengeance of false poetic pretenses," for the sanitized paradise of classicism (or its romantic revision) is not the place of the modern poet's intercourse (Wohlfarth 1970, 165–89). The narrator demystifies the social and esthetic hierarchies in which he no longer believes, while his friend hangs onto them. They live in a transitional period, the dawning of industrialization, during which such visionaries as Victor Hugo, who published *Les Contemplations* in 1856 (the year before *Les Fleurs du Mal* and *Madame Bovary* appeared), and Jules Michelet maintained their cultural ascendency.

The modern poet does not repudiate his vocation as such, but only an exalted, idolatrous view of his person, his powers, and his role. He seals his conversion abruptly, in rush-hour traffic. Hastily crossing a busy boulevard, "hopping in the mud, through the shifting chaos where death comes galloping from all sides at once," he lets his halo slip "into the mire of the macadam" and accepts the fact, bemused: " 'I considered it less disagreeable to lose my insignia than to break my bones. And anyway, I said to myself, misfortune is good for something. Now I can walk about incognito, commit foul acts, and indulge in debauchery like ordinary mortals. So here I am, just like you, as you can see!' " The halo-less citizen exaggerates; he indulges in "ordinary" joys of living, and not a perverse or excessive *crapule* and other *actions basses*. His "incognito" (like that of Constantin Guys) insinuates him into the present moment.

The seer now defrocked begins his liberated life as an aimless *flâneur*, the Parisian prowler himself. This pedestrian, whom the chaotic urban traffic still terrifies, prefers the security of sidewalks or covered arcades (Benjamin 1969, 155–200). Some details reinforce this historical specificity. Macadam, or asphalt (named after its inventor, the Scottish engineer John L. McAdam, about 1830), was first used in Paris in 1849 (*Grand Larousse universel du XIXe siècle*, s.v. *Macadam*). "Mire" (*la fange*) represents the survival of the old Paris in the new, Haussmannized *boulevards* of the capital. This urban fable renews Baudelaire's call for sculptors to "seize upon nobility wherever it may be found, even in the mire" (*OC* 2:721).

The two final paragraphs reinforce the urban poet's freshly gained modesty, though, typically, not without some ambivalence. The conservative interviewer urges him to retrieve his sanctity: " 'At least you should put up a notice for your halo, or have the police advertise for it.' " No, despite his anxieties, he wants resolutely to participate in the common life and turn his "loss" into a considerable gain, his anonymity. He relinquishes his privilege as a "drinker of quintessences" in order to consume wine, coffee, or beer—and enjoy casual conversations: " 'Good God no! I'm fine here. You're the only one who recognized me. Besides, dignity irks me. And I'm glad to think that some bad poet will pick it up and insolently stick it on his head. Make someone happy, what a delight! [*Faire un heureux, quelle jouissance!*] and especially a happy someone I can laugh at! What about X, or Z! Right! Wouldn't that be funny!' "

"Loss of Halo" reconfirms the sincere part of Baudelaire's 1862 dedication to Arsène Houssaye: "It is above all by frequenting enormous cities, in the intersection of their countless relationships that this obsessive ideal [of the prose poem] came to life." Why, then, does he mock "les heureux," heedless beneficiaries of complacency, "bad poets" like the "magnificent imbecile who . . . concentrated in himself the very essence of France's wit" ("A Joker," no. 4, another Parisian boulevard scene)? No longer a romantic icon, the modern poet remains vulnerable. Original as a creator, as a person subordinate, he still needs others to ratify his ego.

THE ESTHETIC, THE ETHICAL, AND THE RELIGIOUS

Baudelaire's most discerning fable of modern life, "Miss Scalpel" (no. 47), recapitulates, and then surpasses, the conflict between "ethical" realism and "esthetic" solipsism. For several reasons it was not published by the *Revue Nationale*—although it was announced three times—during Baudelaire's lifetime. Two worlds of personal integrity, two obsessions (or *idées fixes*) confront one another—one insane, the other stubbornly rational. The fable's format is the most explicitly dialogical of the collection, and yet the stroller meets a crazed woman whose direct speech dominates his narrative. Her initiative—also exceptional in the collection —serves further to accentuate his abortive conversation with her and all previous parallel monologues. This time, however, the narrator definitively rejects delusions, further penetrating the meaning of human suffering, as he relinquishes his pride before divine mystery. [10]

This radical religious fable, more poignantly than "The Fairies' Gifts" (no. 20), challenges the very notion of a just universe. Both the stroller and Miss Scalpel are tantalized by the macabre. "Bistouri," her nickname, means surgical knife, and her mania for operations parodies the Christian doctrine of suffering as purification or retribution, which informs *Les Fleurs du Mal* from "Bénédiction" (Blessing, *FM*, no. 1) on, and which popular religious prejudice routinely assumes. Her madness serves no apparent goal, whereas the narrator suggests that his "taste for horror" should "convert [his] heart, like a cure at knife point." He in fact succeeds.

It is a strange and touching adventure. The narrator-*flâneur* cautiously involves himself with a female peripatetic, a prostitute, a distorted image of the widowed mother. She is prey to a compulsion to nurture medical doctors, and to be treated by them, even though she has no physical symptoms. Miss Scalpel, in fact, is a hypochondriac who seeks to control a little corner of her mortality and now she tries to absorb the socially alienated wanderer into her *mental* alienation, like the prostituted poet of

"Crowds" (no. 12), or the observer of "A une passante" (To a passerby [*FM*, no. 111, added in 1861 in "Tableaux parisiens"]). But he asserts his reality principle: " 'No. I'm not a doctor. Let me go [*Laissez-moi passer*].' " Merely curious at first, he does not view this woman as a fellow human being: "I passionately love mystery, because I always hope to untangle it. So I allowed myself to be dragged off by that companion, or rather by that unhoped-for enigma."

The narrator is an enthusiastic detective and the true interpreter of this Parisian parable, but at the beginning, as often, he remains emotionally detached. He relates her "hovel" only to literary descriptions by the seventeenth-century satirical poet Mathurin Régnier. He considers her at first to be a "comical creature" (*la bouffonne créature*), a grotesque; she may be a prostituted artist, as Donald Aynsworth suggests, but hers is not a profitable commerce. The price she extracts is not money but *her* pleasure; she extorts the man's inner, as well as verbal, consent to her fiction that he is a doctor: " 'Make yourself at home, my friend, get comfortable. It'll bring back the hospital and the good times of youth. —Ah there! now where did that white hair come from? You weren't like that, not too long ago, when you were an intern under doctor L——. I remember that you were the one who helped him with the major operations. Now there's a man who loves to cut, hack and saw!' " Miss Scalpel's sadism stands revealed, contradicting her overt benevolence and generosity. Staunchly realistic, the *flâneur* will not play her game. Although she points to his graying hair, and thus to their common subordination to time, he resists her attempts to forge his identity. They share no truth. This second portrait of the narrator's physical traits recalls the fourth man of "Portraits of Mistresses" (no. 42), who also reflects photographs of Baudelaire at middle age, especially the one inscribed to Poulet-Malassis: "To my dear Auguste, the only creature whose laughter has brightened my Belgian sojourn" (Pichois and Ruchon 1961, photographs numbered 57–58).

Then, for the first and only time in *The Parisian Prowler*, the woman, who mirrors the narrator's narcissism, now attempts aggressively to absorb him into hers. She doggedly denies his reality when she switches her address from *vous* to *tu*. But he angrily resists her imperialistic delusion. This futile "dialogue" summarizes all the stroller's previous failures to communicate:

> A few moments later, addressing me by the familiar *tu*, she repeated her antiphon, and said, "You are a doctor, aren't you, my kitten?"
>
> That unintelligible refrain made me leap to my feet. Furious I yelled, "No!"
>
> "Surgeon, then?"
>
> "No! no! unless it would be to cut off your head! You damned holy ciborium of Saint Mackeral!"
>
> "Wait," she replied, "you'll see."

The narrator's lethal threat distracts our attention (and his) from the woman's shocking self-deception. But the skeptical man is also a perverse "artist," taking the Prince's part against her "too perfect idealization" (no. 27).

Miss Scalpel magnifies his own solipsism. His defensive threat carries an ironic message about his own hidden wish to mimic her role, and so, as before, he locates the struggle in *her* head. His criminal impulse reflects the same chaotic desires expressed by decapitating his muse, both figuratively and literally, in "The Gallant Marksman" (no. 43). The benevolent but deluded prostitute is a mirror of his own "empty bottle," which the narrator of "The Wild Woman and the Affected Coquette" (no. 11) had threatened to throw out the window. Her words are a meaningless antiphon of his own self-communion.

The perverted female "artist"—whose sexual obsessions are hardly disguised—reinforces her delusions with portraits. First a collection of "lithographs by Maurin, which for several years you could find displayed along the Quai Voltaire," and which evoke the uprisings of 1848, the historical foil to her scenario: " 'Look, here's K., the one who denounced to the government the insurgents he was treating at his hospital.' " Then the new "age of mechanical reproduction" arises before our eyes as she displays her *photographs* of young doctors (Benjamin 1969, 217–51. Cf. "Salon de 1859," on photography, *OC* 2:614–19).

He now steers her toward reality. He had been good enough to accompany her and listen, but out of curiosity, not from sympathy with her fantasy. And he threatened to kill her! He rejects her "love," because it exacts an excessive price—his autonomy:

> "When we meet again, you'll give me your portrait, won't you, darling?"
>
> "But," I replied, in turn following, me as well, my obsession, "why do you believe I'm a doctor?"

His refusal, reinforced by a question, like that of a psychoanalyst, urges her into a consensus about facts. He wants both to understand critically and to love, to accept her and to be accepted for who he truly is. Ironically, she believes that the stroller might be a doctor "because [he is] so nice and so good to women!" For his part, he admits the opposite: " 'Strange logic!' I said to myself." Strange indeed! The guest is hardly benevolent.

Is Miss Scalpel the mother—or nurturing lover—he has pursued throughout the collection? If she does unmask *his* hidden scenario—to recover a mother who coddles her little boy—why then does he not revere this slightly older, though still lovely woman? The "poet of modern life" has matured beyond the childish design to sleep with his maid ("Vocations," no. 31); he controls his ambivalence and will not imitate the poverty-stricken intern who excites her ambiguously maternal invitation. " 'After all, I'm a beautiful enough woman, though not too young. I told him, "Come see me, come see me often. And with me, don't worry. I don't need money." ' " The stroller—now firmly ensconced in reality—refuses to "create [her] famous role," act out her script.

He faces his most basic ethical choice when the dialogue reaches a dead end. He steadfastly maintains his reality principle and refuses to lie. Rather, he seeks surgically to open her mind and probe her wound, as might a relentless theoretician who ignores the emotional results of a systemic skepticism:[11]

> "Can you remember the time and the situation when this so peculiar passion arose in you?"
>
> With difficulty I made myself understood; finally I succeeded. But then she replied very sadly, and even, as far as I can remember, averting her eyes, "I don't know... I don't remember."

She resists his psychoanalytic scalpel, protecting her subjective self submerged in dreams of infinite possibility. Her eyes avoid his objective gaze and she voices the sadness of finitude and disillusion, as had the voyager of "Already!" (no. 34) returning to land: "sad, inconceivably sad, like the priest whose divinity is snatched away." Might she become rational if the narrator can open her distorting window? We suspect that reality would consume her.

The conversation has ended as has the story. Now a powerful epilogue points to the mystery which energizes the entire collection. The narrator's outburst of passion for truth carries no irony, no bitterness, but compassion, righteous perplexity at the enormity—and senselessness—of undeserved pain. An extraordinary "prayer"—which I quote in full—marks his boldest insight into the powers and the limits of human understanding:

> What weirdness you find in big cities, when you know how to walk about and look! Life swarms with innocent monsters. — Lord, my God! You, the Creator, you, the Master; you who made Law and Freedom; you, the sovereign who lets things happen, you, the judge who forgives; you who are abounding in motives and causes, and who have perhaps placed a taste of horror in my mind in order to convert my heart, like a cure at knife point; Lord, take pity, take pity on madmen and madwomen! O Creator! Can monsters exist in the eyes of the only One who knows why they exist, how they *were made* and how they might have been able *not to be made?*

The moral philosopher, in his marrow, experiences metaphysical absurdity, the inaccessibility of ultimate meaning. He can answer the mad woman's anguish only by addressing God the

Creator over a dozen times, for he believes that people suffer for good reason.

Conventional wisdom assumes that human distress reflects the will of a divine lawgiver and is proper retribution for sins committed. But Miss Scalpel harms no one. Unable to distinguish fantasy from reality, she exercises no free choice. The torment of the insane, those "innocent monsters," refutes the divine order.

The modern poet, overwhelmed by injustice, with fear, trembling, and ethical anguish, questions the raw, brute mystery of existence. He faces the alternative of despair or faith—unable to embrace either. He has touched the limits of religious thinking; carrying art and ethics to their fullest he finds them insufficient to his quest for justice and truth.

Yet his thinking is free of idolatry; he does not replace the enigma with a facile dictum. Helpless and dismayed, he surrenders his pride by acknowledging that he is but a creature as he realizes that the human and the Absolute are incommensurable. His reverential yet assertive humility acknowledges that intelligence can be glorious, but in confronting the fundamental whys of existence, like Job, he is humbled and awed.

At the same time, his energetic response presupposes his own freedom and self-awareness. The religious content of this anguished prayer remains ambiguous, however. We do not know if Baudelaire, interpreting his own fable, would ratify the existence of a God who listens and cares. Whatever the answers, the narrator struggles to penetrate undeserved and irremediable injustice in a radically new manner: from God's perspective. Beyond his ken lies a possible reason, a vision transcending his, "aux yeux de Celui-là seul qui sait pourquoi ils existent, comment ils *se sont faits* et comment ils auraient pu *ne pas se faire*."

So ends the series of theoretical fables introduced by "Portraits of Mistresses" which murder the "perfect" woman. That sequence is unified by the expression "to kill Time" and the actions which, brutally, reject the world as it exists, imperfect. The *duels* between Ideal and Real—or between Art and Nature (no. 3)—end in the death either of the artist, as in the earliest fables, or in the murder, by the artist, of the Ideal herself. The narrator's multiple consciousness, his simultaneous awareness of incompatible realities, becomes so intense that madness or murder becomes the only *logical* solution. But that is not the final act.

Although it reaches a wisdom, most appropriate, I believe, to our post-Auschwitz, post-Hiroshima age, "Miss Scalpel" ends with unanswered questions. The implicitly situational or explicit irony of previous fables reaches its extreme frontier. This radical religious fable affirms the sanctity of every human being and reinforces our compelling drive to comprehend life's "logic of the Absurd" (no. 20). Yet meaninglessness is not the answer. Humanity is an amalgam of grandeur and misery, "sorrow and madness," like the "artificial and voluntary" Fool who bemoans his impotence while lauding his spiritual ambitions: "However I am made, I as well, to understand and to feel immortal Beauty!" (no. 7). The wiser narrator now directs his words beyond effigies to the Creator who, also, does not answer; but neither does he look away. He is invisible, hidden, mystery itself.

9

CONCLUDING FABLES

Literature as Friendship

No one resolves the Parisian prowler's metaphysical and ethical perplexities. The concluding fables from "Portraits of Mistresses" on (nos. 42–50) magnify the impossible battle between idealism and disillusion. Viewed from above, the narrator's itinerary begins in alienation and its compensatory or escapist dreams ("The Stranger," no. 1), progressing through the seductively poetic empathy of "Widows" (no. 13), to the lethal absolutism of "The Temptations" and "A Heroic Death" (nos. 21, 27). The middle fables such as "The Thyrsus" and "Already!" (nos. 32, 34) posit the realistic amalgam personified by the streetwise poet of "Loss of Halo" (no. 46) who accepts his fallen finitude.

The final four recapitulate each impasse—without, ultimately, silencing the narrator's compassion or righteous outrage. "Miss Scalpel" (no. 47) marks both a culmination and a beginning. This parable of impenetrable otherness lucidly confronts the mystery of universal injustice. "Any where out of the world" and "Let's Beat Up the Poor!" (nos. 48, 49) recapitulate battles with esthetic and ethical theory. The first one summarizes *the esthetic impasse*, despotic desire unable to cure mankind's inherent dissatisfaction. The penultimate fable summarizes *the ethical impasse*, a principle of equality that violates elemental decency, parodying the sadistic "moralities" of "The Bad Glazier," "The Wild Woman and the Affected Coquette" (nos. 9, 11), and "The Gallant Marksman" (no. 43), among others. Before his affirmative conclusion, the poet relinquishes any claim to master fate.

THE ESTHETIC IMPASSE: AUTONOMY VERSUS DESPAIR

"Any where out of the world" fulfills to the extreme the narrator's "craving for disguises and masks, hatred of home, and a passion for traveling" ("Crowds," no. 12), as prepared by "Invitation to the Voyage," "Solitude," "Plans," and especially "Vocations" (nos. 18, 23, 24, 31). The lasting appeal of "Any where out of the world" comes from its forceful echoing of idealized worlds from *Les Fleurs du Mal* and the other "esthetic" fables; but it also decisively confesses to the anguish that finds no home, despite our persistent desire for one.

The fable's bilingual title (quoted from the English poet Thomas Hood) is itself an exotic challenge and it develops the consequences of a fallible human condition, one which Mallarmé would soon illustrate in his poem "Les Fenêtres" (Windows). Baudelaire defines his symbolism: "This life is a hospital in which every patient is haunted by the desire to change beds. This one wants to suffer in front of the stove, and that one believes he will recover next to the window" (cf. Godfrey 1982). Although imagination can enjoy two sorts of escape, one inward, the other cosmic, our emotional turmoil is endless: "It seems that I would always be content where I am not, and I constantly discuss that question of relocation [*déménagement*] with my soul."

The fable weaves an enticing tapestry of "prose" and "poetry" which, however, distinguishes the realist from the dreamer. In a one-way dialogue, the narrator urges his "poor benumbed soul" to consider several havens: the warm maritime city of Lisbon which features, as in "Rêve parisien" (Parisian dream [*FM*, no. 102, "Tableaux parisiens," lines 6–12]), a treeless "landscape made of light and mineral, and of liquid to reflect them!" The passive hedonism of "Beautiful Dorothy" (no. 25) might be recovered in Holland, that "beatific land," as in both verse and prose versions of "Invitation to the Voyage" or Batavia, where "the spirit of Europe is married to tropical beauty" (no. 48).

Specifics do not make fantasy any more plausible. No dialogue develops and the realist asks: " 'Might my soul be dead? So you have reached that degree of stupor where you can take pleasure only in your affliction [*que tu ne te plaises que dans ton mal*]?' " The only *logical* solution to this impossible quest for "beatitude" is self-destruction: " 'let's flee toward the countries which are the analogies of Death.' "

Why have generations of readers taken the last paragraph so literally, reveling in its irresponsibility? How do we interpret the soul's one and only answer, which evokes the title for the first time? Is the escapist choice unqualified? "At last, my soul explodes, and wisely she shouts at me, 'Anywhere! Anywhere! provided it is out of this world!' " The soul's "explosion" reiterates all previous protests, but its "wisdom" is ironic; constant "déménagements" only veil its frustrated yearning for stability. After all, the first sentence had introduced mental movement as a possible cure. The repeated title makes a crucial distinction: "Anywhere out of *this* world"—not out of *the* world—as stated in both the English and French titles. This life might still be accepted and transformed.

"Any where out of the world" asserts the ambivalent drive to discover a perfect state of being (*bien être*, line 5) in *this* world, while it reinforces the irony of "A Heroic Death" (no. 27), which typifies the risks of extremist solutions. The Prince, "a *true* artist, rather indifferent toward people and morality, . . . was *truly* insatiable for voluptuous pleasures"; the Fool, a political as well as artistic extremist, could not reconcile his devotion to justice ("the *ideas* of fatherland and freedom") with his "*perfect* idealization" (italics added). All these fables demonstrate the futility of confusing our mental and social dimensions. One cannot *live* in "a paradise excluding any idea of tomb and destruction" (no. 27).

THE ETHICAL IMPASSE: THEORY VERSUS PRACTICE

The penultimate fable, "Let's Beat Up the Poor!" demystifies the dogma of equality with the same spiritual rigor that "Miss Scalpel" questions the dogma of divine justice. Like "The Bad Glazier" (no. 9), "The Counterfeit Coin" (no. 28), and "The

Rope" (no. 30), it ferociously demonstrates the persistence of unconscious evil. Even a mother mourning her suicidal son might confuse greed and economic self-preservation. Ethical theory can be foolishly literal and self-contradictory, as caricatured in "The Mirror" (no. 40). What is human dignity before the law? What is just before God? "Let's Beat Up the Poor!" reminds us that "the immortal principles of '89" can be practiced destructively (cf. Maclean 1988, 161–76; Monroe 1987, 112–24).

The poet of modern life may or may not be a reactionary, but he is not a true believer. He mocks the self-satisfaction of people who, like Homais, worship "the God of Socrates, of Franklin, of Voltaire and of Béranger! [and hypocritically] support the *Profession de foi du vicaire savoyard* and the immortal principles of 89!" (*Madame Bovary*).[1] He rejects the naive or anachronistic expectations of his century's romantic childhood. Its creed of inevitable social and scientific progress did not survive the revolutions of 1830 and 1848 or Louis Napoleon's 1851 coup d'état. Accordingly, "Let's Beat Up the Poor!" opens with a caustic analysis of the ideological shift:

> For two weeks I had shut myself up in my room, and I had surrounded myself with the books fashionable at that time (sixteen or seventeen years ago); I speak of books dealing with the art of making nations happy, wise, and rich, in twenty-four hours. I had thus digested—swallowed, I mean—all the ramblings of all those managers of public happiness—of those who advise all the poor to become slaves, and those who persuade them that they are all dethroned kings.—It will not be considered surprising that I was then in a state of mind bordering on vertigo or idiocy.

This contemporary tale confronts the political present. Written about 1865—but published only in the 1869 posthumous edition—the narrator may be alluding to Baudelaire's "intoxication in 1848 . . . Literary intoxication; memories of readings" (*Mon coeur mis à nu, OC* 1:679; cf. ibid., 707). In any case, he feels no sympathy with its utopianism and, like Flaubert's masterpiece of historical condescension, *Sentimental Education*, he critically observes a process of *abstraction:* "Yet I thought that I sensed, shut deep within my intellect, the dim seed of an idea better than all the old wives' formulas I had recently perused in the encyclopedia. But it was only the idea of an idea, something infinitely hazy."

The narrator will impulsively "apply" an ethical idea, just as the solitary of "The Bad Glazier" had "madly" applied an esthetic one. By now the irony of these metatextual charades is quite recognizable. But for the first time in the collection, the narrator labels his strategy as Socratic.[2] The Parisian's "good Angel, or a good Demon" (the word "Demon" occurs six times), is one of his conflicting selves: "The difference between the Demon of Socrates and mine is that Socrates' one appears to him only to forbid, warn, suggest, persuade. That poor Socrates had only a prohibitive Demon; mine is a great approver, mine is a Demon of action, or Demon of combat."

The story, as cruel and zany as a Monty Python sketch, demonstrates the potential violence of theory. The "charitable" narrator will act out, in both the psychological and literary senses, this tough-minded aphorism: "'He alone is equal to another, if he proves it, and he alone is worthy of freedom, if he can conquer it.'" The stroller goes to a cheap café (*un cabaret*) for a drink, and before entering, he meets an aged vagrant who, like the old acrobat (no. 14) and the poor family (no. 26), arouses his pity with "one of those unforgettable looks that would topple thrones, if mind could move matter, and if a hypnotist's eyes could ripen grapes." This humorous comparison prepares the parody.

Then the narrator launches another merciless mystification. Instead of responding gently, he attacks the old fellow, starting another fratricidal war, as in "The Cake" (no. 15), also occasioned by poverty and hunger. However, the contrast between the sadistic lyricism and the jarring technical terms signal a parodic detachment:

> Immediately, I pounced on my beggar. With a single punch, I shut one eye, which became, in a second, as big as a ball. I broke one of my nails smashing two of his teeth . . . .
>
> Having next, with a kick directed to his back, forceful enough

> to break his shoulder blades, floored that weakened sexagenarian, I grabbed a big tree branch lying on the ground, and I beat him with the obstinate energy of cooks trying to tenderize a beefsteak.

The final comparison makes it impossible to take this aggression completely in earnest. The graphic description (most of which I omit), exciting our disgust or perverse delight, is as comical as Rabelais's medical dilations on the Pichrocholian wars. Baudelaire uses a lot of big words. The adverb "perpendicularly" had reinforced the irony of "The Bad Glazier" (no. 9). The phrase "les omoplates [de] ce sexagénaire affaibli" nudges us in a similar manner.

At the battle's turning point, the narrator translates his lesson. He also reveals that he is a Socratic ironist who confirms his theory corporeally. This method of enlightenment anticipates Franz Kafka's short story or parable "In the Penal Colony," in which an "inscriber" engraves an all-too-literal judgment into the flesh of a criminal. Here the "thesis" arouses its "antithesis," as would a classical syllogism:

> Suddenly, —Oh miracle! Oh delight of the philosopher who verifies the excellence of his theory! —I saw that antique carcass turn over, straighten up with a force I would never have suspected in a machine so peculiarly unhinged. And, with a look of hatred that seemed to me a *good omen*, the decrepit bandit flung himself on me, blackened both my eyes, broke four of my teeth, and, with the same tree branch, beat me to a pulp. —By my forceful medication, I had thus restored his pride and his life.

The attacker's Spartan therapy works, even unto its ridiculous extreme. The beggar indeed proves himself willing and able to "conquérir sa liberté." But several stylistic signals—the italicized *de bon augure*, the anatomical term *omoplates* (shoulder blades) for the colloquial *épaules* (shoulders), the victim turned into mashed steak—make us question the "jouissance du philosophe qui vérifie l'excellence de sa théorie!"

Symmetry of details seals the parody, as Marie Maclean has noticed: "The narrator is now 'knocked out' for a second time, getting, as is fit, *two* black eyes instead of the beggar's one, and *four* broken teeth instead of the beggar's two, not to mention being persuaded by the same persuader" (1988, 171). The tree branch passed back and forth, might symbolize natural morality, a practical ethics of compassion—now repeatedly, and equally, violated.

"Let's Beat Up the Poor!" grotesquely caricatures egalitarian propaganda, not democratic values as such. Although he condenses his references, the narrator associates himself with Zeno of Elea, a Socrates-like "sophist" who founded dialectics, and Zeno of Citium, the founder of Stoicism, who taught under the Painted Portico (or *Stoa Poikile*) in Athens.[3] The pugilistic "ethicist" embodies abstract equality—a risky technique for those who do not share your metalinguistic wit:

> Then, I made a mighty number of signs [*force signes*, another pun?] to make him understand that I considered the debate [*la discussion*] settled, and getting up with the self-satisfaction of a Stoic sophist, I told him, "Sir, *you are my equal!* Please do me the honor of sharing my purse. And remember, if you are a true philanthropist, you must apply to all your colleagues, when they seek alms, the theory I had the *pain* to test upon your back."
>
> He indeed swore that he had understood my theory, and that he would comply with my advice.

The tenderized "philosopher's" pompous declaration: "Monsieur, *vous êtes mon égal!*" echoes the narrator's other two-edged assertions of equality, brotherhood, or justice. This conclusion maintains the self-parody by renewing the cliché "to have the *pleasure* of doing [something]"—paralleling the vicious solitary who bludgeons the "bad" glazier's back for not providing rose-colored glass to "make life beautiful."

A manuscript variant, omitted by all editors, would have compromised this witticism. The contentious jibe "What do you think of that, citizen Proudhon?" too ideologically specific, would have restricted the fable's dialogical openness (Kopp, 357–59; *OC* 1:1350). It is safe to conclude that Baudelaire's other polemics against democracy contain appreciable irony (Godfrey 1981–82) and that ideology as such, not beggars, is his true target. One need only recall "The Eyes of the Poor" (no. 26), among several ethical fables, which directly asserts the narrator's compassion (Mauron 1966, 43–60).

LITERATURE AS FRIENDSHIP

The Parisian Prowler ends with a surprising contrast, "The Good Dogs," published three times before it entered the posthumous edition, and gratefully dedicated to the Belgian animal painter Joseph Stevens. The editors of the 1869 collection, sensitive to its sincere lyricism, added a verse epilogue—a sonnet about Paris—which scholars now recognize as the projected closure of the 1868 edition of *Les Fleurs du Mal*, which Baudelaire never lived to complete. The closing fable's prepublication history reinforces my judgment that the author himself—who placed this title last on the "Lemer Packet" list and in his autograph table of contents—reserved it as a fit finale.

The most explicitly autobiographical fable, "The Good Dogs" cites more authors, living and ancestral, than any of the others, emphasizing its kinship with an artistic community. Baudelaire's friends, during his stay in Brussels, recognizing its biographical origin, appreciated the "prose poem" as a reciprocal act. The anonymous introduction to its first publication (*Indépendance belge*, June 1865) explained how it was composed by "M. Charles Baudelaire, on the occasion of a vest given to him by M. Joseph Stevens, provided that he write something about poor people's dogs." The same note accompanied its second appearance (*Petite Revue*, 27 October 1866; reproduced verbatim in the *Grand Journal* of 4 November 1866), this time signed by the author's loyal though bankrupt associate, Poulet-Malassis, who added that the piece expresses "thanks to a friend who had bestowed upon him a [*suggestive*] vest" (Kopp, 359–61).

The poet's dedication of this final piece and other major works to prominent colleagues—*Les Fleurs du Mal* to Théophile Gautier, three of the "Tableaux parisiens" to Victor Hugo, the original *Presse* collection to Arsène Houssaye, "The Rope" to Edouard

Manet, and "The Thyrsus" to Franz Liszt—establish a solidarity between author and reader. The choice of Joseph Stevens as recipient is exceptional, however. The names of Gautier, Hugo, Houssaye, Liszt, and Manet lent Baudelaire prestige, yet his ambivalence toward them (with the exception of Liszt) renders the dedications ambiguous, and certainly problematic (Chambers 1985). His unabashedly sincere inscription to Joseph Stevens, on the other hand, authorizes a nonironic interpretation of "The Good Dogs"—as does Baudelaire's dedication to Franz Liszt of "The Thyrsus" (no. 32), his mature manifesto. Among the rare friends who consoled his Belgian exile were the Stevens brothers: the art dealer, Arthur, and the painters, Alfred and Joseph. Baudelaire even reconciled himself with the family of Victor Hugo—Olympio—expatriated in Brussels in 1865, and became particularly close with mature, middle-aged women "past their prime" in his entourage: Madame Hugo, Madame Paul Meurice, and Madame Edouard Manet (*OC* 2:1503; Adhémar 1958).

Baudelaire's ill-fated stay in Brussels, from April 1864 to July 1866, confirms this fable's structural prominence.[4] It was probably the most miserable period of Baudelaire's chronically miserable life. Unable to sell his literary capital in Paris, the poet fled to Belgium to escape his creditors, where he gave several unsuccessful lectures. He fell into periods of hazardous depression, powerless to repay his debts and fearing total professional failure. His previously dormant syphilis was beginning to destroy his nervous system and he increasingly dreaded mental and physical collapse. In fact "apoplexy" (a stroke) would soon deprive him of the power of speech. "The Good Dogs" surmounts this damnation by identifying the narrator with liberated city dogs who recapitulate his previous avatars.

Like the modern poet of "Loss of Halo" (no. 46), the narrator puts his mask aside and realizes his most cordial self-expression. The quoted invocation names a model, not Buffon, "that painter of pompous nature"—despite Baudelaire's expressed admiration —but Laurence Sterne, whom he had elsewhere praised several times:[5] " 'Descend from heaven, or ascend to me from the Elysian fields, to inspire me on behalf of good dogs, pitiful dogs, with a song worthy of you, sentimental humorist, incomparable humorist!'" Presentness, too, has its predecessors. Buffon's classical rhetoric frames an idealized nature, *la belle nature*, while the English author of *Tristram Shandy*, mounted on his macaroon-eating ass, forecasts the humble and ironic poet of modern life. Baudelaire ignores the "academic muse, that old prude," and her social and esthetic elitism, in favor of the oppressed. Freed from his aura, the Parisian writer identifies with common creatures both itinerant and domestic.

The narrator fulfills his search for fellowship, nuancing the ideologically rigid "equality" he had mocked so many times before. His mongrel "prose poem" is the fit vehicle for his "modern" ethics which focuses upon the downtrodden who lead "a dog's life." The city poet sincerely lends his voice to their silent agony: "I invoke the familiar muse, the city muse, the lively muse, so she will help me sing of good dogs, pitiful dogs, muddied dogs, those everyone shuns, as stricken with plague and vermin, except the pauper whose colleagues they are, and the poet, who considers them with a fraternal eye."

The narrator welcomes "la canaille," as did the ugly Benedicta (no. 37), who summoned him to the real. He now confesses his fraternal (or family, i.e., *familier*) leanings, previously disguised as their antitheses: starting with "The Stranger" (no. 1) who had no family, no nation, and no God, to the "perfectly fratricidal war" in "The Cake" (no. 15). The "*fraternitary* prostitution" in "Solitude" (no. 23) becomes more profoundly ironic in "The Pauper's Toy" (no. 19), in which class antagonists "laughed at each other fraternally, with teeth of *equal* whiteness." Despite the masks, the value persists.

Interpreters can retranslate those Socratic denials and recover his militant defense of the donkey in "A Joker" (no. 4), his first, irrefutably direct ethical assertion. It was not until the end of "Vocations" (no. 31) that we understood how the lone individuals of "Widows" and "The Old Acrobat" (nos. 13 and 14), among others, were "brothers [or sisters] to [him] unknown." Until then, we could only guess, contending, all the while, with repeated examples to the contrary.

Now the narrator, in "doggy language," broadcasts his admiration for intelligence, self-awareness, and above all, loyalty, love, and friendship. So he again repudiates the "happy" ones—vain, self-satisfied canines, "le chien bellâtre . . . ce fat quadrupède," incapable of simple responsiveness.[6] "Fatuous" dogs are "tiresome parasites," "unruly like children, stupid like easy women, sometimes sulky and insolent like servants!" The narrator of "Widows" had used the French *turbulent* to reject the superficial joys of rich people ("that unruliness in a vacuum") as he sympathized with the bereaved mother's isolation from her sole companion, "the child [who] is unruly, selfish, without gentleness and without patience" (no. 13). These "bad dogs" summarize the collection's egotists: vain little Frenchmen (nos. 4, 20), "the implacable Venus" (no. 7), the fickle, stupid public (nos. 8, 14), corrupting Parisian society (nos. 10, 21), insensitive self-indulgent mistresses (nos. 11, 26, 42–45), and naive philanthropists (nos. 23, 28, 30, 49). Greyhounds typify those who do not possess "enough flair in their pointed muzzles to follow a friend's trail, nor enough intelligence in their flat heads to play dominos!"

By contrast, two lyrical paragraphs celebrate the collection's heroes of the everyday. These dogs are denizens of the urban jungles, "dans les plis sinueux des vieilles capitales" (in the sinuous ravines of old capitals), portrayed in "Tableaux parisiens" ("Les Petites Vieilles" [*FM*, no. 91, line 1]). The narrator now turns advocate, as if representing in court the community with which, as "stranger," he had but stealthily identified:

> Back to their silky and padded dens! I sing of the muddied dog, the poor dog, the homeless dog, the stroller dog, the acrobat dog, the dog whose instinct, like that of the poor, of gypsies and actors, is marvelously goaded by necessity, such a good mother, true patroness of minds!
>
> I sing of catastrophic dogs, of those who wander, alone, in the sinuous ravines of huge cities, and of those who tell abandoned people, with winks and witty eyes, "Take me along, and out of our two miseries perhaps we'll create a kind of happiness!"

These noble canines redeem all previous victims. The "muddied dog" (*le chien crotté*), too poor to rent a carriage, dirtied in his walks, had appeared as the glass peddler (no. 9), the struggling writer (no. 10), and people impoverished (nos. 2, 13, 15, 19, 26, 28, 30, 35, 49). The homeless dog (*le chien sans domicile*) summarizes solitaries (nos. 1, 22, 23), gypsies and wanderers (nos. 6, 24, 31, 41, 48), and the city's ambulatory schizophrenics (nos. 22, 47). The *flâneur* dog reenacts the narrator's various strolls, travels, fantasies, and stories (nos. 12, 13, 15, 17–19, 24, 33, 35, 41, 47). While the acrobat dog (*le chien saltimbanque*) remains a traditional personification of the artist (nos. 3, 7, 14, 20, 21, 27, 31, 36). All these "catastrophic dogs" redeem those, evoked in the coda of "The Double Room" (no. 5), who submit to Time's *double aiguillon:* "the poor, the gypsy and the actor [*histrion*] [whose instinct is] goaded by necessity" (*aiguillonné par la nécessité* [no. 50]).

"The Good Dogs" celebrates their drive for companionship. These city dwellers have integrated their competing demands. Normal existence is arduous, precarious, yet these tough canines manage to enjoy "business meetings, love meetings." Emotionally free, they negotiate economic distress while preserving their elemental delights: "Through fog, through snow, through mud, during biting dog-days, in streaming rain, they go, they come, they trot, they slip under carriages, urged on by fleas, passion, need, or duty. Like us, they got up early in the morning, and they seek their livelihood or pursue their pleasures." The past tense—"Comme nous, ils se sont levés de bon matin"—suggests that, now, the narrator can successfully both write and love. But did he ever face the day with such gusto? Did he ever "chercher [sa] vie ou [courir à ses] plaisirs" with confidence? Even the liberated poet of "Loss of Halo" (no. 46) was intimidated by carriages. If only the loners of "The Double Room," "To Each His Chimera" (nos. 5 and 6), "At One O'Clock in the Morning" (no. 10), and "Solitude" (no. 23), emulating these city dogs, could have delighted equally in work and play.

Yet, this momentous change in tone ratifies the narrator's wisdom. He had repeatedly expressed his frustration, with outrage or bitter sarcasm, at social inequality or the stupidity of the powerful. Those defensive attacks and perilous mystifications now give way to just enough irony (smiling) to convey acceptance: "How often have I contemplated, smiling and moved, all those four-footed philosophers, obliging slaves, submissive or devoted, that the republican dictionary could just as well qualify as *public benefactors*, if the republic, too absorbed with the *happiness* of people, had time to care for the *honor* of dogs!" The 1789 Revolution, despite its stated goals of Liberty, Equality, Fraternity, could not institutionalize the ideals conceived by the *philosophes*, two-footed or otherwise. Its propagandists used the terms *officieux* and *obligeant* as euphemistic substantives meant to designate the servant class (Kopp, 366). Supporters of democracy, he admonishes, should introduce more actions than décor. Politics must build upon the person's inner integrity. "The triumphal barking" of Belgian dogs hitched onto wagons, for example, "bears witness to the haughty pleasure they feel in competing with horses."

The "more civilized" artistic dogs, dependent upon managers, portray the narrator's own professional poverty. Even these employed vagabonds assert their dignity, and the poet defends their right to the soup they have earned. He details a Joseph Stevens painting, *A Clown's Room* (*Intérieur du Saltimbanque*), described in one of his Belgian manuscripts (*OC* 2:964), as he protests against the exploitation of cultural workers: "Don't you think it fair that such zealous actors take to the road only after loading down their stomachs with powerful and solid soup? And will you not grant a little sensuality to those poor devils who all day have to confront the public's indifference and the unfairness of a director who takes the largest share and who alone eats more soup than four actors?"

Finally stepping outside literature, Baudelaire thanks Joseph Stevens, "the painter," who had given "the poet" a "*suggestive* vest" (in the words of Poulet-Malassis). They had met in Brussels, at an English tavern on the Villa Hermosa. The author of Parisian eclogues (see "Paysage" [Landscape (*FM*, no. 86)] from "Tableaux parisiens"), continues the tradition of Virgil and Theocritus, "who would expect, as payment for their alternating chants, a fine cheese, a flute made by the best, or a goat with swollen udders." Baudelaire's act of gratitude generates the collection's most fecund images: "The poet who has sung of pitiful dogs has received as reward a beautiful vest, whose color, both rich and faded, provokes thoughts of autumn suns, of the beauty of mature women and of Indian summers."

The prose poem itself is inspired by friendship fulfilled. Images of transition combine—as evocations of the widowed mother and Miss Scalpel had done—ripeness, anticipatory grief, and passionate hope. The refrain that structures its finale—

> un beau gilet,
> d'une couleur,
> à la fois riche et fanée,
> qui fait penser aux soleils d'automne,
> à la beauté des femmes mûres
> et aux étés de la Saint-Martin

—touches the pulse of the poet's deepest yearnings. The narrator himself is a "Thoroughbred" (no. 39), a middle-aged man who "loves as one loves in autumn," who is worn out but maintains "new fire in [his] heart." His maturity is an Indian summer, a miraculously warm autumn day (about 11 November) which rehearses, right before the deadly cold, Spring's eternal resurrection. The graying poet (see "Miss Scalpel," no. 47), "reaching his mind's autumn" ("L'Ennemi" [The enemy], *FM*, no. 10), stokes his embers before impending snows, like the lonely old woman (no. 2), the bachelor-widow (no. 13) and all those who toil, solitary, behind shut windows (no. 35).

The Parisian in exile, in the final refrain, consummates an "exchange" that is both esthetic and ethical, stepping out of his text, as it were, to thank the friend who supported and inspired him. Like the "divine Aretino," a sixteenth-century Italian poet who would blackmail the powerful with his licentious satires, he "will never forget how impetuously the painter shed his vest on behalf of the poet." (Aretino, with a keen sense of self-irony, dubbed himself the "divine." This reference contrasts with the narrator's—and Baudelaire's—expressed sincerity toward

Joseph Stevens, acknowledging his Socratic masks while reconciling them with this truly reciprocal gesture.) These distinct arts exchange their common biographical inspiration as the book ends: "And every time the poet dons the painter's vest, he is compelled to think of good dogs, of philosophical dogs, of Indian summers, and of the beauty of women quite mature."

The altered order of images in this closing refrain fathoms their hidden depth. "Dogs" replaces "autumn suns" in the list of lyrical subjects, and the sequence "mature women" and "Indian summers" is reversed: now the superlative "des femmes très-mûres" receives the final, and decisive, emphasis. Women who have lived and loved can conquer Time. Whether or not they represent Baudelaire's mother or simply a contemporary of the forty-five-year-old poet, the last word, *très-mûre,* makes of mortality—and his acceptance of human fallibility—the seal of his wisdom and his art.

AN OPEN CONCLUSION

Does Baudelaire's lyrical presence in "The Good Dogs" definitively harmonize the poet-narrator's conflicts? Do its melodious refrains obscure the radical skepticism of the preceding three fables? Is this celebration of literature as friendship a retreat from terrifying glimpses of irremediable noncommunication and cosmic injustice? Did Baudelaire, who wrote and organized his table of contents about two years before he died, revert, by this arrangement, to a sentimental evasion of philosophical or literary dead ends? Should I, as an avowedly humanistic critic, translate the itinerary traced throughout *The Parisian Prowler* as a journey from detached curiosity, through horror, to compassion and love?

To do so would appear to respect the integrity of the collection—if it were conceived as a medieval divine comedy from hell, through purgatory, to ultimate Redemption. But its hero is not the Olympian visionary of Hugo's *Les Contemplations,* receiving direct messages from the Beyond. He is a postromantic Parisian stroller, a metaphysical bachelor—childless and deprived of home, country, and transcendent guidance. *The Pari-*

sian Prowler is not a bildungsroman but an undulating string of ofttimes heterogeneous pieces. We cannot deny the autonomy of separate fables which may contradict one another, and tensions within individual texts also prevent us from abstracting a lesson from the whole.

Baudelaire's "fables of modern life" encompass both the limits and the powers of his art—of lyricism, plastic grace, and ethical idealism—and point beyond art. These parables and tales successfully absorb the romantic search for the infinite into a tension-filled realism, conveying a beauty that mixes transient and eternal, frailty and spiritual grandeur. *The Parisian Prowler* stands at the threshold of our modernity, as it depicts ways of thinking and living beyond ideologies—romantic or modern—paving the way for Rimbaud and Mallarmé, who created a literature beyond literature, and for others who experience art as but one means among many to redeem or alleviate affliction.

Baudelaire's quest for the Absolute—be it justice, truth, beauty, or God—maintains both ethical realism and a hunger for metaphysical certainty. Yet he never accepts inherited answers. His modern fables reconcile the purity of contemplation with social values, but without sentimental, didactic, or self-deceiving utopian machines. His skepticism, his inability to believe, his neurotic conflicts with people who might have helped or loved him the most, electrify this polyphonic literature which refuses to collapse the sacred—ultimate truth—into the conventional wisdom of his age. The poet's relentless reverence for what is inspires his critical and esthetic works and makes them, in practice, one.

APPENDIX 1

A Critical Postscript

This book answers two of the most common distortions of Baudelaire:

The first distortion emphasizes Baudelaire's escapist or "supernaturalist" themes to the detriment of their dialectical counterpoint, ethical concern. That approach stresses his characters' alienation, their contempt for bourgeois morality, and unusual modalities of consciousness provoked by drugs or dreaming. Baudelaire's self-destructive and often outrageous behavior, his neurotic (yet often systematically ironic) need to "mystify" the public, fostered this reputation. But over a century of scholarly criticism helps us to scrutinize the texts more carefully.

Some influential editors cite intertexts to support this "esthetic" stereotype. Robert Kopp's critical edition of *Petits Poèmes en prose* adduces two analogous examples to justify his view that Baudelaire the author stands behind the cloud reveries at the end of "The Stranger." Imitating the commentaries with which H. Lemaître accompanies his earlier edition, Kopp neglects to quote in its entirety a stanza from "Le Voyage" that seems to praise the arbitrary dreams motivating the existential quest. Instead of dwelling upon the contradictions that structure the poem and the fable, both commentators reduce the dialectic to a simple affirmation of freedom through fantasy. Both omit line 68 which acknowledges that fantasy can never cure the mind's perpetual dissatisfaction:

> Les plus riches cités, les plus grands paysages,
> Jamais ne contenaient l'attrait mystérieux
> De ceux que le hasard fait avec les nuages.
> *Et toujours le désir nous rendait soucieux!*
>
> (Lines 65–68, italics added)

> (The richest cities, the grandest landscapes, never contained the mysterious attraction of those produced by chance from clouds. *And desire continued to make us anxious!*)

The final line counterbalances, and almost nullifies, the positive value of the travelers' persistent need to contemplate clouds. The inward journey appears to free them from anguish; but the brief, exclamatory sentence reminds us, and them, that limitless reverie can at best only divert anxiety.

H. Lemaître and R. Kopp truncate their second comparison more blatantly. They cite an important passage from Baudelaire's "Salon of 1859" which injects an ethical reflection into intense cloud reveries. The poet-critic's rhythmical evocation of Eugène Boudin's landscapes suddenly stops. The writer then condemns such excursions as artistically produced narcotics that reinforce, rather than dispel, a solitude to be feared. Here is the complete conclusion of this long paragraph, itself almost a prose poem, that demonstrates Baudelaire's amalgamation of perspectives:

> In the end, all these clouds, with their fantastic and luminous forms; these ferments of gloom; these immensities of green and pink, suspended and added one upon the other; these gaping furnaces; these firmaments of black or purple satin, crumpled, rolled or torn; these horizons in mourning, or streaming with molten metal—in short, all these depths and all these splendors rose to my brain like a heady drink or like the eloquence of opium. It is rather an odd thing, but never once, while examining these liquid or aerial enchantments, did I think to complain of the absence of man. . . .
>
> [*H. Lemaître and R. Kopp end their citations here to bolster their image of Baudelaire the "stranger" who celebrates amorality and expanded consciousness.*]
>
> But I must take care not to allow the abundance of my pleasure to dictate a piece of advice to the world at large, any more than to M. Boudin himself. It would really be too dangerous. . . .
>
> [*Now I could stop the citation here in order to reduce the author's irony, his* ethical *ambiguity!*]
>
> Let him remember that man is never loath to see his fellows (as

> was observed by Robespierre, who was well versed in the *humanities*); and if he wants to win a little popularity, let him take care not to imagine that the public has arrived at an equal enthusiasm for solitude.
>
> (Baudelaire *Art in Paris*, 200; *OC* 2: 666. Cf. *Les Paradis artificiels*, *OC* 1: 455)

There are several tensions in this rich development which the poet's lyrical style—and an editor's scissors—cannot dissipate. The esthetic ecstasy does not deaden his sense of social responsibility. Quite the contrary. Consciously and quite ostentatiously, Baudelaire censors his temptation to remain aloft. He decisively repudiates naively free imagination.

The entire paragraph from the "Salon of 1859," when studied in full, like the early prose poems, combines lyrical self-expression and acute self-criticism. Its "lesson," if any, is complex: the artist, released from the world through intense reveries of color and shape, still treasures social virtues. Yet, irony prevents any moralistic reduction of the conflict. History certainly tells us that Robespierre's application of the *humanities*—italicized within parentheses to underline the contradiction—would hardly provide a model of civic virtue! Baudelaire as art critic condemns neither the esthetic nor the ethical in this wonderful evocation of the landscape paintings he was translating for his bourgeois public.

A similar resistance to the ethical also underlies the resistance *of* some contemporary theories. The second, more sophisticated distortion sees Baudelaire as a precursor to present-day deconstruction—so symptomatic of our philosophical and academic dilemmas. This Baudelaire anticipates the bold and terrifying view of literature as inevitable aporia, the death of interpretation. Recent interpreters—matured students of Paul de Man, new historicists, and some Marxist-oriented readers—have gone far beyond this preoccupation with the negative. But it will still be useful to trace one of their early models.

Paul de Man so interprets Baudelaire's attempts to surpass his own dialectics of reality and imagination, basing his insights, in large part, on "De l'essence du rire." De Man asserts that a narrator's irony intrudes upon his written illusion in order, on one level, "to prevent the all too readily mystified reader from confusing fact and fiction and from forgetting the essential negativity of the fiction" (de Man 1983, 219). I agree, except that I do not share de Man's skepticism. Baudelaire's modern fables quite lucidly tackle this delicate problem of textual illusion, but not with "essentially negative" results.

However, it is a tribute to de Man's professional rigor that he himself, almost tempted, he admits, to ironize upon his own pessimism, successfully locates Baudelaire's ultimate faith beyond literature. This passage is remarkable for its lyrical intelligence and forthright confession of defeat:

> Schlegel's rhetorical question "What gods will be able to rescue us from all these ironies?" can also be taken quite literally. For the later Friedrich Schlegel, as for Kierkegaard, the solution could only be a leap out of language into faith. Yet a question remains: certain poets, who were Schlegel's actual, and Baudelaire's spiritual, contemporaries, remained housed within language, refused to escape out of time into apocalyptic conceptions of human temporality, but nevertheless were not ironic. In his essay on laughter Baudelaire speaks, without apparent irony, of a semimythical poetic figure that would exist beyond the realm of irony. . . . Could we think of certain texts of that period—and it is better to speak here of texts than of individual names—as being truly meta-ironical, as having transcended irony without falling into the myth of an organic unity or bypassing the temporality of all language? And, if we call these texts "allegorical," would the language of allegory then be the overcoming of irony? Would some of the definitely non-ironic, but, in our sense of the term, allegorical, texts of the late Hölderlin, of Wordsworth, or of Baudelaire himself be this "pure poetry from which laughter is absent as from the soul of the Sage"? It would be very tempting to think so, but, since the implications are far-reaching, it might be better to approach the question in a less exalted mood, by making a brief comparison of the temporal structure of allegory and irony (de Man 1983, 222–23).

Paul de Man asks the right questions but abandons them, unwilling to test some compelling ethical and religious hypotheses. Why did this gifted interpreter and theoretician so arbitrarily censor his thinking?

Why should he so abruptly shelve the basic ideas and life witness of Kierkegaard and others? Why did de Man retreat, refusing to examine the consequences, in whatever mood, of his own—quite correct—insight into the "leap out of language into faith"—or into the world?

Why should he suppress the issue of commitment and replace this momentous speculation with a dry technical discussion, "a brief comparison of the temporal structure of allegory and irony"—as significant as it is? De Man, scrupulous but dogmatic, simply confesses his restrictive assumptions—not held by Baudelaire. The poet did not succumb to this theoretical futility as his fables insert the reader—with his or her reality—into a literary dialogue (cf. Goodheart 1984, 111–35, 169–72). Otherwise, why read? Why write books of interpretation?

APPENDIX 2

Prepublication History

The two following sections will help readers compare Baudelaire's definitive organization of *The Parisian Prowler* and the prepublication history of the "prose poems" as they appeared, before the 1869 posthumous edition, in newspapers and periodicals. The author's 1865 memorandum (MS. 9022, Bibliothèque littéraire Jacques Doucet in Paris), forming the definitive ordering, generally preserves the chronology of their prepublication (found in Kopp, 418–22; *OC* 1:1305–1307).

SECTION A

Contents of the 1869 posthumous edition, *Petits Poèmes en prose* (with *Les Paradis artificiels*), edited by Charles Asselineau and Théodore de Banville, vol. 4 of Baudelaire's *Oeuvres complètes* (Paris: Michel Lévy frères). All subsequent French editions and my translation *The Parisian Prowler* follow this numbering:

A Arsène Houssaye
1. L'Etranger
2. Le Désespoir de la vieille
3. Le *Confiteor* de l'Artiste
4. Un plaisant
5. La Chambre double
6. Chacun sa chimère
7. Le Fou et la Vénus
8. Le Chien et le Flacon
9. Le Mauvais Vitrier
10. A une heure du matin

11. La Femme sauvage et la petite-maîtresse
12. Les Foules
13. Les Veuves
14. Le Vieux Saltimbanque
15. Le Gâteau
16. L'Horloge
17. Un hémisphère dans une chevelure
18. L'Invitation au voyage
19. Le Joujou du pauvre
20. Les Dons des Fées
21. Les Tentations, ou Eros, Plutus et la Gloire
22. Le Crépuscule du soir
23. La Solitude
24. Les Projets
25. La Belle Dorothée
26. Les Yeux des pauvres
27. Une mort héroïque
28. La Fausse Monnaie
29. Le Joueur généreux
30. La Corde
31. Les Vocations
32. Le Thyrse
33. Enivrez-vous
34. Déjà!
35. Les Fenêtres
36. Le Désir de peindre
37. Les Bienfaits de la lune
38. Laquelle est la vraie?
39. Un cheval de race
40. Le Miroir
41. Le Port
42. Portraits de maîtresses
43. Le Galant Tireur
44. La Soupe et les nuages
45. Le Tir et le cimetière
46. Perte d'auréole
47. Mademoiselle Bistouri

48. Any where out of the world. N'importe où hors du monde
49. Assommons les pauvres!
50. Les Bons Chiens

Epilogue

SECTION B

All publications of Baudelaire's "prose poems" before the 1869 posthumous edition. I include original titles, with original numbering, such as they appeared in various periodicals. Asterisks indicate the number of times a work was previously published.

1855. Included in the literary anthology *Fontainebleau.—Hommage à C. F. Denecourt.—Paysages—Légendes—Souvenirs—Fantaisies*, with contributions by Charles Asselineau, Philibert Audebrand, Théodore de Banville, Baudelaire, Victor Hugo, Nerval, and many others. Paris: Hachette: "Les Deux Crépuscules"

A Fernand Desnoyers (dedicatory letter)

Poems: Le Soir

Le Matin

Prose: Le Crépuscule du soir

La Solitude

24 August 1857, *Le Présent:* "Poèmes nocturnes"

Le Crépuscule du soir*

La Solitude*

Les Projets

L'Horloge

La Chevelure

L'Invitation au voyage

"La Suite prochainement." However, *Le Présent* did not publish any more "poèmes nocturnes."

1 November 1861, *Revue Fantaisiste:* "Poèmes en Prose"

1. Le Crépuscule du soir**
2. La Solitude**
3. Les Projets*
4. L'Horloge*
5. La Chevelure*

6. L'Invitation au voyage*
7. Les Foules
8. Les Veuves
9. Le Vieux Saltimbanque

"La Suite à la prochaine livraison." There were no further issues of the *Revue Fantaisiste.*

26 August 1862, *La Presse,* first series: "Petits Poèmes en prose"

A Arsène Houssaye (dedicatory letter)

1. L'Etranger
2. Le Désespoir de la vieille
3. Le *Confiteor* de l'artiste
4. Un Plaisant
5. La Chambre double
6. Chacun la sienne ("Chacun sa chimère")
7. Le Fou et la Vénus
8. Le Chien et le flacon
9. Le Mauvais Vitrier

"La Suite demain."

27 August 1862, *La Presse,* second series:

10. A Une Heure du matin
11. La Femme sauvage et la petite maîtresse
12. Les Foules*
13. Les Veuves*
14. Le Vieux Saltimbanque*

"La Suite prochainement."

24 September 1862, *La Presse,* third series:

15. Le Gâteau
16. L'Horloge**
17. Un Hémisphère dans une chevelure. Poème exotique** ("La chevelure")
18. L'Invitation au voyage**
19. Le Joujou du pauvre
20. Les Dons des fées

"La Suite prochainement." See next entry.

Prepared for 27 September 1862, *La Presse*, fourth series. This last sequence was composed in proofs but *not published*. Asterisks are thus in parentheses.

21. Les Tentations, ou Eros, Plutus et la Gloire
22. Le Crépuscule du soir (***)
23. Les Projets (**)
24. La Solitude (***)
25. La Belle Dorothée
26. Les Yeux des pauvres

10 June 1863, *Revue Nationale et Étrangère:* "Petits Poèmes en prose"

Les Tentations, ou Eros, Plutus et la Gloire
La Belle Dorothée

14 June 1863, *Le Boulevard:* "Poèmes en prose"

1. [No title: Les Bienfaits de la lune]
2. Laquelle est la vraie?

10 October 1863, *Revue Nationale et Étrangère:* "Petits Poèmes en prose"

1. Une Mort héroïque
2. Le Désir de peindre

10 December 1863, *Revue Nationale et Étrangère:* "Petits Poèmes en prose"

Le Thyrse (A Franz Liszt)
Les Fenêtres
Déjà!

7 February 1864, *Le Figaro:* "Le Spleen de Paris. Poèmes en prose"

La Corde (A Edouard Manet)
Le Crépuscule du soir***
Le Joueur généreux
Enivrez-vous

"Sera continué."

14 February 1864, *Le Figaro*

Les Vocations
Un Cheval de race

"Sera continué."

2 July 1864, *La Vie Parisienne*
Les Yeux des pauvres (without author's signature)

13 August 1864, *La Vie Parisienne*
Les Projets** (signed "C.B.")

1 November 1864, *L'Artiste:* "Petits Poèmes en prose"
Une Mort héroïque*
La Fausse Monnaie
La Corde*

25 December 1864, *Revue de Paris:* "Le Spleen de Paris. Poèmes en prose"
1. Les Yeux des pauvres*
2. Les Projets***
3. Le Port
4. Le Miroir
5. La Solitude***
6. La Fausse Monnaie*

21 June 1865, *L'Indépendance Belge:*
Les Bons Chiens (A M. Joseph Stevens)

1 June 1866, *Revue du XIXe Siècle:* "Petits Poèmes lycanthropes"
1. La Fausse Monnaie**
2. Le Diable* (Le Joueur généreux)

12 June 1866, *L'Evénement:* "Le Spleen de Paris"
La Corde (A Edouard Manet)**

27 October 1866, *La Petite Revue:*
Les Bons Chiens* (A M. Joseph Stevens)

4 November 1866, *Le Grand Journal:*
Les Bons Chiens** (A M. Joseph Stevens)

(*Baudelaire died: 31 August 1867*)

31 August 1867, *Revue Nationale et Étrangère:*
Les Bons Chiens***

7 September 1867, *Revue Nationale et Étrangère:*
L'Idéal et le Réel* (Laquelle est la vraie?)

14 September 1867, *Revue Nationale et Étrangère:*
Les Bienfaits de la lune* (A Mademoiselle B.)

21 September 1867, *Revue Nationale et Étrangère:*
Portraits de maîtresses

28 September 1867, *Revue Nationale et Étrangère:*
Any where out of the world. N'importe où hors du monde

11 October 1867, *Revue Nationale et Étrangère:*
Le Tir et le cimetière

1869. The following fables and the verse "Epilogue" were published for the first time in the Posthumous edition, vol. 4 of Baudelaire's *Oeuvres complètes* (Paris: Michel Lévy frères):
Le Galant Tireur
La Soupe et les nuages
Perte d'auréole
Mademoiselle Bistouri
Assommons les pauvres!
Epilogue (not included in the handwritten table of contents)

NOTES

PREFACE

1. *The Parisian Prowler* (Athens: University of Georgia Press, 1989). This title, "Le Rôdeur parisien," appears only in a letter Baudelaire wrote to Arsène Houssaye, dated Noël 1861 (CPl 2:197); cf. Pichois's discussion of all the titles Baudelaire considered without ever deciding: *OC* 1:1298–1301, and Guiette 1969, 109–116. Soupault (1963, 101–23); Nies (1964); Hubert (1970); and Violato (1982) confirm my judgment.

2. My expression "fables of modern life" is inspired by Baudelaire's famous essay "Le Peintre de la vie moderne," written about 1858–1860 and published in *Le Figaro* in 1863. I have chosen the term "fable" to characterize Baudelaire's prose poems, although, technically, they include a number of subgenres. The fable is normally a story whose allegorical meaning is translated at the end, in a "morality"; whereas the parable tells a story whose message—usually religious—remains implicit. My terminology is heuristic.

3. The first edition had placed one hundred poems into titled sections; the second edition changes the general organization and individual sections, radically modifying its overall meaning. See Mossop 1961; Houston (forthcoming), who analyzes the architectural changes and their philosophical significance; Kaplan 1979; 219–31; Kaplan 1985, 103–25; and the elegant article of Lawler 1985, 287–306.

4. The term "theoretical fable" was introduced in a lecture at Brandeis University by Professor Alicia Borinsky and will be part of a chapter on Borges and Cortázar in her book now in preparation.

5. Appendix 2 lists the fables with their French titles as they appear in the definitive posthumous edition and all prepublications.

6. Cf. the earlier version of the essay, entitled "Du vin et du

hachisch" (1851), in which Baudelaire describes Hoffmann's "psychological barometer" which anticipates the fables' complex narrator: "Esprit légèrement ironique tempéré d'indulgence; esprit de solitude avec profond contentement de moi-même; gaieté musicale, enthousiasme musical, tempête musicale, gaieté sarcastique insupportable à moi-même, aspiration à sortir de mon *moi*, objectivité excessive, fusion de mon être avec la nature" (*OC* 1:378–79). See also chap. 8, n. 3.

7. See Monroe 1987; and Maclean 1988; cf. Pierssens 1984 for a preliminary study of the conventional ethical standards, and naive philanthropic utopianism, against which Ducasse (and Baudelaire) direct their polemics. For such a study, I would prefer Jauss's method of delimiting an era's "horizon of expectations" (see "Literary History as a Challenge to Literary Theory," in Jauss 1982, 3–45).

1. INTERPRETING THE PROSE POEMS: AN AMALGAM BEYOND CONTRADICTIONS

1. My numbering follows the definitive order of *The Parisian Prowler* unless otherwise noted.

2. "Du Vin et du hachisch comparés comme moyens de multiplication de l'individualité" appeared in the *Messager de l'Assemblée*, March 1851; the revised, expanded version, "Le Poème du hachisch," appeared 30 September 1858 in the *Revue contemporaine*. "L'Ecole païenne" appeared in the 22 January 1852 issue of *La Semaine théâtrale*.

3. Cf. Baudelaire's definitive condemnation of didactic literature in *Notes nouvelles sur Edgar Poe* (1857): "Le vice porte atteinte au juste et au vrai, révolte l'intellect et la conscience; mais, comme outrage à l'harmonie, comme dissonance, il blessera plus particulièrement certains esprits poétiques; et je ne crois pas qu'il soit scandalisant de considérer toute infraction à la morale, au beau moral, comme une espèce de faute contre le rhythme et la prosodie universelle" (*OC* 2:33–4). Baudelaire reproduced this and other paragraphs in his 1859 essay on Théophile Gautier (*OC* 2:112–14).

4. My detailed examination of shifts between the first two editions of *Les Fleurs du Mal* parallels important insights developed by Barbara

Johnson who, in *Défigurations du langage poétique* (1979), traces the poet's deconstruction of lyricism to the prose poems; see my review in *French Forum* 6, no. 3 (September 1981): 284–85. Cf. Burton 1988.

5. "Form" substitutes a finite symbol for reality, be it an absolute or a simple human fact. Cf. Paul Tillich, *The Dynamics of Faith* (New York: Harper Torchbooks, 1957), chap. 3, "Symbols of Faith."

6. We touch upon the danger of even conceptually distinguishing the "esthetic" from the "ethical." Baudelaire himself was quite aware that moral emotions might be confused with esthetic pleasures: "Le goût de la protection, un sentiment de paternité ardente et dévouée peuvent se mêler à une sensualité coupable que le hachisch saura toujours excuser et absoudre" ("Le Poème du hachisch" [1858], *OC* 1:433; and the entire section 4). See below, chap. 4.

7. See the essay of Abraham Joshua Heschel on Reinhold Niebuhr, "The Confusion of Good and Evil," in *The Insecurity of Freedom* (New York: Farrar, Straus, and Giroux, 1965).

8. Baudelaire felt he depended on Houssaye for his livelihood. See *OC* 1:1307–11, 1325; CPl 2, letters of 14 September, October–November 1860; January, 20 December, Noël 1861; 15 May, 18 August, 22 September, especially 2 October 1862. For an example of Houssaye's abusiveness see Edwards 1987, 72–77. See also Barbara Johnson's analysis of Baudelaire's dedication as a prose poem, (1979, 24–29).

9. Terdiman (1985) and Monroe (1987) come to grips with the historical and stylistic problems.

What I consider to be the false problem of poetic prose makes it practically impossible for Suzanne Bernard (1959), in her influential study, to evaluate, or even to notice, the appropriate complexity of these diverse "texts." The most lucid and useful of such discussions is that of Tzvetan Todorov: "The fact is that Baudelaire is not really writing poetry without verse or simply seeking a kind of music of meaning. He is rather writing prose poems, that is, texts which are in their conception based on the meeting of opposites. It is as though Baudelaire had derived the themes and structure of nine-tenths of these texts from the name of the genre" (T. Todorov, "Poetry without Verse," in Caws and Riffaterre 1983, 64; see esp. pp. 61, 64–66). But any binary conceptualization of the genre ignores its true complexity. See chap. 2, n. 8; chap. 5, n. 13.

10. Houssaye's piece appeared in his 1850 collection of *Poésies complètes*. For the complete text see Baudelaire, *OC* 1:1309–11.

11. Baudelaire explains in *Notes nouvelles sur Edgar Poe:* "Je dis que si le poète a poursuivi un but moral, il a diminué sa force poétique. . . . La Vérité n'a rien à faire avec les chansons" (*OC* 2:333; see also "*Les Misérables* de Victor Hugo" [1862], *OC* 2:217–24).

12. Cf. Said 1975; see Godfrey 1984 for more direct applications to Baudelaire.

13. The emblem of the "thyrsus" condenses Baudelaire's most sophisticated reflections on imagination in *Les Paradis artificiels* (1860). The dedication asserts that "notre individualité" is composed of "un amalgame indéfinissable" of spiritual and natural elements (*OC* 1:399); the image comes from Thomas De Quincey (see *OC* 1:515). Cf. Johnson 1979, 62–65; Todorov in Caws and Riffaterre 1983, 69–70. Richard Klein (1971) was perhaps the first to define this dimension of Baudelaire.

14. All unattributed quotations are taken from the fables under discussion. Specific line references follow the French Kopp edition, which numbers the texts.

15. A notice published in *Le Figaro* of 7 February 1864, signed by Gustave Bourdin but probably inspired by Baudelaire, points to the fables' true complexity: "Tout ce qui se trouve naturellement exclu de l'oeuvre rythmée et rimée, ou plus difficile à y exprimer, tous les détails matériels, et, en un mot, toutes les minuties de la vie prosaïque, trouvent leur place dans l'oeuvre en prose, où l'idéal et le trivial se fondent dans un amalgame inséparable" (cited in Kopp, lxiii). Baudelaire himself, constrained by the stereotypical antithesis between the two genres, tried, unsuccessfully, to name a category sui generis.

16. I interpret ennui as the nineteenth-century equivalent of the *taedium vitae* or *acedia* of monastic tradition, a form of deep depression, which functions in Baudelaire's works, as I see it, as a paradoxical defense against anxiety. Ennui is paradoxical because it alleviates the pain of anxiety, temporarily, while quelling the desire, the self-assertive energy, that makes us want to live. The Devil, in "Le Joueur généreux" (no. 29), calls it "cette bizarre affection de l'Ennui, qui est la source de toutes nos maladies et de tous nos misérables progrès." Cf. Kuhn 1976;

Kaplan 1978, 294–306; and of course the initial poem of *Les Fleurs du Mal*, "Au lecteur."

17. See *Mon coeur mis à nu*, no. 1: "La vaporisation et la centralisation du moi. Tout est là" (*JI*, 51; *OC* 1:676). Bersani (1977) correctly considers Baudelaire's "two postulations" as "a notion crucial to the idealism of the early poems of *Les Fleurs du Mal*, [which] are actually functions of each other" (p. 95), and thus, as such, a superficial notion.

18. The touching poem, "Les Petites Vieilles," was added to the 1861 edition of *Les Fleurs du Mal* as was the entire section "Tableaux parisiens." See Kaplan 1980, 233–48.

19. Cf. "Les Dons des fées," no. 20.

20. See "Le Peintre de la vie moderne," section 9, "Le Dandy," *OC* 2:709–12; Baudelaire's putative "dandysm" was in large part a polemic position. See sections 10 and 11 of the essay; cf. Lemaire 1978, esp. the section, "Baudelaire, le dandy et le poète," 114–24; and Moers 1960. Most relevant is Sima Godfrey's suggestive article, "The Dandy as Ironic Figure" (1981–82, 21–33).

2. FABLES OF THE HUMAN CONDITION: DUALITIES AND TRAGIC COURAGE

1. Most critics have been satisfied with these dualisms. See Ruff 1955; for more nuanced views see Milner 1967 and Emmanuel 1967.

2. As early as 1851, in "Du vin et du hachisch," Baudelaire describes this "solitude de la pensée": "De temps en temps la personnalité disparaît. L'objectivité qui fait certains poètes panthéïstiques et les grands comédiens devient telle que vous vous confondez avec les êtres extérieurs" (*OC* 1:393; see the entire section 4 for Baudelaire's most concise analysis of inebriation). See my analysis of "Une Mort héroïque" (no. 27) in chap. 3.

3. The two final sections of "Le Poème du hachisch," "L'Homme-Dieu," and "Morale," anticipate this entire movement and condemn the sin which the fable only ambiguously suggests: "contrefaisant d'une manière sacrilège le sacrement de la pénitence, à la fois pénitant et confesseur, . . . il avait tiré de sa condamnation une nouvelle pâture pour son orgueil" (*OC* 1:435–36).

4. See chap. 1 and discussion of "Hymne à la Beauté," no. 21 in the 1861 version of "Spleen et Idéal," which denounces the idealist esthetic of "La Beauté" (*FM*, no. 17) in favor of a modest, ethical contribution: "[rendre] l'univers moins hideux et les instants moins lourds."

5. Baudelaire's review of Charles Asselineau, "La Double Vie" (published 9 January 1859 in *L'Artiste*) defines a dynamic notion of the *homo duplex*—the person "always double, action and intention, dream and reality; always one harming the other, one usurping the other's domain" (*OC* 2:87).

6. Cf. "La Mort des amants" defines the atmosphere: "Un soir fait de rose et de bleu mystique" (line 9). Cf. Kopp, 197–98.

7. See the passage cited in appendix 1 on Boudin's landscapes, evocations of Delacroix, and *Artificial Paradises* (*OC* 1:377–441).

8. Suzanne Bernard, in her foundational study of the prose poem, astoundingly judges that here Baudelaire has committed "une erreur esthétique" (1959, 131). This insensitivity to his irony—derived from her simplistic formalistic bias—discredits most of her judgments. See chap. 1, n. 9; chap. 5, n. 13.

9. The phrase "Chaque homme porte en lui sa dose d'opium naturel, incessamment secrétée" is from the prose poem, "L'Invitation au voyage" (no. 18). See chap. 5 for an analysis. We cannot tell from the text of "La Chambre double" whether or not the initial vision was stimulated by drugs. What matters is the dramatic contrast between the two worlds —real and artificial—of the person's life. Baudelaire maintained that drug-induced ecstasy was simply an extreme form of imagination.

10. Marxist criticism has made important contributions to our understanding of Baudelaire's prose poems: first and foremost, Benjamin 1973; also Caers 1973; Blanchard 1985; Terdiman 1985; Ahearn 1986. See chap. 7 and my analysis of "Perte d'auréole" (no. 46).

11. In *Les Fleurs du Mal*, the poet suggests that self-destruction—mental as well as physical—is the seductively ever-present solution to despair, starting with the introductory poem, "Au lecteur": "Il rêve d'échafauds en fumant son houka" (line 38). But the 1861 version of the final section, "La Mort," and especially "Le Voyage," convey a heroically tragic acceptance of life's normal uncertainties and risks. See Kaplan 1979.

12. Jean Prévost discovered a model in one of Goya's *Caprichos:*

"In the engraving, these men are carrying monstrous donkeys [on their shoulders], with half-human heads (those heads are very much like Meryon's chimeras or gargoyles) and Baudelaire made *Chimeras* out of them. . . . Goya's symbol was simple: poor Spain laboring under the oppression of fools: the men are condemned to carry donkeys. . . . Goya's thought remains within his visions. On the contrary, Baudelaire goes beyond. He glimpsed in that drawing the immense truth that each of us carries his Chimera" (1953, 155–56). Prévost's further comparison of Baudelaire's poem "Le Jeu" (*FM*, no. 96, "Tableaux parisiens") introduces a more nuanced perspective. The modern fable surpasses these "models" with self-analysis.

13. Baudelaire added this important comment to his translation of De Quincey, in "Un Mangeur d'opium": "La lutte et la révolte impliquent toujours une certaine quantité d'espérance, tandis que le désespoir est muet. Là où il n'y a pas de remède, les plus grandes souffrances se résignent" (*OC* 1:496). Baudelaire's "stoicism" should be studied in detail; see Clapton 1931, cited by Kopp, 202–203; and "Assommons les pauvres!" (no. 49), examined in chap. 9.

3. FABLES OF THE ARTISTIC QUEST: SACRIFICES TO THE ABSOLUTE

1. See also Starobinski's beautiful illustrated book, *Portrait de l'artiste en saltimbanque* (Geneva: Skira, 1970). Kopp gives an excellent summary of nineteenth-century images of the *saltimbanque*, 233–38.

2. The "pivotal sentence" of "Le Fou et la Vénus" appears in lines 14–15 (out of 30 in the Kopp edition); in "Le *Confiteor* de l'artiste," lines 16–18 (out of 28); in "La Chambre double," lines 47–49 (out of 91).

3. Baudelaire writes of Leconte de Lisle in the *Revue fantaisiste* (15 August 1861): "Le caractère distinctif de sa poésie est un sentiment d'aristocratie intellectuelle, qui suffirait, à lui seul, pour expliquer l'impopularité de l'auteur, si, d'un autre côté, nous ne savons pas que l'impopularité, en France, s'attache à tout ce qui tend vers n'importe quel genre de perfection" (*OC* 2:177).

4. Cf. *Mon coeur mis à nu*, no. 34: "Le Français est un animal de basse-cour, si bien domestiqué qu'il n'ose franchir aucune palis-

sade. Voir ses goûts en art et en littérature. C'est un animal de race latine; l'ordure ne lui déplaît pas dans son domicile, et en littérature, il est scatophage. Il raffole des excréments. Les littérateurs d'estaminet appellent cela le *sel gaulois*" (*OC* 1:698); see also, Baudelaire's essay on Théophile Gautier, with terminology closer to the fable (*OC* 2:106).

5. Kopp quotes a passage from Gérard de Nerval's preface to his translation of Goethe's *Faust:* "[l'amour d'une jeune fille] c'est la pomme d'Eden qui au lieu de science n'offre que la jouissance d'un moment et l'éternité des supplices" (Kopp, 213).

6. Henri Lemaître's literal interpretation is typical: "C'est bien le satanisme qui est au coeur de la perversité, même sous la forme de la mystification la plus méchante et la plus vulgaire" (45).

7. This important essay was published in 1855 but was probably written as early as 1846: see Pichois, "La date de l'essai de Baudelaire sur le rire et les caricaturistes," reprinted in Pichois 1967, 80–94; also Hiddleston n.d., 85–98. See Tatar 1980 for a useful entry into such a comparative study.

8. Paul de Man analyzes Baudelaire's irony in poststructuralist terms: "The ironic language splits the subject into an empirical self that exists in a state of inauthenticity and a self that exists only in the form of a language that asserts the knowledge of this inauthenticity. This does not, however, make it into an authentic language, for to know inauthenticity is not the same as to be authentic" ("The Rhetoric of Temporality," in de Man 1983, 214); perhaps not, I would say, but it comes close enough; see de Man 1983, 210–26, for far-reaching analyses with which I will not encumber this book.

9. See "Un Mangeur d'opium": "le génie n'est que l'enfance nettement formulée, douée maintenant, pour s'exprimer, d'organes virils et puissants" (*OC* 1:498).

10. Kierkegaard develops his most detailed analysis of esthetic overstimulation in the first volume of *Either/Or* (1972, esp. 43–134, "The Immediate Stages of the Erotic or The Musical Erotic," on Mozart's *Don Juan*). Baudelaire's essay on Wagner illustrates *his* susceptibility to this mode of imaginative ecstasy.

11. Cf. "Salon de 1859": "le Beau est *toujours* étonnant" (*OC* 2:616); cf. "Exposition universelle" (1855): "*Le beau est toujours bizarre*" (*OC* 2:578; Baudelaire's italics).

4. POETRY VERSUS COMPASSION: CONVERSION TO THE ETHICAL?

1. Baudelaire first refers to "la tyrannie de la face humaine" in his essay on Thomas De Quincey: "Notre auteur avait trop aimé la foule, s'était trop délicieusement plongé dans les mers de la multitude, pour que la face humaine ne prît pas dans ses rêves une part despotique. Et alors se manifesta ce qu'il a déjà appelé, je crois, *la tyrannie de la face humaine*" (*OC* 1:483; cf. ibid., 470; Baudelaire's italics).

2. See Kopp, 214–18, for plausible autobiographical references. Critics have correctly seen this fable as an *examen de conscience*, a moral self-evaluation that extends verse texts on the same theme: "Ce poème en prose et *L'Examen de minuit* [first published in February 1863] constituent des doublets" (*OC* 1:1117). The poem characterizes the poet as a "prêtre orgueilleux de la Lyre, / Dont la gloire est de déployer / L'ivresse des choses funèbres" (lines 27–29) and it ends with a negative image: "—Vite soufflons la lampe, afin / De nous cacher dans les ténèbres!" (lines 31–32). But Pichois prejudices his interpretation of the fable by comparing it with this pessimistic verse. A more appropriate comparison might be made with the pivotal poem of the final section of the 1861 *Fleurs du Mal*, "La Fin de la journée." There the poet separates himself from the hostile Other, but enjoys positive benefits as his mind plunges into the "rafraîchissantes ténèbres."

3. A broader view of Baudelaire's writings reveals how prayer might become a selfish "réservoir de force" (quoted by Blin 1948, 88–90). The moving *Hygiène* in no. 7 retains the ambiguity of prayer as both self-assertion (through magical manipulation of the divinity) and submissiveness: "Je me jure à moi-même de prendre désormais les règles suivantes pour règles éternelles de ma vie: Faire tous les matins ma prière à Dieu, *réservoir de toute force et de toute justice*, à *mon père*, à *Mariette et* à *Poe*" (*OC* 1:673; cf. ibid., 671, 705).

4. Kopp (28) points out that neither its first publication in *La Presse* (27 August 1862) nor Baudelaire's uncorrected clipping had quotation marks.

5. Among Baudelaire's numerous misogynistic pronouncements in *Mon coeur mis à nu:* "La femme est *naturelle*, c'est-à-dire abominable" (*OC* 1:677); "Le Peintre de la vie moderne": "Le mal se fait sans effort,

naturellement, par fatalité; le bien est toujours le produit de l'art" (*OC* 2:715); see the entire section, "Eloge du maquillage," which, in my view, suggests that Baudelaire may sometimes apply such attitudes (certainly authentically felt) in a polemic context. Much has been written on Baudelaire's belief in original sin and its connection with his misogyny: see Blin 1948, 47–50; Vouga 1957; Leakey 1969; Bassim 1974.

6. See Henri Lemaître's formulation: "Si l'on devait choisir un seul des poèmes en prose pour en faire le symbole concentré de l'esthétique baudelairienne du genre, peut-être devrait-on faire choix de celui-ci : la jouissance esthétique de la foule, l'équivalence poétique de la *multitude* et de la *solitude* sont l'une des principales sources de ces poèmes en prose (la *multitude* est prose tandis que la *solitude* est poésie" (57n.). Cf. "Le Peintre de la vie moderne," sec. 3, "L'Artiste, homme du monde, homme des foules et enfant" (*OC* 2:687–94). See Kopp, 212–26, for sources in Poe and Guys. The fable, according to my analysis, takes a critical stance toward urban estheticism and is all the more "modern" for it.

7. See among *Fusées*, no. 1: "L'amour, c'est le goût de la prostitution. Il n'est même pas de plaisir noble qui ne puisse être ramené à la Prostitution. Dans un spectacle, dans un bal, chacun jouit de tous. Qu'est-ce que l'art? Prostitution. . . . L'amour veut sortir de soi, se confondre avec sa victime, comme le vainqueur avec le vaincu, et cependant conserver des privilèges de conquérant" (*OC* 1:649–50). See my chap. 5, the analysis of "The Temptations" (no. 21).

8. Martin Buber explains in another context: "[empathy] means, if anything, to glide with one's feeling into the dynamic structure of an object . . . the absorption in pure estheticism of the reality in which one participates" (1965, 97).

9. See the modification by Rubin (1985–86) of Starobinski's analysis of the clown, and Ritter 1982, 48–55; see Kaplan 1980, a preliminary version of the present discussion.

10. The hyperbole "unforgettable" (*inoubliable*), which anticipates the eyes of the beggar of fable no. 49, contrasts with "the forgetful public" (*le monde oublieux*) that ignores its "brilliant entertainer."

11. See *Mon coeur mis à nu*, no. 44: "Il est impossible de parcourir une gazette quelconque . . . sans y trouver à chaque ligne les signes

de la perversité humaine la plus épouvantable. . . . Tout journal, de la première ligne à la dernière n'est qu'un tissu d'horreurs . . . une ivresse d'atrocité universelle" (*OC* 1:705–706).

12. Only the adjectival form *accordant* appears in the nineteenth-century dictionaries edited by Boiste and Littré, and the *Petit Robert.*

13. Mauron (1966, 49–55) analyzes Baudelaire's "superimposed" images of the widow and the old acrobat. Claude Pichois imagines the young, widowed Mme Baudelaire seated with her little boy in the Luxembourg gardens about 1827–28 (*OC* 1:1308).

14. Henri Lemaître: "Comme pour servir de point d'orgue rhythmique au mouvement ascendant du poème, c'est un alexandrin qui en marque le terme. On pourra même noter que cet alexandrin final est précédé (à condition de ne pas compter les *e* muets, ce qui est normal dans un poème *en prose*) d'une suite de trois demi-alexandrins : cette organisation en forme strophique de la fin du poème ne doit pas être purement fortuite, et le recours à un rhythme virtuellement versifié (qui, de plus, obéit aux règles classiques de la césure au sixième pied) achève et couronne l'apparition de cette figure de *passante*" (69–70; cf. Kopp, 233).

15. My thanks to Virginia Marino for her phrasing of these matters.

5. THE MODERN FABLE IS BORN: THE ESTHETIC AND ITS ONTOLOGICAL FALLACY

1. The order of presentation remained the same in every subsequent version, except for slight variations in the 1862 *La Presse* proofs. The substantive variants in individual pieces are more significant than this temporary change of publication sequence.

2. Writing of Théodore Rousseau's landscapes in the "Salon de 1846," Baudelaire anticipates this sort of unchecked reverie: "Il y mêle beaucoup de son âme, comme Delacroix; c'est un naturaliste entraîné sans cesse vers l'idéal" (*OC* 2:485). The "Salon de 1859" introduces a stricture: "Tout le charme qu'il sait mettre dans ce lambeau arraché à la planète ne suffit pas toujours pour faire oublier l'absence de construction" (*OC* 2:662; cf. ibid., 964). Baudelaire seems to have sharpened his critical standards in a manner that anticipates the fables' self-analytic dimension.

3. *Mon coeur mis à nu*, no. 32: "Théorie de la vraie civilisation. Elle n'est pas dans le gaz, ni dans la vapeur, ni dans les tables tournantes, elle est dans la diminution des traces du péché originel" (*OC* 1:697). See Vouga 1957.

4. But even these lyrical cycles are structured dialectically. The idealizing groups are framed with such disenchanted pieces as "Hymne à la Beauté" and "Je t'adore à l'égal de la voûte nocturne" (*FM*, nos. 21, 24) and "Ciel brouillé" and "L'Irréparable" (*FM*, nos. 50, 54), which enhance the paradox announced by the section title: "Spleen et Idéal." See analysis below and Kaplan 1985.

5. Henri Lemaître correctly notes the conclusion's self-parody, although he adds an inappropriate, stereotyped remark on Baudelaire's "dandysm": "L'auto-ironie de cette fin est bien la forme baudelairienne et dandyste de la litote; avec, cependant, le souvenir littéraire de la 'pointe' chère aux précieux" (81n.).

6. "But this baring [*mis à nu*] by the prose poem of the essentially narcissistic character of the subject's delight [*jouissance*] constitutes not a modification but an *explanation* of the relations between sender and receiver in the verse poem" (Johnson 1979, 47; see the entire chapter, "La chevelure et son double," 31–55).

7. Compare "Laquelle est la vraie?" (no. 38) and "Le Désir de peindre" (no. 36) with "Un Cheval de race" (no. 39) and the closing image of the concluding fable (no. 50), "Les Bons Chiens": "la beauté des femmes très-mûres."

8. Analyze these complex insights from *Mon coeur mis à nu*, no. 36: "Goût invincible de la prostitution dans le coeur de l'homme, d'où naît son horreur de la solitude. —Il veut être *deux*. L'homme de génie veut être *un*, donc solitaire" (*OC* 1:700). This is Kierkegaard's "single one." See also the final sentence of "La Solitude" (no. 23): "Le bonheur dans le mouvement et dans une prostitution que je pourrais appeler *fraternitaire*." Also see references in *JI*, 204–209, on the ambivalence of the term "prostitution."

9. See Kaplan 1980; Stamelman 1983, 390–409; and Kaplan 1984.

10. See Arthur Rimbaud: "J'ai fait la magique étude / Du bonheur, qu'aucun n'élude" ("O saisons, ô châteaux . . .", *Nouveaux classiques Larousse*, ed. Etiemble, p. 17); see Rimbaud, *Une saison en enfer*, the

section "Délires II," in which he quotes the same poem to repudiate bourgeois complacency.

11. From *OC* 2:1329. The Pichois edition, following the 1855 text, puts the entire text in quotation marks. Cf. Kopp, 70, "Les Foules," and next paragraph.

12. This variant can be found in Kopp, 73–74. The Pichois version (*OC* 1:1331–32), taken from the 1857 *Le Présent*, has the entire text in quotation marks and substitutes *poignard* for *poison* in the last line. A misprint?

13. The negative evaluations Suzanne Bernard (1959) makes of Baudelaire's revisions of "Les Projets" in 1862 misconstrue its deliberately obvious ironies: "Tout ce décor un peu factice n'existait pas en 1857, non plus en 1861 : c'est à travers le seul paysage intérieur que vagabondait l'imagination du poète. Chose plus grave, la conclusion est différente : plus banale, moins 'baudelairienne'" (118). "Ces transformations dans le sens de la platitude trahissent ce que trahissent aussi beaucoup de poèmes de la dernière période: un essoufflement, un tarissement de l'imagination créatrice . . . , une sorte d'enlisement aussi dans le prosaïsme que la conception même de son recueil condamnait Baudelaire à affronter sans cesse" (119). It is remarkable how close she comes to understanding how Baudelaire systematically enhanced the self-critical dimension of his fables, but her stereotypical definition of "prose poem" as stylistic contradiction blinds her to it.

14. Paul de Man uses Baudelaire to define his less supple conception of modernity: "The distinctive character of literature thus becomes manifest as an inability to escape from a condition that is felt to be unbearable. . . . This modernity, which is fundamentally a falling away from literature and a rejection of history, also acts as the principle that gives literature duration and historical existence" (1983, 162). I don't know if de Man would agree that Baudelaire is not victimized by self-deception, but he formulates in nondualistic categories what I consider to be one of the modern fables' germinal insights: "the three movements of flight, return, and the turning point at which flight changes into return and vice versa, exist simultaneously on levels of meaning that are so intimately intertwined that they cannot be separated. When Baudelaire, for example, speaks of 'représentation du présent,' of 'mé-

moire du présent,' of 'synthèse du fantôme,' or of 'ébauche finie,' his language names, at the same time, the flight, the turning point, and the return. Our entire argument lies compressed in such formulations" (ibid., 163).

6. THE ETHICAL AND UNIVERSAL ABSURDITY: A DRIVE TOWARD DIALOGUE

1. "Le Mauvais Vitrier" (no. 9) describes "un courage de luxe pour exécuter les actes les plus absurdes et souvent les plus dangereux," and speaks of the "absurdes volontés" of Demons. Satan in "Le Joueur généreux" (no. 29) tells the narrator of "l'absurdité des différentes philosophies qui avaient jusqu'à présent pris possession du cerveau humain."

2. The more structured of these prepublication series can guide our interpretation of the final ordering, in particular those which appeared in two issues of the *Revue Nationale et Étrangère:* (1) 10 October 1863: "Une Mort Héroïque," "Le Désir de peindre" (nos. 27 and 36 of the PE), and (2) 10 December 1863: "Le Thyrse," "Les Fenêtres," "Déjà!" (nos. 32, 35, 34 of the PE). To the first group—which is unified by the theme of esthetic idealism—I would add "La Fausse Monnaie," "Le Joueur généreux," "La Corde," "Les Vocations" (nos. 28, 29, 30, 31 of the PE)—all published in 1864—which point to a possible reconciliation of fate and freedom.

3. First published in *Le Monde Littéraire*, 17 April 1853; reprinted in 1855, 1857, and 1869 (the Pichois edition reproduces the last version); see pp. 1429–32 for variants and commentaries.

4. *Le Figaro* of 7 February 1864 published this sequence, with important introductory remarks signed G. Bourdin, under the title "Le Spleen de Paris. Poèmes en prose": "La Corde" (dedicated to Edouard Manet), "Le Crépuscule du soir"***, "Le Joueur généreux," "Enivrez-vous." The next issue (14 February) published only "Les Vocations," and "Un Cheval de race." Asterisks signify times previously published.

5. This change was not reproduced in *L'Evénement* of 12 June 1866 nor in the PE: see *OC* 1:1338–39. The next quotation is from Kopp, 100.

6. See above, n. 4.

7. The term was developed by French anthropologist Lucien Lévy-Bruhl; cf. Blin 1939, chapter entitled "Le Sens de la participation esthétique," 189–207.

8. See also *OC* 1:594; and "Un Mangeur d'opium," ibid., 499; "Peintre de la vie moderne," *OC* 2:714; and the remarkable letter of 23 April 1860 to Poulet-Malassis, CPL 2:30–31.

9. "Les Bohémiens en voyage" (*FM*, no. 13) provides a model for the boy's spiritual disinterestedness; like the anxious sea voyagers, he begins "Le coeur gros de rancune et de désirs amers" (final poem of *FM*, no. 126, line 6). Another "true traveler," he seeks novelty without specific goals: "les vrais voyageurs sont ceux-là seuls qui partent / Pour partir" (lines 17–18).

7. THEORETICAL FABLES OF REALITY: THE ONTOLOGICAL PARADOX OF LITERATURE

1. See my preface, note no. 4 referring to Professor Alicia Borinsky's use of this term.

2. Here is the list Baudelaire announced in a letter to Julien Lemer in February 1865 but did not send until July of that year: "Perte d'auréole," "Mademoiselle Bistouri," "Any where out of the world," "Assommons les pauvres" (apparently without an exclamation point), "Les Bienfaits de la lune," "Laquelle est la vraie?" "La Soupe et les nuages," "Le Galant Tireur," "Le Tir et le cimetière," "Portraits de maîtresses," and finally "Les Bons Chiens."

3. The passage on Rousseau is crucial: "L'enthousiasme avec lequel il admirait la vertu, l'attendrissement nerveux qui remplissait ses yeux de larmes, à la vue d'une belle action ou à la pensée de toutes les belles actions qu'il aurait voulu accomplir, suffisaient pour lui à donner une idée superlative de sa valeur morale. Jean-Jacques s'était enivré sans hachisch" ("Le Poème du hachisch," 1858, *OC* 1:436). Robert Kopp recalls previous instances of ecstasy celebrated (though he does not emphasize their ultimate failure): "The Stranger becomes intoxicated contemplating clouds, the dreamer of 'The Double Room' by absorbing laudanum, the stroller of 'Cake' by enjoying a majestic site, the narrator of 'The Clock' by collapsing into his beautiful Felina's eyes, Fancioulle by identifying with the role he incarnates, etc. As for virtue, Rousseau

got drunk on it even without the help of drugs, for which Baudelaire does reproach him" (314).

4. Cf. Gaston Bachelard, *La Flamme d'une chandelle* (Paris: Presses Universitaires de France, 1961).

5. The only other fable containing the word *légende* is in fact "Les Veuves": "Les innombrables légendes de l'amour trompé, . . . du dévouement méconnu, des efforts non récompensés," etc. "Les Petites Vieilles" (*FM*, no. 91) more explicitly reveals the poet's "intoxication with virtue": "Je goûte à votre insu des plaisirs clandestins: / Je vois épanouir vos passions novices . . . / Mon âme resplendit de toutes vos vertus" (lines 76–77, 80). See quotation above, about Jean-Jacques Rousseau.

6. The 1863 *Revue Nationale* publication italicizes "ce que"; Kopp, 111; cf. *OC* 1:1342.

7. See also *OC* 2:455–56; note pp. 1307–1308, from the section, "De l'idéal et du modèle." He paraphrases this paragraph in "Le Peintre de la vie moderne," written about 1860 (*OC* 2:685).

8. R. Kopp's commentary to "Les Bienfaits de la lune" cites a prescient quotation, reported by René Piot, about Delacroix's reaction after Baudelaire read this prose poem to him: "Sachez, mon petit clerc, . . . que le jour où les peintres auront perdu la science et l'amour de leur outil, les théories stériles commenceront. Car ne sachant plus écrire leur pensée avec des formes et des couleurs, ils l'écririront avec des mots et les littérateurs les auront" (Kopp, 323).

9. Henri Lemaître incorrectly states that *Le Boulevard* first published "Laquelle est la vraie?" without a title, pp. 181, 248n. Instead, the piece numbered 1 was untitled ("Les Bienfaits de la lune"); see Kopp, 116, 421; cf. *OC* 1:1344.

10. Compare Delacroix's negative reaction (*OC* 2:1376, n. 3).

11. The 25 December 1864 issue of the *Revue de Paris* included, under the title "Le Spleen de Paris. Poèmes en prose," this numbered sequence: "1. Les Yeux des pauvres*; 2. Les Projets***; 3. Le Port; 4. Le Miroir; 5. La Solitude***; 6. La Fausse Monnaie*." Asterisks indicate the number of times previously published.

8. FINAL EXECUTIONS OF IDEALISM: THE ESTHETIC, THE ETHICAL, AND THE RELIGIOUS

1. The four degrees of love are: (1) naïveté, "the age of Cherubino," a stock character in Beaumarchais's *Le Mariage de Figaro*, who represents adolescent infatuation; (2) the search for beauty as a choice; (3) the climacteric third period in which beauty itself is not enough and must be "seasoned with perfumes, ornaments, etc." (fable no. 42); (4) absolute calm.

2. These italics, found in the manuscript, were not reproduced in the first *Revue Nationale* publication (21 September 1867), nor in the PE. See Kopp, 126; *OC* 1:1346.

3. Baudelaire's analysis of Delacroix reflects his own complex self-portrait: "Eugène Delacroix était un curieux mélange de scepticisme, de politesse, de dandysme, de volonté ardente, de ruse, de despotisme, et enfin d'une espèce de bonté particulière et de tendresse modérée qui accompagne toujours le génie" ("L'Oeuvre et la vie d'Eugène Delacroix," 1863, *OC* 2:756). See also preface, n. 6.

4. See the highly suggestive essay "Baudelaire, or Infinity, Perfume, and Punk," in Kristeva 1987, 318–40. My thanks to Manya Steinkoler for this reference.

5. See also "L'Héautontimorouménos" (*FM*, no. 83) which summarizes this self-destructive irony: "Je suis de mon coeur le vampire, / —Un de ces grands abandonnés / Au rire éternel condamnés / Et qui ne peuvent jamais sourire!" (lines 25–28). Or the "phare ironique" of "L'Irrémédiable" which follows.

6. The manuscript capitalizes Time and Life; Kopp, 128.

7. Riffaterre 1978; "La métaphore filée dans la poésie surréaliste," in Riffaterre 1979, 217–34.

8. This ending was censored, for apparent obscenity, or hostility against religion (Kopp, 338). I suspect that the editors were as much threatened by its repudiation of the idealized Poet as by its slang. Compare with "Perte d'auréole" (no. 46), which deflates the poet humorously.

9. My interpretation is congruent with Marxist insights into the "loss of aura" perpetrated by the bourgeoisie and industrial capitalism. See Klein 1970; Wohlfarth 1970; Benjamin 1973, 152–54; Caers 1973, for

an outline of Lucien Goldmann's structural analysis; Blanchard 1985; Terdiman 1985; and Ahearn 1986.

10. My use of "Mademoiselle Bistouri" to summarize the narrator's attempts to reconcile the esthetic, the ethical, and the religious is supported by François Mauriac's choice of its final phrase as an epigraph to *Thérèse Desqueyroux*, a novel as Baudelairean as it is Catholic. But my use of the term "religious," as noted in my preface, is hardly orthodox. My interpretation was inspired by the remarkable paper of Herbert Fingarette, "The Meaning of the Law in the Book of Job" (1978, 1581–1617). See also Otto [1923] 1958; Massin 1944, 1–41, for nuanced theological approaches. For a previous version of the present analysis see Kaplan 1985. Cf. Aynsworth 1982; Maclean 1988, 141–60.

11. See Goodheart 1984; also see Bernheimer 1982: "This is the kind of defensive maneuver I find typical of the hyperrationalistic strategies of deconstructive criticism. Feelings are 'inscribed' as mere linguistic figures. The physical relationships of bodies are dissected to provide the pieces for intellectual play. A militant theory of uncertainty announces its aporia within a critical apparatus that functions with all the surety of a well-oiled machine" (5). I would only add—and Bernheimer's book demonstrates that he would agree—that deconstructive criticism placed in a fuller context leads to fundamental insights.

9. CONCLUDING FABLES: LITERATURE AS FRIENDSHIP

1. "Mon Dieu, à moi, c'est le Dieu de Socrate, de Franklin, de Voltaire et de Béranger! Je suis pour la *Profession de foi du vicaire savoyard* et les immortels principes de '89!" (*Madame Bovary* [Paris: Garnier-Flammarion, 1966], p. 112).

2. Baudelaire's letter to Sainte-Beuve (2 January 1866) reinforces this internal analysis of "Assommons les pauvres!": "Vous avez plus que jamais l'air d'un confesseur et d'un accoucheur d'âmes. On disait, je crois, la même chose de Socrate; mais les sieurs Baillarger et Lélut ont déclaré, sur leur conscience, qu'il était fou" (CP1 2:562–64; quoted by Lemaître, 216–17; and Kopp, 356–57). Other such projections of the narrator's antisocial urges have appeared in "The Double Room" (no. 5) when the dreamer exclaims: "What benevolent demon has thus

surrounded me with mystery, silence, peace and aromas?" In "The Bad Glazier" (no. 9) "malicious Demons slip into" the narrator and pervert his compassion entirely. "Solitude" (no. 23), which, as does "Let's Beat Up the Poor!" questions "a prostitution that I might call *fraternitary*," admits that "the Demon gladly frequents arid places." And of course the Satans of "The Temptations" and "The Generous Gambler" (nos. 21, 29) occasion his most equivocal assertions of cynical opportunism.

3. Marcel Ruff explains the reference: "Baudelaire semble ici avoir confondu Zénon, le fondateur du stoïcisme, qui enseignait sous le Portique (*stoa*) du Pécile, à Athènes, avec Zénon d'Elée, fondateur de la dialectique et célèbre pour avoir nié le mouvement par les "sophismes" de la fléche immobile dans les airs, d'Achille ne pouvant rattraper la tortue, etc." (Baudelaire, *Oeuvres complètes*, 1968, 183 n.).

4. See the last part of Enid Starkie's well-documented biography, *Baudelaire* (1957, 467–574); and especially Claude Pichois and Jean Ziegler, *Baudelaire. Biographie* (1987, 501–87); and Raymond Poggenburg, *Charles Baudelaire: Une micro-histoire* (1987).

5. In *La Fanfarlo*, *OC* 1:554; "Présentation de *Révélation magnétique*," *OC* 2:247. In the "Salon de 1859," Baudelaire, appreciating a religious painting by Legros, makes an association with Sterne in a way that reinforces the impression of sincerity in "Les Bons Chiens": "Cependant l'esprit du vrai critique, comme l'esprit du vrai poète doit être ouvert à toutes les beautés; avec la même facilité il jouit de la grandeur éblouissante de César triomphant et de la grandeur du pauvre habitant des faubourgs incliné sous le regard de son Dieu. . . . Par une association mystérieuse que les esprits délicats comprendront, l'enfant, grotesquement habillé qui tortille avec gaucherie sa casquette au temple de Dieu, m'a fait penser à l'âne de Sterne et à ses macarons" (*OC* 2:630).

6. The term *bellâtre*, which denotes a handsome but stupid and fatuous male, is a corruption of true beauty; it consists of *belle* with the suffix of degradation *âtre*, just as the idealized "rose et bleu" in "La Chambre double" (no. 5) turn into "Quelque chose de crépusculaire, *de bleuâtre et de rosâtre*" (italics added).

BIBLIOGRAPHY

WORKS BY BAUDELAIRE

Art in Paris. Trans. Jonathan Mayne. Ithaca: Cornell University Press; New York: Phaidon, 1965.

Correspondance. Ed. Claude Pichois and Jean Ziegler. 2 vols. Paris: Gallimard, Editions de la Pléiade, 1976.

Journaux intimes. Fusées. Mon coeur mis à nu. Carnet. Ed. Jacques Crépet and Georges Blin. Paris: José Corti, 1949.

Oeuvres complètes. Ed. Claude Pichois. 2 vols. Paris: Gallimard, Editions de la Pléiade, 1975, 1976.

Oeuvres complètes. Ed. Marcel A. Ruff. Paris: Editions du Seuil, "L'Intégrale," 1968.

The Painting of Modern Life. Trans. Jonathan Mayne. New York: Phaidon, 1965.

The Parisian Prowler. Trans. Edward K. Kaplan. Athens: University of Georgia Press, 1989.

Petits Poèmes en prose. Ed. Robert Kopp. Paris: José Corti, 1969.

Petits Poèmes en prose. Les Paradis artificiels, in *Oeuvres complètes*, vol. 4. Ed. Charles Asselineau and Théodore de Banville. Paris: Michel Lévy frères, 1869.

Petits Poèmes en prose (*Le Spleen de Paris*). Ed. Henri Lemaître. Paris: Editions Garnier, 1962.

Selected Letters. Trans. Rosemary Lloyd. Chicago: University of Chicago Press, 1982.

SECONDARY SOURCES

Adhémar, Jean. 1958. "Baudelaire, les frères Stevens, la modernité." *Gazette des beaux-arts*, February, 248–53.

Bibliography

Ahearn, Edward J. 1986. "Marx's Relevance for Second Empire Literature: Baudelaire's 'Le Cygne.'" *Nineteenth-Century French Studies* 14, nos. 3–4:269–77.

Aynesworth, Donald. 1982. "Humanity and Monstrosity in *Le Spleen de Paris:* A Reading of 'Mademoiselle Bistouri.'" *Romanic Review* 72, no. 2 (March): 209–21.

Bakhtin, Mikhail. 1984. *Problems in Dostoevsky's Poetics*. Minneapolis: University of Minnesota Press.

Bassim, Tamara. 1974. *La Femme dans l'oeuvre de Baudelaire*. Neuchâtel: A la Baconnière.

Bataille, Georges. 1957. "Baudelaire." In *La Littérature et le mal*. Paris: Gallimard: 37–68.

Benjamin, Walter. 1969. *Illuminations*. Trans. Harry Zohn. New York: Schocken.

———. 1973. *Charles Baudelaire: A Lyric Poet in the Era of High Capitalism*. Trans. Harry Zohn. London: NLB.

Bernard, Suzanne. 1959. *Le Poème en prose de Baudelaire jusqu'à nos jours*. Paris: Nizet.

Bernheimer, Charles. 1982. *Flaubert and Kafka: Studies in Psychopoetic Structure*. New Haven: Yale University Press.

Bersani, Leo. 1977. *Baudelaire and Freud*. Berkeley: University of California Press.

Blanchard, Marc Eli. 1985. *In Search of the City: Engels, Baudelaire, Rimbaud*. Saratoga, Calif.: Anma Libri.

Blanchot, Maurice. 1949. "L'Echec de Baudelaire." In *La Part du feu*. Paris: Gallimard.

Blin, Georges. 1939. *Baudelaire*. Paris: Gallimard.

———. 1948. *Le Sadisme de Baudelaire*. Paris: Corti.

Bonnefoy, Yves. 1980. *L'Improbable et d'autres essais*. Enlarged edition. Paris: Mercure de France.

———. 1988. *La Vérité de parole*. Paris: Mercure de France.

Booth, Wayne C. 1974. *A Rhetoric of Irony*. Chicago: University of Chicago Press.

Buber, Martin. 1965. *Between Man and Man*. New York: Macmillan.

Burton, Richard. 1988. *Baudelaire in 1859: A Study of Poetic Creativity*. Cambridge: Cambridge University Press.

Caers, Agnes Krutwig. 1973. "La Vision du monde dans les *Petits poèmes en prose.*" *Revue de l'Institut de Sociologie* 3–4:625–39.

Cargo, Robert T. 1971. *Concordance to Baudelaire's "Petits Poèmes en prose."* University: University of Alabama Press.

Caws, Mary Ann, and Hermine Riffaterre, eds. 1983. *The Prose Poem in France.* New York: Columbia University Press.

Cellier, Léon. 1977. *Parcours initiatiques.* Neuchâtel: A la Baconnière.

Chambers, Ross. 1977. "*Frôler ceux qui rôdent*": le paradoxe du saltimbanque." *Revue des sciences humaines* 42, no. 167:347–63.

———. 1980–81. "'Je' dans les *Tableaux parisiens* de Baudelaire." *Nineteenth-Century French Studies* 9, nos. 1–2:59–68.

———. 1984. "Du temps des 'Chats' au temps du 'Cygne.'" *Oeuvres et critiques* 9:11–26.

———. 1985. "Baudelaire et la pratique de la dédicace." *Saggi e ricerche di letteratura francese* 24:121–40.

Clapton, G. T. 1931. "Baudelaire, Sénèque et saint Jean Chrysostome." *Revue d'histoire littéraire de la France*, April–June.

Clark, T. J. 1984. *The Painting of Modern Life: Paris in the Art of Manet and His Followers.* Princeton: Princeton University Press.

De George, Fernande M. 1973. "The Structure of Baudelaire's *Petits poèmes en prose.*" *L'Esprit Créateur* 13, no. 2 (Summer): 144–53.

Delacroix, Maurice. 1977. "Un poème en prose de Charles Baudelaire: '*Les yeux des pauvres.*'" *Cahiers d'analyse textuelle* 19:47–65.

Delaney, Susan. 1984–85. "Paroles gelées." *UCLA French Studies* 2–3:49–69.

De Man, Paul. 1983. *Blindness and Insight.* 2d ed., rev. Minneapolis: University of Minnesota Press.

Edwards, Peter J. 1987. "Une version inconnue du poème en prose 'L'Horloge.'" *Bulletin baudelairien* 22, no. 2 (December): 72–77.

Emmanuel, Pierre. 1967. *Baudelaire.* Collection "Ecrivains devant Dieu." Paris: Desclée de Brouwer.

Fairlie, Alison. 1967. "Observations sur les 'Petits poèmes en prose.'" *Revue des sciences humaines*, July–September, 449–60.

———. 1981. *Imagination and Language: Collected Essays on Constant, Baudelaire, Nerval, and Flaubert.* Cambridge: Cambridge University Press.

Fingarette, Herbert. 1978. "The Meaning of the Law in the Book of Job." *Hastings Law Review* 29, no. 6 (July): 1581–1617.

Fondane, Benjamin. 1947. *Baudelaire et l'expérience du gouffre*. Paris: Seghers.

Freud, Sigmund. 1917. "Mourning and Melancholia." *Standard Edition of the Complete Psychological Works* 14:237–60.

Friedman, Geraldine. 1989. "Baudelaire's Theory of Practice: Ideology and Difference in 'Les yeux des pauvres.'" *PMLA* 104, no. 3 (May): 317–28.

Godfrey, Sima. 1981–82. "The Dandy as Ironic Figure." *Sub-Stance*, no. 36:21–32.

———. 1982. "Baudelaire's Windows." *L'Esprit Créateur* 22, no. 4 (Winter): 83–100.

———, ed. 1984. *The Anxiety of Anticipation, Yale French Studies*, no. 66.

———. 1985. "'Mère des souvenirs': Baudelaire, Memory and Mother." *L'Esprit Créateur* 25, no. 2 (Summer): 32–44.

Goodheart, Eugene. 1984. *The Skeptic Disposition in Contemporary Criticism*. Princeton: Princeton University Press.

Guiette, Robert. 1969. "Le titre des *Petits poèmes en prose*." In *Modern Miscellany Presented to Eugène Vinaver*, ed. Lawrenson, Sutcliffe, Gadoffre, 109–16. Manchester: Manchester University Press. (Reprinted in *Romanica Gandensia* 13:165–72.)

———. 1972a. "Baudelaire et le poème en prose." *Romanica Gandensia* 13:147–56.

———. 1972b. "Vers et prose chez Baudelaire." *Romanica Gandensia* 13:157–63.

Guisan, Gilbert. 1948. "Prose et poésie d'après les *Petits poèmes en prose*." *Etudes de lettres. Bulletin de la Société des Etudes de Lettres*, no. 70 (February). Lausanne: Imprimerie de la Concorde: 87–107.

Hiddleston, J. A. 1985. "'Fusée,' Maxim, and Commonplace in Baudelaire." *Modern Language Review* 80, no. 3 (July): 563–70.

———. N.d. "Baudelaire et le rire." *Etudes baudelairiennes* 12:85–98.

———. 1987. *Baudelaire and "Le Spleen de Paris."* Oxford: Clarendon Press.

Houston, John Porter. 1980. *French Symbolism and the Modernist Move-*

ment: A Study of Poetic Structures. Baton Rouge: Louisiana State University Press.

———. Forthcoming. "Two Versions of *Les Fleurs du Mal* and Ideas of Form." In *The Ladder of High Designs*, ed. David Lee Rubin and Doranne Fenoaltea. Charlottesville: University Press of Virginia.

Hubert, Renée Riese. 1966. "La Technique de la peinture dans le poème en prose." *CAIEF* 18:169–78.

———. 1970. "Intimacy and Distance in Baudelaire's Prose-Poems." *Texas Studies in Literature and Language* 12:241–47.

———. 1970a. "Contexts of Twilight in Baudelaire's 'Petits poèmes en prose.'" *Orbis Litterarum* 25:352–60.

Jauss, Hans Robert. 1982. *Toward an Aesthetics of Reception.* Trans. Timothy Bahti. Minneapolis: University of Minnesota Press.

Jenny, Laurent. 1976. "Le Poétique et le narratif." *Poétique* 28:440–49.

Johnson, Barbara. 1979. *Défigurations du langage poétique. La seconde révolution baudelairienne.* Paris: Flammarion.

———. 1980. *The Critical Difference: Essays in the Contemporary Rhetoric of Reading.* Baltimore: Johns Hopkins University Press.

———. 1987. *A World of Difference.* Baltimore: Johns Hopkins University Press.

Jouve, Pierre Jean. 1958. *Tombeau de Baudelaire.* Paris: Seuil.

Kaplan, Edward K. 1978. "The Courage of Baudelaire and Rimbaud: The Anxiety of Faith." *French Review* 52, no. 2 (December): 294–306.

———. 1979. "Baudelaire and the Battle with Finitude: 'La Mort,' Conclusion of *Les Fleurs du Mal.*" *French Forum* 4, no. 3 (September): 219–31.

———. 1980. "Baudelaire's Portrait of the Poet as Widow: Three *Poèmes en prose* and 'Le Cygne.'" *Symposium* 34, no. 3 (Fall): 233–48.

———. 1984. *Mother Death: The Journal of Jules Michelet, 1815–1850.* Amherst: University of Massachusetts Press.

———. 1985. "Modern French Poetry and Sanctification: Charles Baudelaire and Yves Bonnefoy." *Dalhousie French Studies* 8 (Spring–Summer): 103–25.

———. 1987–88. "The Writing Cure: Gaston Bachelard on Baudelaire's Ambivalent Harmonies." *Symposium* 61, no. 4 (Winter): 278–91.

Kierkegaard, Søren Abbaye. 1954. *"Fear and Trembling" and "The Sickness Unto Death."* Trans. Walter Lowrie. Princeton: Princeton University Press.

———. 1962. *Works of Love*. Trans. Howard Hong and Edna Hong. New York: Harper Torchbooks.

———. 1965. *The Concept of Irony*. Trans. Lee M. Capel. Bloomington: University of Indiana Press.

———. 1972. *Either/Or*. Trans. Walter Lowrie, with revisions by Howard Johnson. 2 vols. Princeton: Princeton University Press.

Klein, Richard. 1970. "'Bénédiction'/'Perte d'auréole': Parables of Interpretation." *MLN* 85, no. 4 (May): 515–28.

———. 1971. "Straight Lines and Arabesques: Metaphors of Metaphors." *Yale French Studies* 45:64–86.

Kristeva, Julia. 1987. *Tales of Love*. Trans. Leon Roudiez. New York: Columbia University Press.

Kuhn, Reinhard. 1976. *The Demon at Noontide: Ennui in Western Literature*. Princeton: Princeton University Press.

Lawler, James. 1985. "The Order of 'Tableaux parisiens.'" *Romanic Review* 3 (May): 287–306.

Leakey, F. W. 1969. *Baudelaire and Nature*. Manchester: Manchester University Press.

Lemaire, Michel. 1978. *Le Dandysme de Baudelaire à Mallarmé*. Montreal: Presses de l'Université de Montréal.

Maclean, Marie. 1988. *Narrative as Performance: The Baudelairean Experiment*. London and New York: Routledge.

Massin, Jean. 1944. "Baudelaire devant la douleur," in *Hier et demain*, 1–41. Paris: Sequana.

Mauron, Charles. 1966. *Le Dernier Baudelaire*. Paris: Corti.

Mehlman, Jeffrey. 1974. "Baudelaire with Freud." *Diacritics* (Spring): 7–13.

Metzidakis, Stamos. 1986. *Repetition and Semiotics*. Birmingham, Ala.: Summa Publications.

Milner, Max. 1967. *Baudelaire. Enfer ou ciel, qu'importe?* Paris: Plon.

———. 1980. "Baudelaire et la théologie." In *Romantisme et religion*, ed. Baude, Munch. Paris: Presses Universitaires de France.

Moers, Ellen. 1960. *The Dandy*. London: Seike and Warburg.

Monroe, Jonathan. 1987. *A Poverty of Objects: The Prose Poem and the Politics of Genre*. Ithaca: Cornell University Press.

Mossop, D. J. 1961. *Baudelaire's Tragic Hero*. Oxford: Oxford University Press.

Muecke, D. C. 1969. *The Compass of Irony*. London: Methuen.

Nies, Fritz. 1964. "Der Poet als Flâneur und der 'Zyklische' Charakter der 'Petits poèmes en prose.'" In *Poesie in prosaischer Welt: Untersuchungen zum Prosagedicht bei Aloysius Bertrand und Baudelaire*, 259–86. Heidelberg: Carl Winter.

Otto, Rudolf. [1923] 1958. *The Idea of the Holy*. Trans. J. W. Harvey. New York: Oxford University Press.

Pachet, Pierre. 1976. *Le Premier venu. Essai sur la politique baudelairienne*. Paris: Denoël.

Pichois, Claude. 1967. *Baudelaire: Etudes et témoignages*. Neuchâtel: Editions de la Baconnière.

Pichois, Claude, and François Ruchon. 1961. *Iconographie de Baudelaire*. Geneva: Cailler.

Pichois, Claude, and Jean Ziegler. 1987. *Baudelaire. Biographie*. Paris: Julliard.

Pierssens, Michel. 1984. *Lautréamont. Ethique à Maldoror*. Lille: Presses Universitaires de Lille.

Pizzorusso, Arnaldo. 1971. *Da Montaigne a Baudelaire*. Rome: Bulzoni Editore.

Poggenburg, Raymond. 1987. *Charles Baudelaire: Une micro-histoire*. Nashville: Vanderbilt University Press.

Politzer, Heinz. 1962. *Franz Kafka: Parables and Paradoxes*. Ithaca: Cornell University Press.

Prévost, Jean. 1953. *Baudelaire: Essai sur l'inspiration et la création poétiques*. Paris: Mercure de France.

Ricoeur, Paul. 1965. *Fallible Man*. Trans. Charles Kelbley. Chicago: Regnery.

Riffaterre, Michael. 1978. *Semiotics of Poetry*. Bloomington: University of Indiana Press.

———. 1979. *La Production du texte*. Paris: Seuil.

Ritter, Naomi. 1982. "Baudelaire and Kafka: The Triangular Circus Scene." *Comparatist* 6:48–55.

Rubin, Vivien L. 1985–86. "Two Prose Poems by Baudelaire: *Le Vieux Saltimbanque* and *Une mort héroïque*." *Nineteenth-Century French Studies* 14, nos. 1–2:51–60.

Ruff, Marcel. 1955. *L'Esprit du mal et l'esthétique baudelairienne*. Paris: Armand Colin.

Said, Edward W. 1975. *Beginnings: Intention and Method*. New York: Basic Books.

Sartre, Jean-Paul. 1947. *Baudelaire*. Paris: Gallimard.

Soupault, Philippe. 1963. *Profils perdus*. Paris: Mercure de France.

Stamelman, Richard. 1983. "The Shroud of Allegory: Death, Mourning, and Melancholy in Baudelaire's Work." *Texas Studies in Literature and Language* 25, no. 3 (Fall): 390–409.

Starkie, Enid. 1957. *Baudelaire*. London: Faber and Faber.

Starobinski, Jean. 1967. "Sur quelques répondants allégoriques du poète." *Revue d'histoire littéraire de la France* 67 (April–June): 402–12.

Stierle, Karlheinz. 1980. "Baudelaire and the Tradition of the *Tableau de Paris*." *New Literary History* 11, no. 2 (Winter): 345–62.

Swain, Virginia. 1982. "The Legitimation Crisis: Event and Meaning in 'Le Vieux Saltimbanque' and 'Une mort héroïque.' " *Romanic Review* 73, no. 4 (November): 452–62.

Tatar, Maria. 1980. "E. T. A. Hoffmann's 'Der Sandmann': Reflection and Romantic Irony." *MLN* 95:585–608.

Terdiman, Richard. 1985. *Discourse/Counter-Discourse: The Theory and Practice of Symbolic Resistance in Nineteenth-Century France*. Ithaca: Cornell University Press.

Violato, Gabriella. 1982. "Sui *Petits poèmes en prose:* Orientamenti di lettura." *Saggi e ricerche di letteratura francese* 21:243–82.

Vouga, Daniel. 1957. *Baudelaire et Joseph de Maistre*. Paris: Corti.

Wing, Nathaniel. 1975. "The Poetics of Irony in Baudelaire's *La Fanfarlo*." *Neophilologus* 59, no. 2 (April): 165–89.

———. 1979. "Effects and Affects of Theory: Reading Bersani on Baudelaire and Freud." *Diacritics* (December): 13–27.

———. 1986. *The Limits of Narrative: Essays on Baudelaire, Flaubert, Rimbaud, and Mallarmé*. Cambridge: Cambridge University Press.

Wohlfarth, Irving. 1970. "'Perte d'auréole': The Emergence of the Dandy." *MLN* 85:165–89.

Wright, Barbara, and D. H. T. Scott. 1984. *"La Fanfarlo" and "Le Spleen de Paris."* London: Grant and Cutler.

INDEX

Baudelaire's fables are listed by their English titles and his poems and essays under the French.

Index